Reimagining School Leadership

TRANSFORMING EDUCATION THROUGH CRITICAL LEADERSHIP, POLICY AND PRACTICE

Series editors: **Stephanie Chitpin, Sharon D. Kruse and Howard Stevenson**

Transforming Education Through Critical Leadership, Policy and Practice is based on the belief that those in educational leadership and policy-constructing roles have an obligation to educate for a robust critical and democratic polity in which citizens can contribute to an open and socially just society. Advocating for a critical, socially just democracy goes beyond individual and procedural concerns characteristic of liberalism and seeks to raise and address fundamental questions pertaining to power, privilege, and oppression. It recognizes that much of what has gone under the name of "transformational leadership" in education seeks to transform very little, but rather it serves to reproduce systems that generate structural inequalities based on class, gender, race, (dis)ability, and sexual orientation.

This series seeks to explore how genuinely transformative approaches to educational leadership, policy, and practice can disrupt the neoliberal hegemony that has dominated education systems globally for several decades, but which now looks increasingly vulnerable. The series will publish high-quality books, both of a theoretical and empirical nature, that explicitly address the challenges and critiques of the current neoliberal conditions, while steering leadership and policy discourse and practices away from neoliberal orthodoxy toward a more transformative perspective of education leadership. The series is particularly keen to "think beyond" traditional notions of educational leadership to include those who lead in educative ways – in social movements and civil society organizations as well as in educational institutions.

Reimagining School Leadership: Sustaining Improvement Through and Beyond Uncertainty

EDITED BY

DAVID E. DEMATTHEWS
University of Texas at Austin, USA

AND

SHARON D. KRUSE
Washington State University Vancouver

United Kingdom – North America – Japan – India – Malaysia – China

Emerald Publishing Limited
Emerald Publishing, Floor 5, Northspring, 21-23 Wellington Street, Leeds LS1 4DL

First edition 2024

Editorial matter and selection © 2024 David E. DeMatthews and Sharon D. Kruse.
Individual chapters © 2024 The authors.
Published under exclusive licence by Emerald Publishing Limited.

Reprints and permissions service
Contact: www.copyright.com

No part of this book may be reproduced, stored in a retrieval system, transmitted in any form or by any means electronic, mechanical, photocopying, recording or otherwise without either the prior written permission of the publisher or a licence permitting restricted copying issued in the UK by The Copyright Licensing Agency and in the USA by The Copyright Clearance Center. Any opinions expressed in the chapters are those of the authors. Whilst Emerald makes every effort to ensure the quality and accuracy of its content, Emerald makes no representation implied or otherwise, as to the chapters' suitability and application and disclaims any warranties, express or implied, to their use.

British Library Cataloguing in Publication Data
A catalogue record for this book is available from the British Library

ISBN: 978-1-83797-411-5 (Print)
ISBN: 978-1-83797-410-8 (Online)
ISBN: 978-1-83797-412-2 (Epub)

Printed and bound by CPI Group (UK) Ltd, Croydon, CR0 4YY

INVESTOR IN PEOPLE

Contents

List of Figures and Tables   *vii*

About the Editors   *ix*

About the Contributors   *xi*

Chapter 1   The Challenge and Promise of Reimagining School Leadership   *1*
Sharon D. Kruse and David E. DeMatthews

Chapter 2   Building and Sustaining Improvement in Disruptive Times: School Leadership in Aotearoa New Zealand   *13*
Michalis Constantinides

Chapter 3   New Approaches to Complex Challenges: Leadership That Matters   *31*
Deidre M. Le Fevre

Chapter 4   Reimagining Leadership for Symmetry: A Framework for Embedding Mutual Respect Into School Improvement Efforts   *49*
Whitney M. Hegseth

Chapter 5   Critically Reflexive School Leadership and the Racial-Discipline Gap: Leading for Racial Justice   *71*
Conor L. Scott and Melinda M. Mangin

Chapter 6   "But How Will This Improve Outcomes?" Tensions and Lessons of Improvement During a Racial Equity Transformation at Copley Public Schools   *89*
Patricia M. Virella

Chapter 7 Leading Through Climate Disasters and Environmental Injustice: Past, Present, and Future *103*
Megan Rauch Griffard, Diamond Ebanks and Jacob D. Skousen

Chapter 8 Mindful Leadership: Cultivating Awareness, Wisdom, and Connection *133*
Sharon D. Kruse and David E. DeMatthews

Chapter 9 Conclusion: Reflections and Lessons Learned *151*
David E. DeMatthews and Sharon D. Kruse

Index *159*

List of Figures and Tables

Chapter 4
Fig. 4.1.   A Framework for Examining Interactions Between Schools and Mutual Respect in Classrooms.   52

Chapter 7
Fig. 7.1.   Practical Steps to Lead Through Disaster.   125

Chapter 4
Table 4.1.   Definitions and Examples of Mutual Respect in Practice.   53
Table 4.2.   Interrelated Priorities When Leading for Symmetry.   59

Chapter 7
Table 7.1.   Scholarship on the Student Outcomes Following a Natural Disaster.   107
Table 7.2.   Scholarship on the Role of School Leadership Following a Natural Disaster.   113

Chapter 8
Table 8.1.   Burnout and Mindfulness Contrasted.   137

About the Editors

David E. DeMatthews, PhD, is an Professor in the Department of Educational Leadership and Policy at the University of Texas at Austin and holds a courtesy appointment in the Department of Special Education. Prior to arriving at UT-Austin, DeMatthews was an Assistant Professor at the University of Texas at El Paso. He began his career in education working as a teacher, campus leader, and district administrator in Baltimore City Public Schools and the District of Columbia Public Schools. DeMatthews' research focuses on equitable and inclusive school improvement, with an emphasis on leadership and policy. More specifically, he aims to understand how districts and schools create equitable and inclusive schools at the intersections of race, social class, language, and other markers of identity. Given the importance of stable school leadership to school improvement processes, he has also cultivated a stream of research focused on principal career pathways, job-related stress and burnout, and turnover. He has published over 150 research articles in academic journals, book chapters, research reports, and editorials in media outlets. DeMatthews' research has been published in *Educational Researcher, Educational Administration Quarterly, AERA Open, Teachers College Record, Educational Policy, Journal of Educational Administration, Urban Education, Journal of School Leadership, Journal of Research on Leadership Education,* and *Leadership and Policy in Schools*. DeMatthews authored several books, including, *Community Engaged Leadership for Social Justice: A Critical Approach in Urban Schools* with Routledge. He regularly appears as a commentator on education policy issues in national and regional media outlets. DeMatthews' work and ideas have been featured in prominent media outlets including *The New York Times, Washington Post, USA Today, Associated Press, ABC News, Education Week, The Hill, The Dallas Morning News, Houston Chronicle,* and other regional outlets.

Sharon D. Kruse, PhD, is an Academic Director and Professor of Educational Leadership at Washington State University. Her scholarship broadly addresses two concerns: (1) to help teachers and school leaders better understand the key role leadership plays in schools and (2) to explore how education is currently structured and influenced by social and organizational complexity. Kruse's interests in education and organizational change are an extension of her desire to encourage district and school improvement, the development of communal leadership, and social justice through institutional and systemic reform. Her recent books include *Mindful Educational Leadership: Contemplative, Cognitive,* *and Organizational Systems and Practices* (Routledge); *Educational Leadership, Organizational Learning, and the Ideas of Karl Weick: Perspectives on Theory and Practice* (with Bob Johnson, Routledge); and *A Case Study Approach to Educational Leadership* (with Julie Gray, Routledge). Kruse is past editor of the Journal of Research on Leadership Education and past Director of the UCEA Center for the Study of Academic Leadership.

About the Contributors

Michalis Constantinides, PhD, is a Lecturer (Assistant Professor) in Educational Leadership and Management and the program leader for the MEd Educational Leadership at the School of Education, University of Glasgow. He received his Doctorate in Educational Leadership from University College London, Institute of Education. His research, teaching, and outreach focus on the organization and management of education systems and educational change with a particular focus on network-based continuous improvement. He has been working with schools and communities of schools at cross-national levels (England, Scotland, and New Zealand) promoting school-university partnerships and collaborations within a framework of shared values and aspirations. Michalis is also a member of the lead design team of US-based scholars in developing a new series of massive open online courses on *Transforming Education in an Interconnected World*. The aim is to create an "on-ramp" for teachers, leaders, parents, and community members as collaborators in improvement research.

Diamond Ebanks, PhD, earned her Doctorate from the Environment, Ecology and Energy Program at the University of North Carolina at Chapel Hill. Her community-based research focuses on the intersection of race, social vulnerability, and the movement of water, including both excess water (flooding) and the lack thereof (drought). Her areas of focus in research, teaching, and service are: environmental justice, race and disasters, qualitative methods, and diversity and equity. In her research, she seeks to understand the different ways marginalized communities advocate against vulnerability-making processes from outside influences and top-down "solutions." In the environmental classes she teaches, she asks students to identify the ways their identities – visible or invisible – contribute to how they understand and respond to different environmental issues. In her advocacy, she leverages the resources and privileges she has so they can be best used by others in their community struggles.

Megan Rauch Griffard, PhD, is an Assistant Professor in the Educational Policy and Leadership program at the University of Nevada, Las Vegas. She is delighted to be returning to her alma mater (MEd, 2014). Her research focuses on the role of school leaders in personnel working conditions, retention, and turnover. She is also interested in disruptions to schooling, such as natural disasters and pandemics. Griffard earned her Doctorate in Education from the University of North Carolina at Chapel Hill. In addition to her master's in education from UNLV,

Griffard holds a BA from Boston College and an MS from Northwestern University. Dr Griffard is also a former Clark County School District teacher.

Whitney M. Hegseth, PhD, is a Visiting Fellow of educational leadership at Boston College. Her anthropological and comparative research is focused on system-level supports for marginalized youth, so that they are equipped with the necessary confidence and skills to uphold a more just, democratic society. At present, Whitney examines leadership at the meso-level; she conducts comparative studies of educational systems, focusing on interactions between these systems, their environments, and classroom practice. Her publications consider how to (re)build educational systems for equity, antiracist practice, holistic student development, and mutual respect, and are geared toward scholars (e.g., *Educational Researcher, Anthropology and Humanism*), practitioners (e.g., *Oxford Research Encyclopedia of Education*), and policymakers (e.g., *the Brookings Institution*). Two recent awards demonstrate Whitney's rising presence in her field: the Outstanding Graduate Student Research Award from AERA's Educational Change SIG in 2023, and the Outstanding Dissertation Award from AERA's Systems Thinking SIG in 2022. Prior to Boston College, Whitney was trained in Educational Leadership, Policy, and Innovation (University of Michigan, PhD), International and Comparative Educational Policy (Stanford University, MA), and Sociocultural Anthropology (UC Berkeley, BA). She was a Research Analyst at Empirical Education, Inc. in Palo Alto, CA, and a K-12 teacher in France, Singapore, and the United States. Across these varied academic and professional experiences, Whitney has spent the past 15 years working on two interrelated topics: 1) how to improve our assumptions and treatment of young people; and 2) systemic school improvement.

Deidre M. Le Fevre, PhD, is a Professor in educational leadership at the University of Auckland, New Zealand. She began her career teaching in elementary and secondary schools in New Zealand and the United Kingdom before moving into academia. Her Doctorate is from the University of Michigan and she previously held positions at the University of Michigan and Washington State University, USA. Dr Le Fevre is currently the Academic Director for graduate programs in educational leadership at the University of Auckland where she leads a team of international researchers focusing on leadership, policy, and schooling improvement. She has led major international research grants focusing on leadership, equity, professional learning, and organizational improvement and serves on several international journal editorial boards. Dr Le Fevre has had the privilege of supporting many exceptional leaders across sectors and countries. She is committed to improving education. Her current research foci include the development of leaders' interpersonal capabilities, promoting effective process of change, and enabling professional learning that has a positive impact. She has published extensively and enjoys the ongoing challenge of seeking to understand the complexities of learning, teaching, leadership, and organizational improvement.

Melinda M. Mangin, PhD (she/her), is a Professor in the Graduate School of Education at Rutgers University where she teaches and conducts research related to teacher leadership and transgender identities in the context of PreK-12 schools. Mangin's scholarship is informed by her previous experience as a public high school Spanish teacher in New York City and North Carolina. She is a frequent speaker on the topic of teacher leadership and transgender children, presenting at national conferences, local schools, and teacher education preparation programs. Dr Mangin is the author of *Transgender Students in Elementary School: Creating an Affirming and Inclusive School Culture* (2020) and co-editor with Mario Suárez of *Trans Studies in K-12 Education: Creating an Agenda for Research and Practice* (2022). Dr Mangin's research and scholarship are supported by the Spencer Foundation.

Conor L. Scott is a practicing school administrator and doctoral candidate in the Graduate School of Education at Rutgers University. His research examines culturally responsive school leadership, the relationship between educational policy and school administration, and the role that school leaders play in alternately reproducing and dismantling inequities in school. Mr Scott has been an educator for more than 12 years. He has held roles as a social studies teacher, learning disabilities teacher-consultant, supervisor of special services, and assistant principal. Mr Scott employs critical race theory as a lens for understanding, critiquing, and improving educational systems, structures, and practices. As a researcher and future professor, Mr Scott aims to mobilize the knowledge needed to build more equitable school environments.

Jacob D. Skousen, EdD, earned his Doctorate from Boise State University in 2015 and joined the UNLV faculty UNLV in 2019. He also has a Master of Arts degree in Curriculum and Instruction with an emphasis in bilingual education, and a Master of Education degree in Educational Leadership and Administration. Dr Skousen is an Assistant Professor in educational policy and leadership in the Department of Educational Psychology, Leadership, and Higher Education. Prior to UNLV, Dr Skousen spent three years as an Assistant Professor in educational leadership and policy studies at the University of Northern Colorado. As a researcher, having had 15 years as a practitioner in P-12 education, as a teacher, instructional coach, and principal, he works to bridge theory and practice. Dr Skousen has a research agenda focused on leadership development and equity.

Patricia M. Virella PhD is an Assistant Professor in the Department of Educational Leadership at Montclair State University. Dr Virella's research focuses on implementing equity-oriented leadership through leader responses, organizational transformation, and preparation. Dr Virella also studies equity-oriented crisis leadership examining how school leaders can respond to crises without further harming marginalized communities.

Chapter 1

The Challenge and Promise of Reimagining School Leadership

Sharon D. Kruse[a] and David E. DeMatthews[b]

[a]Washington State University, USA
[b]University of Texas at Austin, USA

Abstract

This introductory chapter underscores the urgent need to reimagine school leadership in the face of unprecedented challenges and uncertainties, including the COVID-19 pandemic, ongoing struggles for racial justice, and declining trust in public institutions. The chapter argues that traditional, top-down leadership approaches no longer sufficiently meet the complex needs of students, families, and communities and advocates for paradigm shift toward more collaborative, adaptive, and equity-centered leadership practices. Leadership practices are suggested that build inclusive school communities, foster a culture of continuous learning, and prioritize the holistic well-being of every student are highlighted as crucial. Readers are challenged to rethink the very purpose and goals of education, moving beyond narrow measures of academic achievement to encompass the development of the whole child. Three key themes are introduced: (1) school characteristics and structures for facing future challenges, (2) leadership practices to initiate and support new organizational perspectives, and (3) innovative school organizations addressing crises and implications. The chapter asserts that transforming school leadership requires a fundamental rethinking of the structures, policies, and incentives that shape the work of educational leaders. Therefore, school leaders must be equipped with the knowledge, skills, and dispositions to lead for social justice, build culturally responsive school communities, and create transformative spaces where all students can thrive. This bold vision requires leaders to approach their work with humility, curiosity, and courage as they navigate the complexities of educational leadership in the 21st century.

Reimagining School Leadership, 1–11
Copyright © 2024 Sharon D. Kruse and David E. DeMatthews
Published under exclusive licence by Emerald Publishing Limited
doi:10.1108/978-1-83797-410-820241001

Keywords: Equity; adaptability; school transformation; education leadership; cultural responsiveness

Introduction

The COVID-19 pandemic, ongoing struggles for racial justice, and a growing sense of mistrust in public institutions have created significant barriers for school leaders in their efforts to improve schools. The sudden shift to remote learning during the pandemic exposed and exacerbated existing inequities in access to technology, internet connectivity, and supportive learning environments at home (Wharton-Beck et al., 2024; Zhao & Watterston, 2021). Additionally, the disproportionate impact of the virus on low-income communities and communities of color highlighted systemic health disparities and the need for schools to provide comprehensive support services beyond academics (Gee et al., 2023; Wharton-Beck et al., 2024). The racial justice protests of 2020, sparked by the deaths of George Floyd, Breonna Taylor, and other Black Americans, brought systemic racism and police brutality to the forefront, prompting many school leaders to reevaluate their approaches to diversity, equity, and inclusion. Furthermore, declining trust in public institutions, including schools, has made it more challenging for leaders to build consensus and support for improvement initiatives among students, families, and community members (Kavanagh et al., 2020). In the face of unprecedented challenges and uncertainties, it has become increasingly clear that the top-down, hierarchical, and compliance-oriented models of leadership that have long dominated our schools are no longer sufficient to meet the complex needs of our students, families, and communities. However, the current context also provides an important opportunity to critically consider and reimagine the future of school leadership.

The disruption caused by the pandemic has highlighted the need for more flexible, adaptable, and resilient leadership practices that can respond effectively to rapidly changing circumstances. The renewed focus on racial justice has underscored the importance of culturally responsive and antiracist leadership approaches that prioritize equity and address the unique needs and experiences of marginalized students and families. The erosion of trust in public institutions has created an urgent imperative for school leaders to engage in authentic community engagement, build strong relationships with stakeholders, and foster a sense of shared purpose and collective responsibility for student success. In this volume, we call for a reimagination of school leadership as a collaborative, adaptive, and equity-centered endeavor that prioritizes building collective capacity, fostering inclusive school communities, and addressing the unique needs and experiences of marginalized students and families. We contend this requires a fundamental rethinking of the goals and purposes of education, beyond narrow measures of academic achievement, to encompass the holistic development and well-being of every student.

We assert that while school leadership is critical to advancing student achievement and other educational equity initiatives, contemporary approaches to leadership and improvement are increasingly insufficient in a rapidly changing and unpredictable world. The research has long contended that traditional top-down, hierarchical leadership models that prioritize standardization, compliance, and accountability are ill-suited to the complex challenges facing schools today (Leithwood, 2021; Marshall, 1995; Murphy & Meyers, 2008). Instead, as researchers (DeMatthews et al., 2021; Rodela & Rodriguez-Mojica, 2020; Santamaría & Jean-Marie, 2014) have argued, school leaders must embrace more collaborative, distributed, and adaptive leadership practices that empower teachers, students, and families to cocreate solutions and drive continuous improvement. This requires a shift toward more relational, trust-based, and community-centered approaches to leadership that prioritize building collective capacity, fostering a sense of belonging and inclusivity, and leveraging the diverse strengths and perspectives of all members of the school community. At the heart of this transformation lies a recognition that schools are not just places of learning, but also vital spaces of belonging, healing, and empowerment (Allen et al., 2018; Darling-Hammond et al., 2020; Yosso, 2005). We contend, as do the chapter authors in this volume that transforming schools means actively working to dismantle the systemic barriers and biases that have historically marginalized certain groups of students, and intentionally cultivating a culture of care, compassion, and mutual respect. To do this, school leaders must engage in ongoing self-reflection and growth, confronting their own biases and blind spots and developing the cultural competence and humility needed to lead across differences. Furthermore, they must also be willing to share power and decision-making with students, families, and community members, recognizing that true progress can only be achieved through authentic collaboration and partnership.

It is imperative that educators critically consider current conceptions of school leadership and school improvement throughout the US and around the world with a focus on leading through uncertainty, building sustainability, and advancing student experiences and outcomes beyond narrow quantitative outcome measures such as test scores, graduation rates, and college admission rates. In this volume, we highlight the need to conceptualize innovative frameworks for schoolwork to develop a societal mode of growth that can better recognize and address the complexities of our times. Emerging from how schools' function in uncertainties and emergencies, the chapters explore alternative and innovative trajectories of schools as organizations within their local and regional systems. Of course, transforming school leadership is not just about individual leaders and their practices; it also requires a fundamental rethinking of the structures, policies, and incentives that shape the work of educational leaders. Too often, the pressure to improve test scores, raise graduation rates, and compete in a market-driven educational landscape can distract leaders from the deeper work of building inclusive, equitable, and transformative school communities (DeMatthews, 2018; Rodela & Rodriguez-Mojica, 2020).

To truly reimagine school leadership, leaders must also reimagine the systems and contexts in which leaders operate, creating the conditions and support structures that enable them to lead in more holistic, adaptive, and justice-oriented ways.

Recent contributions to the educational leadership literature have highlighted the need for attention to be paid to the role of leadership within and among diverse school contexts and increasing diversity within the student population (Bass, 2020; Kohli, 2018, 2019; Liang & Liou, 2018; Miller et al., 2011; Rodela & Rodriguez-Mojica, 2020; Santamaría & Jean-Marie, 2014). This research extends and, in many ways, challenges a long-standing tradition of leadership studies that have privileged narratives framed around primary leadership functions. These functions include providing instructional guidance for educators to ensure student growth and learning (Leithwood et al., 2004, Portin et al., 2009), creating and promoting a positive culture built on trust and one that creates a sense of belonging (Leithwood et al., 2020; Supovitz et al., 2010), creating systems that are shared and collaborative (Seashore Louis et al., 2010; Wahlstrom & Louis, 2008), distributive in nature (Cieminski, 2018; Knoeppel & Rinehart, 2008; Leithwood et al., 2004), transformational (Avolio et al., 2009; Bush, 2015; Day et al., 2016), and transformative (Shields, 2010). Yet, while this important and deep literature that has built a strong foundation of knowledge concerning the role of leadership in school improvement, this literature has not sufficiently addressed the limits of traditional approaches to instructional leadership and approaches that do not fully consider the multiple identities of students and the multiple experiences and outcomes that are important to school.

These limitations are particularly salient in the current moment, as school leaders face a myriad of challenges including the ongoing impact of the pandemic, continued racial injustice, and declining trust in public institutions. It must be emphasized that this means rethinking accountability systems that prioritize narrow measures of academic achievement over more holistic indicators of student and school success. To do so requires investing in the professional development and support structures that enable leaders to engage in ongoing learning, reflection, and growth (Kruse, 2023). And it means fostering greater collaboration and partnership between schools, families, and community organizations, recognizing that the work of education is a shared responsibility that extends beyond the walls of the classroom (Auerbach, 2010; DeMatthews, 2018; Khalifa, 2012).

Target Audience and Key Themes

This volume is primarily for education leadership researchers, faculty, graduate students, and school and district leaders seeking to better understand the context, challenges, and opportunities of school leadership in the present and future. The volume is part of the series, *Transforming Education Through Critical Leadership, Policy and Practice*. The series is based on the belief that those in educational leadership and policy-constructing roles have a moral obligation to educate for a robust critical and democratic citizenry, so that citizens may contribute to an open and fair society unafraid to critique different forms of contemporary colonial and neoliberal practices, while, at the same time, proposing alternatives consistent with a critical, socially just democracy. The series aims to publish work that challenges and offers alternatives to the excessive individualism, reductionism, standardization, deficit, and narrowly pragmatic neoliberal agenda that has increased marginalization and disengagement in education.

The content of this book responds to the series challenge and spans multiple contexts within the US and around the world and provides unique insights into how school leaders navigate the complexities of their contexts in ways that promote equity and sustainability. Drawing from international voices, the volume covers three key themes: (1) school characteristics and structures for facing future challenges, (2) leadership practices to initiate and support new organizational perspectives, and (3) innovative school organizations addressing crises and implications. These themes underscore a need for adaptable school structures, forward-thinking leadership approaches, and creative organizational models that can navigate uncertainty and crisis. Moreover, these themes suggest that the future of school leadership must be grounded in a commitment to equity, excellence, and the holistic well-being of every student, and a willingness to challenge the status quo and reimagine what is possible for our schools and communities.

To realize this vision, school leaders must be equipped with the knowledge, skills, and dispositions to lead for equity and social justice, to build culturally responsive and inclusive school communities, and to foster a culture of continuous learning and improvement (Khalifa et al., 2016; Larson & Murtadha, 2002). This requires a reimagining of leadership preparation programs (Bertrand & Rodela, 2018; Young, 2015) and professional development opportunities to better align with the complex realities and demands of 21st century schools (Jean-Marie et al., 2009). It also necessitates a shift in the structures, policies, and incentives that shape the work of school leaders, to create the conditions and support systems that enable them to lead in more innovative, adaptive, and equity-focused ways (Rogers, 2022).

We must approach the work of school leadership with a sense of humility, curiosity, and courage as we navigate the complexities and uncertainties of our times (Kruse, 2023). Leaders must be willing to question our assumptions, challenge the status quo, and imagine new possibilities for what education can and should be. They must be willing to take risks, make mistakes, and learn from our failures, recognizing that growth and progress often emerge from the most difficult and uncomfortable places. And they must be willing to center the voices, experiences, and aspirations of those who have been most marginalized and oppressed by our educational systems, recognizing that true equity and justice can only be achieved when we amplify the power and potential of every student, family, and community.

Ultimately, as these chapters suggest, the future of school leadership is about more than just improving student outcomes or closing gaps on standardized test scores. It is about creating schools that are vibrant, inclusive, and transformative spaces where all students can thrive and reach their full potential, and where the next generation of leaders and change-makers can be nurtured and empowered to create a more just, equitable, and sustainable world. This is the challenge and the opportunity facing school leaders today, and it is one that requires boldness, creativity, and an unwavering commitment to the power of education to transform lives and communities.

In conclusion, in this volume we grapple with the urgent need to transform school leadership in the face of unprecedented challenges and uncertainties. Together, the authors have purposefully attempted to balance theory with exemplars from practices taken from schools across the globe. Collectively, they underscore the limitations of traditional, top-down leadership approaches and advocate for a paradigm shift toward more collaborative, adaptive, and equity-centered practices. By emphasizing the importance of building inclusive school communities, fostering a culture of continuous learning, and prioritizing the holistic well-being of every student, the authors challenge us to rethink the very purpose and goals of education. They argue that school leaders must be equipped with the tools and dispositions to lead for social justice, dismantle systemic inequities, and create transformative spaces where all students can thrive.

Chapter Summaries

The edited book is composed of seven chapters and a conclusion. Each offers insights into school leadership that challenges the status quo. Each is conceptually distinct. Yet, those familiar with social justice theorizing will recognize overlapping constructs and dilemmas. We submit that together they underscore the fundamental links between leadership and equity. Finally, we conclude with a final chapter that explores societal commitment to public education's role in democracy and human potential and the reimagining of school leadership amid current challenges and opportunities.

Chapter 2, written by Michalis Constantinides, revisits, reinforces, and extends our view of the underpinning principles and practices of school leadership in Aotearoa New Zealand. Constantinides presents vignettes from case studies of schools that illustrate the crucial role of the principal in ensuring ongoing improvement and innovation while working in increasingly complex and uncertain environments. The chapter discusses the need to understand the importance of relationships between individuals and groups, actions, contexts, environments, and cultures where processes of interaction shape principals' practices. Features of complexity thinking are used as a lens through which to understand schools as complex adaptive systems and illustrate the importance of the dynamics of the interactions among the agents and elements within the New Zealand educational system. Constantinides concludes by drawing together the implications for leadership that emerge across this chapter.

Chapter 3, written by Diedre LeFevre, explores the challenges of engaging in leadership practices that promote equity and empower students who have traditionally been underserved in schooling continues throughout educational contexts. Complex challenges like this require complex solutions because they have multiple causes and interdependencies and thus requires leaders focus on systemic and sustainable change for improvement rather than taking a "fixing parts" approach. LeFevre focuses on promising approaches to leadership which can support capability in responding to such complex challenges. The chapter addresses four key areas for focus, (1) being comfortable with uncertainty, (2) understanding the role of emotion in leadership and change, (3) knowing how to interrupt problematic narratives, and (4) successfully engaging the views of young people. Implications for reimagining leadership include how to engage with diverse perspectives in decision-making, ways to support people struggling with the uncertainty of change, and how to lead sustainable responses to complex challenges.

Chapter 4, written by Whitney Hegseth, proposes a framework that can assist school leaders in working toward respect that is mutual and integrated with their other school improvement efforts. Hegseth defines mutual respect as the work of intervening on those power asymmetries typically found in classrooms, both between teachers and students, and among diverse groups of students, by way of according children increased equality, autonomy, and equity. Drawing on empirical examples from an ethnographic and comparative study of four elementary schools situated across two educational systems (i.e., Montessori and International Baccalaureate (IB)) and two national contexts (i.e., the United States and Canada), Hegseth highlights the need for a framework for mutual respect. The work of embedding symmetry, particularly in schools, which reflect the racism, classism, sexism, ableism, and heterosexism that is ever-present in broader society, is anything but straightforward. This is because: (1) mutual respect is multidimensional, and these dimensions can reinforce and conflict with one another in unexpected ways; and (2) mutual respect can be operationalized via a school's instructional, organizational, and social practices, again in ways that may conflict or work synergistically. By highlighting the complexity of leading for mutual respect, this framework is a first step toward supporting such efforts in leadership preparation and practice.

Chapter 5, written by Connor Scott and Melinda Mangin, considers school discipline practices and their effects. In recent decades, school discipline has become increasingly characterized by zero-tolerance policies that mandate predetermined punitive consequences for specific offenses. Zero-tolerance policies have not been shown to improve student behavioral outcomes or school climate. Further, these disciplinary policies are applied unevenly across schools and student populations. Despite the well-documented research base that demonstrates that these practices are ineffective, they remain commonplace in K-12 school across the United States. Transformative and culturally responsive educational leadership requires school leaders to examine the historical, societal, and institutional factors that contribute to the racial-discipline gap within their particular schools. This process requires committing to leading for racial justice, self-reflexive practice, and having the courage to boldly name and dismantle practices that do not create equitable outcomes for students on the margins. Drawing on tenets of Critical Race Theory and Culturally Responsive School Leadership to situate the history and proliferation of harmful disciplinary practices, this chapter discusses how critically reflexive school leaders can mobilize restorative practices to dismantle the systems, structures, and practices that reproduce inequities in schools. Scott and Mangin provide aspiring and practicing school leaders with the knowledge needed to reform existing school discipline policies and implement practices that support racial justice.

Chapter 6, written by Patricia Virella, delves into the transformative journey of Copley Public Schools (CPS) toward creating a more inclusive and just learning environment, mainly focusing on racial equity. The district's history of state control due to academic underperformance led to a shift toward antiracist and equitable practices under former superintendent Danielle Crane. In this chapter, Virella emphasizes the importance of achieving racial equity in schools, highlighting how one large urban school district engaged in a multiyear transformational process toward racial equity. The partnership between CPS and a university's educational leadership department was designed to address racial equity through a multiyear plan involving school and district leaders. The approach centered around Vygotsky's Zone of Proximal Development, emphasizing support for professional growth and equitable student outcomes. Virella outlines a detailed plan grounded in research and best practices, focusing on leadership roles in shaping school culture and driving transformation. Lessons learned from the district's racial equity transformation highlight positive outcomes while addressing challenges such as historical practices influencing policies and systemic barriers to improvement. Leaders worked toward forming coalitions of progress, emphasizing the importance of understanding past influences on present environments and the need for informed decision-making to foster racially equitable educational settings.

Chapter 7, written by Megan Griffard, Diamond Ebanks, and Jacob Skousen, discusses the role of school leadership in the face of climate disasters and environmental injustice. These disruptions to schooling are emblematic of increasing global uncertainty. School leaders play a pivotal role mitigating uncertainty following an environmental crisis or disaster through leadership activities that support their communities. However, preparing school leaders for unexpected disruptions to schooling has often been overlooked by preparation programs and professional development. The goal of this chapter is to equip school leaders with an essential understanding of both the influence of disasters and environmental injustice on schools and the tools to respond effectively to these events. First, Griffard et al. contextualizes environmental injustice and inequality as a factor that influences school and student performance, especially for students living below the poverty line and students of color. Next, they synthesize how school leaders have responded to prior instances of climate disasters and environmental injustice. Finally, key considerations for school leaders confronting future occurrences are presented.

Chapter 8 written by Sharon D. Kruse and David E. DeMatthews offers a powerful antidote to the stress and burnout facing many school leaders today. This chapter integrates three key streams of mindfulness research and practice – contemplative, cognitive, and organizational mindfulness – to present a more caring and compassionate model of educational leadership. Drawing on the experiences of focal school leaders, the chapter explores how mindful leadership practices can transform schools by cultivating awareness of self, others, and the larger environment, developing equanimity and resilience in the face of challenges, adopting a stance of curiosity and openness to multiple perspectives, nurturing authentic relationships and emotional attunement, and navigating paradoxes of purpose and identity with wisdom. Rather than a fixed technique, mindful leadership is presented as an ongoing practice and way of being – purposeful, present, and openhearted. By starting where they are and committing to continual growth, educational leaders can become leaders in fostering cultures of well-being and transformative learning. The chapter concludes with suggested mindfulness practices for individuals and organizations to support this lifelong journey. Mindful leadership is ultimately a courageous and pragmatic path to see reality, embrace vulnerability, and wholeheartedly engage in positive change more clearly.

Chapter 9 written by David E. DeMatthews and Sharon D. Kruse conclude the volume. The chapter synthesizes the increasing challenges principals face including the COVID-19 pandemic and increasing political attacks on public education. DeMatthews argues that despite concerns about principal turnover and stress, effective school leadership is critical for navigating current difficulties and enabling schools to be transformative spaces for students and communities to thrive. This edited volume explores how school leadership can be reimagined for greater effectiveness and sustainability in uncertain times, through evidence and insights from leaders in the US and globally. Key implications discussed include revising professional standards to prioritize principals' self-care and long-term, holistic student outcomes beyond standardized testing. Investing in research on principals' job-related stress and health, and providing training on coping strategies. Empowering distributed leadership among school staff and proactive crisis management plans. DeMatthews and Kruse conclude by calling for adequate supports and resources for principals, and a societal commitment to public education's role in democracy and human potential, to enable the reimagining of school leadership amid current challenges and opportunities.

References

Allen, K., Kern, M. L., Vella-Brodrick, D., Hattie, J., & Waters, L. (2018). What schools need to know about fostering school belonging: A meta-analysis. *Educational Psychology Review*, *30*(1), 1–34. https://doi.org/10.1007/s10648-016-9389-8

Auerbach, S. (2010). Beyond coffee with the principal: Toward leadership for authentic school–family partnerships. *Journal of School Leadership*, *20*(6), 728–757.

Avolio, B. J., Walumbwa, F. O., & Weber, T. J. (2009). Leadership: Current theories, research, and future directions. *Annual Review of Psychology*, *60*, 421–449.

Bass, L. (2020). *Caring leadership in schools: Practical wisdom for principals, teachers, and parents*. Springer.

Bertrand, M., & Rodela, K. C. (2018). A framework for rethinking educational leadership in the margins: Implications for social justice leadership preparation. *Journal of Research on Leadership Education*, *13*(1), 10–37. https://doi.org/10.1177/1942775117739414

Bush, T. (2015). Aspiring to leadership: Facilitators and barriers. *Educational Management Administration & Leadership, 43*(6), 855–860.

Cieminski, A. B. (2018). Practices that support leadership succession and principal retention. *Education Leadership Review, 19*(1), 21–41.

Darling-Hammond, L., Flook, L., Cook-Harvey, C., Barron, B., & Osher, D. (2020). Implications for educational practice of the science of learning and development. *Applied Developmental Science, 24*(2), 97–140. https://doi.org/10.1080/10888691.2018.1537791

Day, C., Gu, Q., & Sammons, P. (2016). The impact of leadership on student outcomes: How successful school leaders use transformational and instructional strategies to make a difference. *Educational Administration Quarterly, 52*(2), 221–258.

DeMatthews, D. (2018). Social justice dilemmas: Evidence on the successes and shortcomings of three principals trying to make a difference. *International Journal of Leadership in Education, 21*(5), 545–559.

DeMatthews, D. E., Serafini, A., & Watson, T. N. (2021). Leading inclusive schools: Principal perceptions, practices, and challenges to meaningful change. *Educational Administration Quarterly, 57*(1), 3–48. https://doi.org/10.1177/0013161X20913897

Gee, K., Asmundson, V., & Vang, T. (2023). Educational impacts of the COVID-19 pandemic in the United States: Inequities by race, ethnicity, and socioeconomic status. *Current Opinion in Psychology, 52*. https://doi.org/10.1016/j.copsyc.2023.101643

Jean-Marie, G., Normore, A. H., & Brooks, J. S. (2009). Leadership for social justice: Preparing 21st century school leaders for a new social order. *Journal of Research on Leadership Education, 4*(1), 1–31.

Kavanagh, J., Carman, K., DeYoreo, M., Chandler, S., & Davis, L. (2020). *The drivers of institutional trust and distrust: Exploring components of trustworthiness*. RAND Corporation. https://www.rand.org/pubs/research_reports/RRA112-7.html

Khalifa, M. (2012). A re-new-ed paradigm in successful urban school leadership: Principal as community leader. *Educational Administration Quarterly, 48*(3), 424–467.

Khalifa, M. A., Gooden, M. A., & Davis, J. E. (2016). Culturally responsive school leadership: A synthesis of the literature. *Review of Educational Research, 86*(4), 1272–1311.

Knoeppel, R. C., & Rinehart, J. S. (2008). Student achievement and principal quality: Explaining the relationship. *Journal of School Leadership, 18*(5), 501–527.

Kohli, R. (2018). Behind school doors: The impact of hostile racial climates on urban teachers of color. *Urban Education, 53*(3), 307–333.

Kohli, R. (2019). Lessons for teacher education: The role of critical professional development in teacher of color retention. *Journal of Teacher Education, 70*(1), 39–50.

Kruse, S. D. (2023). *Mindful educational leadership: Contemplative, cognitive, and organizational systems and practices*. Routledge.

Larson, C. L., & Murtadha, K. (2002). Leadership for social justice. *Teachers College Record, 104*(9), 134–161.

Leithwood, K. (2021). A review of evidence about equitable school leadership. *Education Sciences, 11*(8), 377. https://doi.org/10.3390/educsci11080377

Leithwood, K., Harris, A., & Hopkins, D. (2020). Seven strong claims about successful school leadership revisited. *School Leadership & Management*, *40*(1), 5–22.

Leithwood, K., Louis, K. S., Anderson, S., & Wahlstrom, K. (2004). *How leadership influences student learning: Review of research*. The Wallace Foundation.

Liang, J. G., & Liou, D. D. (2018). Transformational leadership and school change: A cross-cultural study. *Leadership and Policy in Schools*, *17*(4), 497–515.

Marshall, C. (1995). Imagining leadership. *Educational Administration Quarterly*, *31*(3), 484–492. https://doi.org/10.1177/0013161X95031003009

Miller, P. M., Brown, T., & Hopson, R. (2011). Centering love, hope, and trust in the community: Transformative urban leadership informed by Paulo Freire. *Urban Education*, *46*(5), 1078–1099.

Murphy, J., & Meyers, C. V. (2008). *Turning around failing schools: Leadership lessons from the organizational sciences*. Corwin Press.

Portin, B. S., Knapp, M. S., Dareff, S., Feldman, S., Russell, F. A., Samuelson, C., & Yeh, T. L. (2009). *Leadership for learning improvement in urban schools*. Center for the Study of Teaching and Policy.

Rodela, K. C., & Rodriguez-Mojica, C. (2020). Equity leadership informed by community cultural wealth: Counterstories of Latinx school administrators. *Educational Administration Quarterly*, *56*(2), 289–320.

Rogers, L. K. (2022). Is role change enough? District organizational supports for principal supervision. *Educational Administration Quarterly*, *58*(4), 527–560.

Santamaría, L. J., & Jean-Marie, G. (2014). Cross-cultural dimensions of applied, critical, and transformational leadership: Women principals advancing social justice and educational equity. *Cambridge Journal of Education*, *44*(3), 333–360.

Seashore Louis, K., Dretzke, B., & Wahlstrom, K. (2010). How does leadership affect student achievement? Results from a national US survey. *School Effectiveness and School Improvement*, *21*(3), 315–336.

Shields, C. M. (2010). Transformative leadership: Working for equity in diverse contexts. *Educational Administration Quarterly*, *46*(4), 558–589.

Supovitz, J., Sirinides, P., & May, H. (2010). How principals and peers influence teaching and learning. *Educational Administration Quarterly*, *46*(1), 31–56.

Wahlstrom, K. L., & Louis, K. S. (2008). How teachers experience principal leadership: The roles of professional community, trust, efficacy, and shared responsibility. *Educational Administration Quarterly*, *44*(4), 458–495.

Wharton-Beck, A., Chou, C. C., Gilbert, C., Johnson, B., & Beck, M. A. (2024). K-12 school leadership perspectives from the COVID-19 pandemic. *Policy Futures in Education*, *22*(1), 21–42. https://doi.org/10.1177/14782103221135620

Yosso, T. J. (2005). Whose culture has capital? A critical race theory discussion of community cultural wealth. *Race, Ethnicity and Education*, *8*(1), 69–91. https://doi.org/10.1080/1361332052000341006

Young, M. (2015). Effective leadership preparation: We know what it looks like and what it can do. *Journal of Research on Leadership Education*, *10*(1), 3–10.

Zhao, Y., & Watterston, J. (2021). The changes we need: Education post COVID-19. *Journal of Educational Change*, *22*(1), 3–12. https://doi.org/10.1007/s10833-021-09417-3

Chapter 2

Building and Sustaining Improvement in Disruptive Times: School Leadership in Aotearoa New Zealand

Michalis Constantinides

University of Glasgow, UK

Abstract

This chapter revisits, reinforces, and extends our view of the underpinning principles and practices of school leadership in Aotearoa New Zealand. It presents extracts from case studies of schools that illustrate the crucial role of the principal in ensuring ongoing improvement and innovation while working in increasingly complex and uncertain environments. The chapter discusses the need to understand the importance of relationships between individuals and groups, actions, contexts, environments, and cultures where processes of interaction shape principals' practices. Features of complexity thinking are used as a lens through which to understand schools as complex adaptive systems and illustrate the importance of the dynamics of the interactions among the agents and elements within the New Zealand educational system. The chapter concludes by drawing together the implications for leadership that emerge across this chapter.

Keywords: New Zealand; relationships; complexity; cultural responsiveness; leadership dynamics

Introduction

New Zealand, also known by its Māori name as Aotearoa, the "Land of the Long White Cloud," has a history of recognizing indigeneity as evidenced by the 1835 Declaration of Independence and the 1840 Te Tiriti o Waitangi

(Treaty of Waitangi).[1] The Treaty acknowledged distinctive rights that flowed from notions of aboriginal title (Durie, 1994) and, to this day, is regarded as the founding document of New Zealand. The principles of the Treaty – partnership, participation, and protection – guide much of the Crown's public policy in relation to Māori (Boulton et al., 2004). Partnership and participation imply interactions, commitment, honor, faith, and respect between Māori and non-Māori and sharing of rights between both parties of the Treaty (Te Puni Kōkiri, 2001). Protection of Māori people, their property, and culture are linked to the third principle of the Treaty which refers to respecting Māori for whom they are and acknowledging their cultural identity.

In the educational context of New Zealand, the founding document is stated in a range of policy documents (e.g., New Zealand Curriculum, Ka Hikitia) emphasizing the need to be responsive to and actively addressing the principles of the Treaty. Schools in New Zealand enjoy high levels of autonomy, elements of which involve increased decision-making about school improvement processes by the principals. The bicultural nature of the education system requires school leaders to be relationally and culturally responsive to diversity and social justice by recognizing their commitment to the principles of Te Tiriti o Waitangi (Treaty of Waitangi) and in their practices. The New Zealand education system is undergoing major systemic reforms with new initiatives aimed at addressing inequities and academic achievement challenges. These new initiatives are intended to provide support and guidance for educators, school governors, and parents and allow schools to be more responsive to the communities they serve (Ministry of Education, 2019). Central to their design is the improvement of educational outcomes for indigenous Māori and Pacific students and young people from low-socioeconomic backgrounds. Yet, achievement disparities between the Māori and Pākehā (Aotearoa New Zealand citizens of European ancestry) students continue to be of concern. Students' performance in OECD/PISA rankings has been steadily declining, and while still above the OECD average, Māori and Pasifika students score lower than the OECD average achievement (Tomorrow's Schools Independent Taskforce, 2018).

The role of educational leadership and more specifically that of the principal has been critical in challenging and addressing inequitable discourses, acting as advocate for those whose voice is not always represented and provide equal opportunities for all. In 2018, a new leadership capability framework was published by the Education Council | Mātatu Aotearoa providing guidelines for leadership development through a set of core capabilities (Wylie & McKinley, 2018). This document was supplemented by The Leadership Strategy for the Teaching Profession of Aotearoa New Zealand (2018) to include, "the growth and development of leadership capability for all registered teachers across English medium and Māori medium settings in New Zealand – in both positional and

---

[1] Founding document of the country written and signed in 1840 as a means of partnership between Māori and the government (represented by the Crown) of New Zealand.

non-positional leadership roles" (Education Council, 2018, p. 4). The key principles are centered on capacity building and a culture of collaboration and relational trust where leaders are expected to become successful agents of change and meet the needs of the learners. More specifically, forms of collaboration imply collective pursuit of shared goals for the students in the broader community, including all phases of education, whereas relational trust is seen as building cohesive, purposeful partnerships, communities, and networks. Despite the aspirational targets, details of practical applications of these leadership strategies with consideration of contextual factors as well as opportunities for leadership preparation are rather limited.

Educational Leadership Landscape in Aotearoa New Zealand

The links between the impact and influence of particular approaches to leadership as well as practices and student outcomes are well evidenced in a large body of literature across different countries (Day et al., 2016; Grissom et al., 2021; Leithwood et al., 2020; Robinson et al., 2008; Silins et al., 2002). However, academic outcome measures do not cover the full social and emotional outcomes that are also valued in many school systems. The paucity of studies linking social, emotional, and cultural student outcomes to the quality of leadership may be a limitation of the current body of research. Statistical analyses of leadership effects on student outcomes need separation of the effects of leadership from the effects of other variables, for instance, differences in students' socioeconomic background, school composition, and prior achievement levels. For example, in the United States, federal, state and school district administrations are responsible for collecting standardized assessments on many of these variables, and the resulting data sets are made available, under certain conditions, to researchers. In contrast, the New Zealand Ministry of Education takes no responsibility for generating and using such data sets, and this is one major reason why there are no large-scale New Zealand studies of the impact of any school-level variable, including leadership, on student outcomes.

As the professional and organizational challenges facing school leaders become increasingly complex, their role features high levels of ambiguity and uncertainty in achieving desired outcomes for all. This is because societal and institutional forces impacting the environment in which they work can still shape the development and interpretation of policies and reforms. Yet, how leaders navigate complex and ambiguous environmental expectations (e.g., regulations from government bodies, stakeholder needs, professional or societal norms) depends on how they act as key agents of change, make sense of their role and how they construct, make meaning, and negotiate tensions and contradictions to respond to the dilemmas that arise in their environment.

Aotearoa New Zealand is going through a big change in the principal population with more than a third of the total principal population being less than 5 years in the role. New Zealand government's external evaluation agency, the Education Review Office (ERO), conducted a mixed-methods study of new principals moving into the role (before being appointed), as well as their first 5 years of being a principal (ERO, 2023). This included a wide range of tools such as: surveys of 596 new principals (representing more than two thirds of all the new principals) and surveys of 317 board chairs/presiding members that work with new principals, in-depth interviews with 21 new principals and 16 key experts in principle pathways and supports as well as secondary analyses of local and international systems, policies, and research evidence around pathways for new and emerging principals. Drawing on previous policy documents published by either the New Zealand Government or the Governments of Australia and the United Kingdom, 11 key areas of principal practice were identified as necessary for New Zealand principals:

(1) Giving effect to Te Tiriti o Waitangi throughout the school (including active implementation of decolonization and antiracism strategies)
(2) Working in partnership with whānau (extended family) Māori, hapū, and iwi to develop a localized curriculum that is inclusive of mātauranga Māori (Māori Knowledge)
(3) Establishing and maintaining a clear shared vision, strategic direction, and goals for the school
(4) Building and maintaining positive, effective relationships with staff and learners (this includes school leadership, teachers, other staff, and learners)
(5) Building and maintaining positive, effective relationships with the school community (this includes with parents and whānau, community groups and networks, relevant agencies, neighboring schools and early learning services/tertiary providers, and others)
(6) Ensuring the delivery of high-quality teaching practice and curriculum across the school (this may involve direct or indirect leadership and oversight)
(7) Working with data to monitor and evaluate teaching and learning
(8) Working closely with diverse families and community groups to promote inclusion for all learners
(9) Managing the school's resources, for example, finances, employment, timetabling, and property
(10) Working effectively with the school's board members
(11) Ensuring the school complies with all legislative and policy requirements

Findings from this study identified five areas that require action to help ensure new principals in Aotearoa New Zealand's schools are set up to succeed:

(1) Establish accessible and sufficient pathways for aspiring leaders to become principals.
(2) Ensure there are sufficient, accessible, and evidence-based development opportunities for aspiring principals.
(3) Support the delivery of accessible and evidence-based development opportunities once new principals start in the role.

(4) Prioritize preparing and supporting principals in small schools.
(5) Ensure Māori aspiring leaders have clear, well-supported pathways into school leadership.

Although leadership professional development is being reevaluated in New Zealand and increasing calls from the Education Council (2018) highlight the importance of creating, developing, and sustaining leadership capabilities for all registered teachers and leaders across English and Māori medium settings, yet there is no systematic professional development in place to support educational practitioners growing leadership skills and dispositions. As a result, the aspirations to build leadership capacity and capability of the New Zealand educational leaders are stated as general principles.

Complexity Perspective in Educational Leadership

The use of complexity science as a lens through which to gain deeper insight into how education operates as a complex system and how different processes unfold in a given education ecology is still in its infancy (Jacobson et al., 2019; Stacey, 2007). A central concept within this perspective is the "complex adaptive system" in which "a diversity of agents... interact with each other, mutually affect each other, and in so doing generate novel, emergent, behavior for the system as a whole" (Lewin, 1999, p. 198). Schools are such "complex adaptive systems," composed of agents and elements. Agents refer to the people within the educational environment that have influence over how change processes unfold, whereas elements constitute the conditions under which the agents act.

As complex adaptive systems, schools are characterized by interdependent elements operating at multiple system levels and the larger systems of which they are a part, interact with and adapt to one another by generating distinct patterns and routines in unpredictable ways, becoming more than the sum of individual parts (Constantinides, 2021; Senge et al., 2012; Shaked & Schechter, 2017). In order to respond to the disruptions and perturbations occurring in their environment, adaptive systems need power and authority to be decentralized, system elements to sustain a productive balance on the edge of chaos, and everyone involved (i.e., students, teachers, principals, and parents) to embrace a core vision framed with shared values, beliefs, policies, and practices. As complex adaptive systems, schools are not capable of shaping the dynamics and leading the whole system independently from others (Kershner & McQuillan, 2016). Instead, systems are "adaptive" in terms of responding to their environment. Similarly, mutual interactions between different school units or components codevelop together as well. This means that the components and their interrelationships are subject to ongoing codevelopment and collaboration. This enables them to "learn" and react effectively in uncertain and dynamic environments while at the same time, they embody their histories (Jacobson et al., 2019). In the same vein, New Zealand schools are deeply embedded in their external environment they interact with, and the history of this interaction affects their development.

Other main complex systems concepts are emergence and self-organization. Emergence is a fundamental construct in complex systems research, which is broadly defined as the formation of new properties or patterns at a system's macro-level from self-organizing interactions of elements at a system's micro-level (Mitchell, 2009). Emergence describes patterns that become evident that are characteristic of whole systems, not of individual elements. Individual elements function separately but interdependently, and the elements are described as self-organizing. An example of a biological system that can be thought of as a complex system is the human brain, with neurons the separate elements (Morowitz, 1995). The aforementioned features are used in the following sections to discuss and navigate the dilemmas of leadership that arise in complex adaptive systems.

Leading in Times of Uncertainty

Leading schools through crises and especially during the COVID-19 pandemic revealed how powerful the role of school leadership has been in successfully navigating through uncertainty. The New Zealand national lockdown was shorter than for many countries, with most schools being completely closed for between 7 and 9 weeks. Schools faced multiple challenges and school leaders had to consider how to lead in complex situations and adapt their leadership approaches. Several studies were conducted regarding leadership practices over lockdown which explored both the challenges and opportunities that arose in the context of New Zealand (Mutch, 2020; Thornton, 2021) and beyond (Hulme et al., 2021; Longmuir, 2021; Striepe & Cunningham, 2021).

One way to understand school principals' role when facing uncertainty is to do it through a sensemaking perspective. This approach considers both the increasingly complex world principals face (Johnson & Kruse, 2019) as well as the complexity of the sensemaking process itself (Gioia et al., 1994). The former involves the efforts of individuals to interpret and understand their ever-changing environment (Maitlis, 2005), whereas the latter involves the interplay between action and interpretation (Weick et al., 2005). A study of 18 principals from across New Zealand conducted by Thornton (2021) found five leadership practices in response to the COVID-19 pandemic crisis. These were: detecting signals through a sensemaking process and responding appropriately; demonstrating empathy and prioritizing well-being; communicating frequently and effectively; leading collaboratively through a community leadership role; and taking opportunities to learn at all stages of the crisis. Sensemaking is a continual process but is thought to be heightened during times of uncertainty and ambiguity. In Thornton's (2021) study, this strategy was particularly highlighted in the early phases of the crisis as an important element that could determine critical decision-making and planning. More specifically, the author argues that school principals in her study were able to detect early signals of the health crisis which in turn enabled the adequate planning and better preparation of the school community by ensuring the availability of digital devices for all students while organizing staff professional learning and having trail online learning days.

Flow of Interaction and Communication

In times of crises, communication becomes a vital tool that can have a significant impact on school's organizational culture. School leaders in the New Zealand studies were able to establish strong channels of communication and convey their expectations to cope with the rapid changes associated with crisis development (Mutch, 2020; Notman, 2015; Thornton, 2021). Examples included regular check-ins with students, staff, and families over well-being and safety issues via two-way communication through several communication channels (e.g., texts, emails, social media). During the delivery of remote learning, principals displayed an empathetic stance toward students and staff via meaningful and sympathetic communication and interaction repeatedly trying to minimize feelings of alienation and isolation among staff members.

In addition, distributed and collegial often in tandem with collaborative leadership emerged as crisis responsive approaches. School principals acknowledged the value of trust and belief in one another and the importance of leadership and collegial willingness to support staff during a crisis. Their adopted "crisis leadership" involved the distribution of leadership to staff, community leadership, involvement in community networks, and keeping families connected and informed about the efforts schools made during crises periods. Working together as a team appeared to foster a sense of belongingness which was found to be critical for better educational outcomes (Notman, 2015; Thornton, 2021). Mutch (2020) highlights the important role of schools in their communities resulting from their close relationships with families and suggests that in times of crisis, this role becomes even more crucial. While in natural disasters, such as earthquakes, schools may offer physical shelter, in the case of the COVID-19 pandemic, this support took the form of coordinating resources and services as well as providing moral support. Mutch (2020, p. 9) advocates for schools to support communities refocus and "model how to move forward with purpose and hope."

People's communication, relationships, and interactions in schools are a critical consideration for appreciating the benefits of complexity sciences and for understanding complex responsive processes. Exploring ways of thinking in terms of complex responsive processes offer a powerful account of how patterns form in the thinking, feeling, and behavior of both individuals and groups, and how both continuity and novelty emerge spontaneously in those patterns as a result of self-organizing processes. Stacey et al. (2000) argue that the loose translation of complexity ideas into the social domain presents "complex systems as objective realities that scientists can stand outside of ... and see their modeling work as a route to increasing the ability of humans to control complex worlds" (Stacey et al., 2000, p. 9). Central to the critique is that no one can step outside the human social systems to which they are applying complexity ideas and see the "system as a whole," school leaders are themselves involved in the local interactions:

> If organizations are metaphorically or analogically like complex adaptive systems, then leaders are agents in those systems ... They are participants unable to step outside ... The dynamics and the emergent behaviour arise through their participation not their acts of design. (Stacey et al., 2000, p. 206)

School leaders are considered part of the flow of interaction and communication between people that constitute the "system." The focus is on the nature of interaction and communication between people. The word "system" is therefore better understood as a shorthand for processes that result in emergent patterns. Individuals or groups experience systemic effects, but no one can step outside those processes. Leaders cannot determine patterns of interaction or choose the future of their school which will emerge from interactions; as in times of crises in New Zealand (e.g., COVID-19, earthquakes), they did not have control. However, school leaders in the aforementioned examples had influence, not as designers but as participants too. This view offers a way of understanding the nature of schools in which leaders act and whose future they seek to influence. It means focusing on the processes which take place through interactions, direct or indirect, between people individually and in groups (e.g., parents, wider community).

Collaboration and Trust as Emergent Processes

Generating new and productive forms of collaboration where trust and confidence are based on an ethic of care, are central to crisis leadership work (Schechter et al., 2022). Leading through crises in the New Zealand context would not have been possible through collaborative processes, which stemmed from how responses to and recovery from crises rely on the relationships between key stakeholders, within and outside the school community. Such processes are oriented to innovation in "complex dynamic environments" and respond to change, adaptation, and emergence in settings where uncertainty and turbulence are challenges. Closely aligned with this phenomenon are Notman's (2015) findings of principalship in the wake of the Christchurch major earthquake in 2011. He explored school leadership through situations of crisis management following a catastrophic earthquake in the city of Christchurch, New Zealand in 2011. Notman (2015, p. 451) highlighted the limited research evidence into the experiences and practices of school leaders in times of crises and found that a sense of "collective cohesion" emerged where school leaders derived support for the intensity of their work from the community around them. The leaders focused on building "a strong sense of group cohesiveness" (Notman, 2015, p. 452) where trust and confidence, based on an ethic of care, were vital to crisis leadership work. In addition, school leaders identified the need to improve the conditions for teaching and learning. This was balanced against the impact of the disruption from the earthquake crisis by working through a reconfiguring process that anticipated a "state of new normal" (Notman, 2015, p. 456). Guided through this process, leaders recognized that they were not seeking to return to the prior status quo, but to adapt and adjust their strategies to the new environments, relationships, and interactions shaped by the shared experiences.

The concept of trust is closely associated with a positive school ethos, improved conditions for teaching and learning and sustained student behavior, engagement, and outcomes (Bryk & Schneider, 2002; Le Fevre & Robinson, 2015) and was necessary for school principals to share their vulnerability, and take risks when uncertainty was high. During a time of ambiguity and urgency in the context of New Zealand, such emerging dispositions and practices were reflected in the principals' capacity to build a sense of caring into their practice and foster relational trust (Mutch, 2020; Notman, 2015). They made sure that schools became safe and nurturing environments for students, staff, and the community. It is also evident from this, and the wider literature on successful school leadership, that successful school leaders provide certainty, hope, guidance, and ensure open and trusted communication within and beyond the school community (Constantinides, 2023; Leithwood et al., 2020).

Recognizing Culturally Relevant and Complex Leadership Practices

The bicultural nature of the education system highlights the importance of culturally relevant pedagogies and situational leadership strategies. Culturally relevant approaches to research advocate for inclusiveness wherein Indigenous ways of knowing and doing are valued (Bishop et al., 2009; Macfarlane, 2015). Durie (2001a) argues that any attempt at measuring better outcomes for Māori means that these outcomes must be defined by Māori. In his address to the Ministry of Education in 2001, Sir Mason Durie proposed a bottom line for Māori education:

> A starting point, and one likely to gain wide approval is that education should be consistent with the goal of enabling Māori to live as Māori. That means being able to have access to te ao Māori, the Māori world – access to language, culture, marae, resources such as land, tikanga, whānau, kaimoana. The extent that the purpose of education is to prepare people for participation in society, it needs to be remembered that preparation for participation in Māori society is also required. If after twelve or so years of formal education a Māori youth were totally unprepared to interact within te ao Māori [the Māori world], then no matter what else had been learned, education would have been incomplete.

A consistent message emerges from the literature, particularly from Māori academics, that there is a need for the education system to meet the needs for Māori, rather than Māori needing to fit the education system (Berryman et al., 2017; Bishop et al., 2009; Macfarlane, 2015). This highlights a concern that the methods for determining Māori educational success are flawed. And that the expectation to simultaneously implement western oriented policies and reforms can lead to a sense of incoherence in the system. This stresses the complexity of New Zealand's education system which implies diversity and also multiple connections between a wide range of elements or part of the whole. Accordingly, a system is to be understood as a set of interacting or interdependent entities forming an integrated whole. Complexity is particularly sensitive to systemic properties and relationships, rejecting the reductionist assertion that complex systems can be wholly understood through the analysis of their constituent parts. Since many systemic properties are emergent, arising from the relationships and interaction of the parts over time, the whole can be said to be "greater than the sum of its parts."

Several culturally relevant frameworks have been developed through Māori lenses so that the various interacting parts of the education system hang together, become more coherent, and enable meaning making to emerge with more clarity and fairness. One example (among others) of culturally responsive frameworks and pedagogies is Durie's (2001b) concept of *mauri ora* demonstrated when a person is engaged in positive relationships with others, feels a sense of belonging, is spiritually and emotionally strong, and is positive and energetic. For Māori, this means that success enables them to walk confidently and with mana in the two worlds of Aotearoa New Zealand. Another example of a framework built on culturally responsive pedagogy is Macfarlane's (2004) *Educultural Wheel* illustrated through relational values and strategies for assisting teachers in establishing a culture of care. These values are expressed as key cultural concept bases for effective classroom and leadership strategies. The first four core values develop and support the realization of the fifth core value, pumawanatanga. The concepts are relational and entwined. None occur without the other and they strengthen each other. They are: whanaungatanga (building relationships), rangatiratanga (teacher effectiveness), manaakitanga (ethic of caring), kotahitanga (ethic of bonding), and pumanawatanga (morale, tone, pulse) – breathing life into the other four values (Macfarlane et al., 2012). Social inclusion is situated at the core of these frameworks aspiring to drive the policy agenda, schooling, and the New Zealand education system and should be central in promoting cohesion in social systems, such as schools, and by extension societies that are increasingly diverse, culturally, and linguistically. When dealing with the increasing complexity of education systems and their subsystems (e.g., teachers, students, parents, policy-making entities, and so on), understanding the nature of interactions and how they operate in the context of an environment is vital. The school-environment system and the subsystems it contains is itself characterized by change and in line with the aforementioned culturally relevant pedagogies. Social change can be explained by the social system developing through a progressive process of transformation to create increasingly complex structures. These structures become stratified in response to specific functional imperatives. Transformation is necessary to allow specialization and specialization leads to more advanced knowledge, but interdependence is essential because the complexity framing maintains the coherence of the whole.

New Zealand-based studies outline how successful practices are enacted in context with cultural responsiveness and socioeducational transformation. In combination with the situational and cultural demands related to their contextual circumstances, culturally responsive principals acknowledge the need to strengthen culturally responsive and relational pedagogies, advance an inclusive school culture and a culture of success for all, especially for indigenous Māori students, and reframe the curriculum to address local needs (Notman, 2020; Notman & Henry, 2011). One primary principal's case in a Māori girls' college highlighted the need for a new principal to reassess the existing school context before implementing changes. The principal was herself Māori and acknowledged the importance of the principle of whakapapa (genealogy) which allowed her to position, contextualize, and nurture the relationships between people in the school and wider community (Notman, 2011). These adaptive communication patterns depended upon her responsiveness toward and awareness of the cultural needs of the school and students. In practice, this responsiveness focused on sound planning and organizational practices, and strong levels of communication with parents and the wider community.

Moreover, Notman (2020) reports on a case study of two secondary coprincipals that identifies adaptive strategies and success factors in a joint leadership role. Despite the challenges in a joint senior leadership position, both coprincipals had been successful at the school because the clarity of vision and values informed their day-to-day practices and behaviors and were considered as some of the core success factors. Nonetheless, it is important to acknowledge that opportunities to distribute leadership practices are reduced in smaller or isolated schools. To become an adaptive system with capacity as a holistic concept (Stoll, 2009), school leaders in the study by Notman (2020) had to take charge of and initiate change. The purpose of capacity building focused on developing knowledge, skills, and qualities of school leaders, who were expected to redesign and nurture their school culture so that staff participation, collaboration, and a sense of individual and collective belonging and ownership of the school's strategic vision would be fostered. "Capacity" in these examples was seen as a quality that allowed people, individually – personal capacity and collectively – school, to learn from the environment around them and to apply this learning to new situations in order to achieve their objectives in an ever-changing context. These objectives were oriented toward making a difference for all students and in all aspects of learning considering the multifaceted nature of capacity building. In a similar vein, drawing on motivation to understand a system's collective response to disequilibrium, McQuillan (2020) argues that without the capacity of system actors to adapt system interactions and outcomes, the status quo will likely endure.

Similarly, Notman and Henry (2011) comment on the ability of successful principals to create holistic development with equal attention to students' academic, social, and cultural development through clearly articulated expectations for curriculum and teaching and learning. The focus on leading learning was seen as a social and situated practice that was often coenacted by principals, teachers, students, and the wider community using cultural, intellectual, and material resources found in their classrooms, schools, and community contexts. In this way, case study principals built on the diverse cultural repertoires of students and their families and embraced culturally responsive approaches that not only recognize but also actively engage students' cultural resources in teaching and learning, allowing them to develop an identity and sense of ownership and belonging.

Culturally responsive and situational approaches are appropriately represented as multiple adaptations made in response to multiple stimuli, both originating in the environment and, internally, in the reflexivity of agency. This emphasis on reflexivity raises questions about how far new skills of recontextualizing can be seen as constitutive. The study of complex adaptive systems is further complicated by the reflexivity of actors (leaders, teachers) capable of absorbing and adjusting to the very knowledge produced about them. Reflexivity in agency and on the interplay of influences should be encouraged so that actors at the micro-level (e.g., schools) can also be attuned to making decisions based on systemic considerations, which is aligned with Goldspink's (2007) argument to leverage on collective intelligence to "develop viable responses to the more perennially difficult aspects of administration" (p. 46). Similarly, Hazy et al. (2007) call for leaders to "enact formal organizational policies and processes for emergence and self-organization to happen" (p. 95) in a complex adaptive system characterized by semiautonomous agents having the capacities to adapt to the changing environment.

In addition, several case studies highlight the need to empower staff to model and drive collective learning to accelerate the transition into a more equitable and sustainable improvement journey (Jacobson & Notman, 2018; Notman, 2020). Principals in these cases embraced shared decision-making and leadership approaches that offered greater opportunities for capacity building through distributed leadership roles. This decentralized and distributed decision-making approach promotes self-organization at the ground level and would echo the dynamics of complex systems. According to Leithwood et al. (2009), complexity science holds "promise for unpacking the nature and consequences of distributed leadership" (p. 6).

Collectively, the findings presented here highlight how school leaders purposefully worked to create and sustain their school communities on elements of trust grounded in cultural relationships that could in turn provide short- and long-term positive outcomes. Existing literature on culturally responsive leadership often explains the ways in which educational leaders "understand, respond, incorporate, accommodate, and ultimately celebrate the entirety of the children they serve" (Khalifa et al., 2016, pp. 6–7). Behaviors displayed by these leaders were relational and holistic and gained their meaning from the web of relationships that made up the school's culture (Khalifa et al., 2016). These exemplar findings are also consistent with the literature on culturally responsive leadership which suggests that leaders who seek to change a school's environment must understand the existing culture before any further action can be taken (Berryman et al., 2017; Khalifa, 2018; Leithwood et al., 2008). As such, from a complexity perspective, reading the broad indicators of school organizational culture matters. Nonetheless, attending to local experiences may prove more productive if these leaders are to understand an organization's culture in ways that contribute to overall organizational well-being (Fullan, 2016; Schein, 2010). When viewed as something generated from within the organization, rather than imposed as a result of leadership choice and action, the construct became more nuanced and, as opposed to the broader understanding and uses, increasingly valuable. Many school leaders in the New Zealand-based studies recognized that in order to enact a culturally responsive pedagogy of relations, they had to replace change-resistant cultures with learning cultures emphasizing the collective responsibility for each other's well-being and learning, including a sense of collective commitment and cultural connectedness. From this standpoint, cultural values are critical to adaptive change. Once leadership becomes an influence process that emerges through interactions at multiple levels across the organization, then relationships among system agents will lead to greater adaptability and creativity (Goldstein et al., 2010).

Implications and Conclusion

This chapter detailed some of the approaches used by school leaders in New Zealand during times of crisis while also addressing cultural, historical, and social educational issues. It revealed the complex nature of school leadership in disrupting the "normalcy" within the New Zealand schooling landscape and in turn amplifying challenges in the modern organizational context forcing an adaptation of "traditional" school leadership practices in the face of increasingly volatile, complex, and ambiguous environments. The research presented in this chapter has important implications for equity, professional learning, and leadership development.

Attention to equity challenges appears to be most effective as impetus for system and cultural change when part of the process led by principals involves many stakeholders who perceive that they equally own the process toward change and prioritize this process over other pressures stemming from their institutional environment (e.g., external accountability, school competition, bureaucratic control). Although Māori students in New Zealand schools are the second largest ethnic group after Pākehā/European students, there are precious few principals and senior leaders within schools who are Māori. This may be one of the factors that to date limits community engagement, cultural responsiveness, and commitment to Māori attainment. Therefore, the importance of relationships may be seen as a key enabler of culturally responsive pedagogies (Berryman et al., 2015; Bishop et al., 2009; Hynds et al., 2011). Initiating and sustaining pedagogical approaches in ways that are just and responsive to the needs of Māori would essentially validate local Māori knowledge systems and sites of cultural significance as being rich learning contexts (Macfarlane et al., 2019). This expectation requires continuous professional development activities and constant consultation with local communities.

The evidence presented in this chapter also suggests that the (cultural) complexity of schooling in New Zealand presents education leaders with an opportunity to build dynamic infrastructures to support their educational establishments in learning and improvement. It requires leaders to see the whole school as a complex structure with many interdependent components prompting increased coordination and collaboration based on elements of trust and cultural connectedness. For school leaders, the implications are clear: adaptive leadership approaches and dispositions are needed in order to respond to manifestly complex and unpredictable situations. These leaders will need the capacity to lead an education profession that is constantly in flux and demonstrate a sophisticated systems and values-centered approach with which staff, students, and the wider community are at the heart of the learning environments. To survive, evolve, and thrive in their changing environments, they must understand themselves, the nature of their boundaries, and the possibilities and constraints within their environment.

References

Berryman, M., Egan, M., & Ford, T. (2017). Examining the potential of critical and Kaupapa Māori approaches to leading education reform in New Zealand's English-medium secondary schools. *International Journal of Leadership in Education, 20*(5), 525–538.

Berryman, M., Ford, T., Nevin, A., & SooHoo, S. (2015). Culturally-responsive contexts: Establishing relationships for inclusion. *International Journal of Special Education, 30*(3), 39–51.

Bishop, R., Berryman, M., Cavanagh, T., & Teddy, L. (2009). Te Kotahitanga: Addressing educational disparities facing Māori students in New Zealand. *Teaching and Teacher Education, 25*(5), 734–742.

Boulton, A., Simonsen, K., Walker, T., Cumming, J., & Cunningham, C. (2004). Indigenous participation in the "new" New Zealand health structure. *Journal of Health Services Research & Policy, 9*(2_suppl), 35–40.

Bryk, A. S., & Schneider, B. L. (2002). *Trust in schools: A core source for improvement.* Russell Sage Foundation Publications.

Constantinides, M. (2021). Understanding the complexity of system-level leadership in the English schooling landscape. *Journal of Educational Administration, 59*(6), 688–701.

Constantinides, M. (2023). Successful school leadership in New Zealand: A scoping review. *Education Sciences, 13*(12).

Day, C., Gu, Q., & Sammons, P. (2016). The impact of leadership on student outcomes: How successful school leaders use transformational and instructional strategies to make a difference. *Educational Administration Quarterly, 52*(2), 221–258.

Durie, M. H. (1994). *Whaiora Māori health development.* Oxford University Press.

Durie, M. (2001a). *A framework for considering Māori educational advancement*. Massey University.

Durie, M. (2001b). *Mauri Ora: The dynamics of Māori health*. Oxford University Press.

Education Council. (2018). *The leadership strategy for the teaching profession of Aotearoa New Zealand: Enabling every teacher to develop their leadership capability*. Education Council.

Education Review Office (ERO). (2023). *'Everything was new': Preparing and supporting new principals*. New Zealand Government.

Fullan, M. (2016). The elusive nature of whole system improvement in education. *Journal of Educational Change, 17*(4), 539–544.

Gioia, D. A., Thomas, J. B., Clark, S. M., & Chittipeddi, K. (1994). Symbolism and strategic change in academia: The dynamics of sensemaking and influence. *Organization Science, 5*(3), 363–383.

Goldspink, C. (2007). Rethinking educational reform—A loosely coupled and complex systems perspective. *Educational Management Administration & Leadership, 35*(1), 27–50.

Goldstein, J., Hazy, J. K., & Lichtenstein, B. B. (2010). *Complexity and the nexus of leadership: Leveraging nonlinear science to create ecologies of innovation*. Palgrave Macmillan.

Grissom, J. A., Egalite, A. J., & Lindsay, C. A. (2021). *How principals affect students and schools*. Wallace Foundation.

Hazy, J. K., Goldstein, J. A., & Lichtenstein, B. B. (Eds.). (2007). *Complex systems leadership theory: New perspectives from complexity science on social and organizational effectiveness* (Vol. 1). ISCE Publishing.

Hulme, M., Beauchamp, G., Clarke, L., & Hamilton, L. (2021). Collaboration in times of crisis: Leading UK schools in the early stages of a pandemic. *Leadership and Policy in Schools*, 1–20.

Hynds, A., Sleeter, C., Hindle, R., Savage, C., Penetito, W., & Meyer, L. H. (2011). Te Kotahitanga: A case study of a repositioning approach to teacher professional development for culturally responsive pedagogies. *Asia-Pacific Journal of Teacher Education, 39*(4), 339–351.

Jacobson, M. J., Levin, J. A., & Kapur, M. (2019). Education as a complex system: Conceptual and methodological implications. *Educational Researcher, 48*(2), 112–119.

Jacobson, S., & Notman, R. (2018). Leadership in early childhood education (ECE): Implications for parental involvement from New Zealand. *International Studies in Educational Administration, 46*(1), 86–101.

Johnson, B. L., & Kruse, S. D. (2019). *Educational leadership, organizational learning, and the ideas of Karl Weick: Perspectives on theory and practice*. Routledge.

Kershner, B., & McQuillan, P. J. (2016). Complex adaptive schools: Educational leadership and school change. *Complicity: An International Journal of Complexity and Education, 13*(1), 4–29.

Khalifa, M. A. (2018). *Culturally responsive school leadership*. Harvard Education Press.

Khalifa, M. A., Gooden, M. A., & Davis, J. E. (2016). Culturally responsive school leadership: A synthesis of the literature. *Review of Educational Research, 86*(4), 1272–1311.

Le Fevre, D. M., & Robinson, V. M. J. (2015). The interpersonal challenges of instructional leadership: Principals' effectiveness in conversations about performance issues. *Educational Administration Quarterly, 51*(1), 58–95.

Leithwood, K., Harris, A., & Hopkins, D. (2008). Seven strong claims about successful school leadership. *School Leadership & Management, 28*(1), 27–42.

Leithwood, K., Harris, A., & Hopkins, D. (2020). Seven strong claims about successful school leadership revisited. *School Leadership & Management, 40*(1), 5–22.

Leithwood, K., Mascall, B., & Strauss, T. (Eds.). (2009). New perspectives on an old idea: A short history of the old idea. In *Distributed leadership according to the evidence* (pp. 1–14). Routledge.

Lewin, R. (1999). *Complexity: Life at the edge of chaos*. University of Chicago Press.

Longmuir, F. (2021). Leading in lockdown: Community, communication and compassion in response to the COVID-19 crisis. *Educational Management Administration & Leadership*. https://doi.org/10.1177/17411432211027634

Macfarlane, A. H. (2004). *Kia hiwa ra: Listen to culture: Māori students' plea to educators*. New Zealand Council for Educational Research.

Macfarlane, A. H. (2015). Restlessness, resoluteness, and reason: Looking back at 50 years of Māori education. *New Zealand Journal of Educational Studies, 50*(2), 177–193.

Macfarlane, A., Macfarlane, S., & Curtis, T. (2019). Navigating kaupapa Māori fields of knowledge. In *Oxford research encyclopedia of education*. https://doi.org/10.1093/acrefore/9780190264093.013.328

Macfarlane, A., Macfarlane, S., & Glynn, T. (2012). In S. Carrington & J. MacArthur (Eds.), *Teaching in inclusive school communities* (pp. 163–188). John Wiley and Sons.

Maitlis, S. (2005). The social processes of organizational sensemaking. *Academy of Management Journal, 48*(1), 21–49.

McQuillan, P. J. (2020). Quantifying the complex adaptive system metaphor: Generating the educational transformation heuristic. *International Journal of Complexity in Education, 1*(2), 95–120.

Ministry of Education. (2019). *Supporting all schools to succeed: Reform of the tomorrow's schools system*. Ministry of Education.

Mitchell, M. (2009). *Complexity: A guided tour*. Oxford University Press.

Morowitz, H. J. (1995). *The mind, the brain and complex adaptive systems*. Taylor and Francis.

Mutch, C. (2020). How might research on schools' responses to earlier crises help us in the COVID-19 recovery process. *Set: Research Information for Teachers, 2*, 3–10.

Notman, R. (2011). *Successful educational leadership in New Zealand: Case studies of schools and an early childhood centre*. NZCER Press.

Notman, R. (2015). Seismic leadership, hope, and resiliency: Stories of two Christchurch schools post-earthquake. *Leadership and Policy in Schools, 14*(4), 437–459.

Notman, R. (2020). An evolution in distributed educational leadership: From sole leader to co-principalship. *Journal of Educational Leadership, Policy and Practice, 35*, 27–40.

Notman, R., & Henry, D. A. (2011). Building and sustaining successful school leadership in New Zealand. *Leadership and Policy in Schools, 10*(4), 375–394.

Robinson, V. M. J., Lloyd, C. A., & Rowe, K. J. (2008). The impact of leadership on student outcomes: An analysis of the differential effects of leadership types. *Educational Administration Quarterly, 44*(5), 635–674.

Schechter, C., Da'as, R., & Qadach, M. (2022). Crisis leadership: Leading schools in a global pandemic. *Management in Education.* https://doi.org/10.1177/08920206221084050

Schein, E. H. (2010). *Organizational culture and leadership.* John Wiley & Sons.

Senge, P., Cambron-McCabe, N., Lucas, T., Smith, B., Dutton, J., & Kleiner, A. (2012). *Schools that learn: A fifth discipline fieldbook for educators, parents, and everyone who cares about education.* Crown.

Shaked, H., & Schechter, C. (2017). *Systems thinking for school leaders: Holistic leadership for excellence in education.* Springer.

Silins, H. C., Mulford, W. R., & Zarins, S. (2002). Organizational learning and school change. *Educational Administration Quarterly, 38*(5), 613–642.

Stacey, R. D. (2007). *Strategic management and organisational dynamics: The challenge of complexity to ways of thinking about organisations.* Pearson Education.

Stacey, R. D., Griffin, D., & Shaw, P. (2000). *Complexity and management: Fad or radical challenge to systems thinking?* Psychology Press.

Stoll, L. (2009). Capacity building for school improvement or creating capacity for learning? A changing landscape. *Journal of Educational Change, 10*(2), 115–127.

Striepe, M., & Cunningham, C. (2021). Understanding educational leadership during times of crises: A scoping review. *Journal of Educational Administration, 60*(2), 133–147.

Te Puni Kōkiri. (2001). *He Tirohanga o Kawa ki te Tiriti o Waitangi: Principles of the treaty as expressed by the courts and the Waitangi Tribunal.* https://www.tpk.govt.nz/en/o-matou-mohiotanga/crownmaori-relations/he-tirohanga-o-kawa-ki-te-tiriti-o-waitangi

Thornton, K. (2021). Leading through COVID-19: New Zealand secondary principals describe their reality. *Educational Management Administration & Leadership, 49*(3), 393–409.

Tomorrow's Schools Independent Taskforce. (2018). *Our schooling futures: Stronger together | Whiria Nga Kura Tuatintini.* https://conversation.education.govt.nz/assets/TSR/Tomorrows-Schools-Review-Report-13Dec2018.PDF

Weick, K. E., Sutcliffe, K. M., & Obstfeld, D. (2005). Organizing and the process of sensemaking. *Organization Science, 16*(4), 409–421.

Wylie, C., & McKinley, S. (2018). *Educational leadership capability framework.* Education Council.

Chapter 3

New Approaches to Complex Challenges: Leadership That Matters

Deidre M. Le Fevre

University of Auckland, New Zealand

Abstract

The challenges of engaging in leadership practices that promote equity and empower students who have traditionally been underserved in schooling continue throughout educational contexts. Complex challenges like this require complex solutions because they have multiple causes and interdependencies. This requires leaders focus on systemic and sustainable change for improvement rather than taking a "fixing parts" approach. This chapter focusses on promising approaches to leadership which can support capability in responding to such complex challenges. The chapter addresses four key areas for focus: (1). being comfortable with uncertainty, (2). understanding the role of emotion in leadership and change, (3). knowing how to interrupt problematic narratives, and (4). successfully engaging the views of young people. Implications for reimagining leadership include how to engage with diverse perspectives in decision-making, ways to support people struggling with the uncertainty of change, and how to lead sustainable responses to complex challenges.

Keywords: Uncertainty; relational practice; emotion; youth voices; educational leadership

Introduction

There is an ongoing challenge to engage in educational leadership practices that promote equity and empower students who have traditionally been underserved in schooling. This worldwide challenge exists within the context of large global issues – including global conflict, climate change, and the effects of poverty on young people – which present the need for urgent and important changes in direction for school leadership. The complex nature of these contextual issues reveals the importance of changing the ways we think, feel, and act (Le Fevre, 2022) in leadership to create schools that can be responsive to the needs of all young people.

Many powerful theories and definitions pertaining to what effective leadership means exist; however, these are often approached in isolation to one another. Historically there has been a tendency to focus on what leaders should do (e.g., they should set clear goals or manage time efficiently) and on what sort of personality type makes a good leader (e.g., being charismatic). Nevertheless, history has shown that maintaining such a narrow focus on specific aspects of leadership is insufficient to bring about and sustain improvements that address enduring and significant challenges in education. It is now recognized that there is a need to explore a more integrated approach to understanding "leadership that matters" if we are to bring about sustained improvement through and beyond uncertainty. As Strom et al. (2021) note, it is critical to stop "focusing on disconnected ways of thinking and being, or onto-epistemologies, that emphasize dualisms, linearity, one-to-one correspondences, and essentialism" (p. 199) as these are inadequate and unhelpful ways to understand the complexities of life and leadership. It is now more important than ever to work at the intersection of the different approaches to leadership and to pay attention to what and how leaders think (their theories and beliefs about leadership, education, and the future), how they feel (what supports them to have courage and take action even when taking action is hard), and ultimately, how they act (what leadership practices they enact). There are no set answers to these questions, as leadership happens within diverse, uncertain, and contested contexts. There are, however, some overarching concepts that are continually developing and changing, and these are explored in this chapter.

School leaders face significant, complex, and ongoing problems which demand they lead in spaces where disagreement, uncertainty, and ambiguity often prevail (Le Fevre, 2022). The French philosopher Renouvir once said that "there is no certainty, there are only people who are certain." The challenges school leaders must navigate and the uncertainty in local and global contexts within which they work are significant. The current global situation has been described as one of volatility, uncertainty, complexity, and ambiguity (Hadar et al., 2020). This has significant implications for how we reimagine school leadership. This chapter draws on research from a range of countries, and the focus is both local and global. It is local from the perspective that effective leadership is contextually bound and responsive to specific community and cultural needs. It is global in the sense that the complex challenges discussed here are inherent to school leadership across many countries.

Processes of leadership are complex and uncertain, as leaders face the multifaceted challenges of leading schools into the unknown. This chapter begins by exploring some of the current challenges of school leadership with a focus on four specific challenges: (a) navigating uncertainty; (b) responding to emotion; (c) interrupting problematic dominant narratives; and (d) engaging the voices of youth. This focus on the challenges of school leaders and leadership is followed by the identification of some key implications for how school leaders can intentionally think, feel, and act to reimagine school leadership in ways that navigate these challenges and meet the needs of students across diverse contexts.

Responding to Complex Challenges

Reimagining school leadership demands an understanding of the nature of the challenges that school leaders' face; it also requires a more developed awareness of the possible ways leaders might navigate these challenges. Education for the future faces enduring issues and questions that have been with us for decades. As well as this education also faces new problems with currently unknown solutions. Providing effective leadership as we face these issues is central to the work of those leading education into the future. The challenges discussed here are inherent to leadership and are not something that can be overcome or worked around in a simplistic way. Rather, effective leadership requires a deep understanding of the complex nature of these overarching challenges and how they play out in the specific contexts in which people lead. This, in turn, can support leaders to navigate these challenges and to reimagine leadership in new ways.

Complex challenges are embedded in complex systems. Schools are complex systems that are embedded within even larger systems (communities, cultures, countries). This makes these challenges systemic, significant, and difficult to navigate. For example, leaders need to engage in interactions with multiple people across multiple systems, and these interactions in themselves create complexity (Mason, 2008). Leading in ways that improve education within complex systems cannot be achieved by focusing on individual issues or people; rather, such leadership can only be attained by "designing better processes for carrying out common work problems and creating more agile mechanisms for sensing and reacting to novel situations" (Bryk et al., 2015, p. 61). As they lead into an unknown future, leaders must be able to focus on effective ways of thinking, feeling, and acting rather than concentrating only on specific responses.

Before exploring the four challenges mentioned earlier, it is important to understand there are no simple answers or "to-do" lists for leaders here. For example, complexity theory reveals how the whole is greater than the sum of its parts (Mason, 2008). This means that, as school leadership addresses or tries to "fix" certain parts of the system, other parts are changing and affecting what they are currently working on. Complexity theory makes transparent that the system is unpredictable, autonomous, and self-organizing (Mason, 2008), constantly bringing forth emergent phenomena. Complex challenges therefore require leaders to focus on systemic and sustainable change for improvement rather than taking a "fixing parts" approach (Gurr et al., 2021). A systems thinking approach is needed because of the interrelated nature of elements and the relationships that are less predictable, deterministic, or linear (Gurr et al., 2021).

A "fixing parts" approach will not work if the goal is to reimagine school leadership in ways that address large, fundamental, and ongoing issues; school leadership improvement is about more than the sum of the individual parts. While it might seem tempting to take a combination of what has been referred to as "best practice" and try to implement these together in different contexts, this is rarely successful (Shaked & Schechter, 2020). Rather than considering the parts in isolation, it is important to consider how the parts "function together in networks of interaction" (Shaked & Schechter, 2020, p. 107). Simply combining best practices does not lead to improvement; this is due to the uncertain and complex nature of education and educational leadership (Gurr et al., 2021). It is important instead to focus on underlying ways of thinking, feeling, and acting that represent leadership "ways of being," rather than homing in more simplistically on specific parts of the system.

The complex challenges faced by school leadership are inherent and enduring. They are inherent in that they are a part of the work of leadership; they are a part of the contemporary realities of the places, cultures, communities, and larger global contexts that schools are situated in. They are enduring because they are not likely to go away. Trying to resolve complex challenges with simple solutions is a common pitfall in school leadership. Complex challenges require complex solutions because they have multiple causes and interdependencies; however, it is human nature to respond to complex problems as though they were simple or routine challenges. Indeed, this temptation to try to solve complex problems with simple solutions has been one of the major pitfalls of leadership internationally for many decades (Heifetz et al., 2009). As a focus develops on how to reimagine school leadership, there also needs to be a focus on how to acknowledge and work with complexity and uncertainty.

The Challenge of Navigating Uncertainty

Educational leaders today face significant, complex, and ongoing crisis "within a landscape of challenges where the notion of uncertainty has become the norm" (Pashiardis & Brajckmann-Sajkiewicz, 2022). This demands they "lead in spaces where disagreement, uncertainty and ambiguity often prevail" (Le Fevre, 2022, p. 166). For example, school leaders work with students, staff, policies, and communities with diverse and sometimes conflicting ambitions for education; they do this amid changing and – as the recent pandemic revealed – sometimes urgent circumstances.

There is a current, pressing challenge to support leaders so that they can better understand the nature of uncertainty, the impact this has on themselves and others, and how to create change through uncertainty. Leadership demands being comfortable with being uncomfortable – being able to work with uncertainty and to overcome the constant "need to know." Indeed, the task of school leaders today is to be able to lead schools into the unknown future. The makes the very nature of leadership uncertain work.

School leaders are responsible for improving outcomes for students. Yet uncertainty also prevails, as some of the most powerful outcomes in education are difficult to measure (Safir & Jamila, 2021). The challenge of "measuring the immeasurable" means there can be a temptation to focus on readily measurable outputs that are easily observable and accessible to assess; however, these are often not the most important aspects of education for students (Safir & Jamila, 2021).

To be an effective leader demands working toward a vision for the future. Indeed, "The transformation of society and education is not possible without the transformation of how we see and imagine our futures" (Milojevic, 2005, p. 13). Reimagining school leadership involves reimagining how we think about the future. However, for too long now, the discourse about schooling, the purpose of schooling, and the future of schooling have been dominated and shaped by the worldviews of dominant cultures in society. It is these dominant cultures that have shaped policies and practices in response to the questions asked by so many: "What do we want in the future? What are our goals and aspirations for young people? What are the goals and aspirations of young people for themselves?" While these remain important questions, it is critical that we move away from only considering answers provided by the dominant voices who are currently controlling the narrative.

In the past, leadership for the future has been explored through a "futures discourse." For example, the "probable future" has been described as that which will most likely happen if people "keep doing what they are doing"; this probable future may not be desirable (Milojevic, 2005). The "preferable future" represents that which is considered desirable by a certain group of people, and this is what often drives policy and resourcing. Such visions and decisions about the future have and remain contestable, however, and dominant cultures once again tend to direct policy and resourcing in directions they value. For Maake et al. (2019), it is therefore not surprising that indigenous leadership has evolved as a radical sociopolitical phenomenon. For Indigenous people, leadership takes on a complexity beyond simplistic definitions of skills. Dominant voices directing policy and resourcing often do so at the expense of minoritized communities, so leadership is instead a "passionate mix of righteous anger, resistance, and a call to arms" (Maake et al., 2019, p. 231).

Leadership through uncertainty will take courage and a new focus if education is to address inequities within and across countries. School leadership faces the challenge of engaging with multiple, changing, and complex definitions of preferred futures in ways that confront existing frames which may no longer serve future generations. This includes engaging with traditionally marginalized voices and communities. Indeed, leadership is also a political act, and, according to Hargreaves (2005),

> Attempts to change education in fundamental ways are ultimately political acts. They are attempts to redistribute power and opportunity within the wider culture. Educational change is not just a strategic puzzle. It is, and should be, a moral and political struggle. (p. 2)

Ultimately, school leadership has a central role to play in reshaping policies and practices so that they are inclusive and also value student outcomes that are emerging and changing. The future is uncertain; therefore, supporting school leadership to navigate uncertainty is critical.

The Challenge of Navigating Emotions

Complex challenges can be emotionally difficult to face and limited attention has been paid to how school leaders feel about these challenges and how they can respond to both their own emotions and the emotions of those they lead. Emotion is part of being human and refers to a wide range of affective processes, including "feelings, moods, affects and well-being" (Boekaerts, 2010, p. 94). These processes are integral to life; contrary to popular opinion, teachers and school leaders cannot simply "leave their emotions at the school door."

Emotions are central to educational leadership (Berkovich & Eyal, 2015). For example, educational leaders may experience positive emotions of joy, happiness, hope, pride, compassion, wonder, and excitement as expressions of their well-being and vocational commitment and achievement (Berkovich & Eyal, 2015; Samier & Schmidt, 2009). At the same time, however, they may also experience negative emotions such as guilt, shame, envy, jealousy, frustration, disappointment, anxiety, anger, fear, embarrassment, and sadness. Indeed, as Blackmore asserted, educational leadership involves "the desire to make a difference…leadership is equally about fear of failure, pain, exhaustion and guilt associated with the ethical dilemmas that leaders confront on a daily basis" (2010, p. 642). There is no doubt that emotion is an integral part of both leadership and the role of being a school leader. Paying attention to this and supporting leaders to recognize the role of emotion, both for themselves and others, is a significant and important challenge (Le Fevre et al., 2020).

Cognition and emotion are interconnected. For many years, researchers considered emotion, cognition, and motivation to be separate processes; however, it is now apparent that they work together in complex and inseparable ways (Cahour, 2013). Add to this the trend of viewing emotion as a somewhat troublesome sign of weakness or instability and it becomes clear why the role of emotion has often been overlooked in understanding school leadership. Discomfort is part of leading and learning to improve (Le Fevre et al., 2020), yet traditional approaches to leadership have tended to focus on what needs to change, with limited attention paid to how people feel. The role of emotion in school leadership is perhaps more important than ever, given the immensity of the contextual issues that school leaders are currently working within. Indeed, there is international evidence that educators and leaders are suffering from the impact of negative emotion, stress, and burnout (Collie, 2021). It is important that school leaders understand the role of emotion in leadership and change; and acknowledge the emotional impact on both themselves and the people they work with and lead. With support, they can navigate these emotions, have a strong sense of well-being, and feel empowered in their work.

School leaders and the educators they work with often respond to the uncertainty surrounding educational change by experiencing a sense of risk and vulnerability (Twyford et al., 2017). For example, leaders may be expected to lead in new ways, which involves having to change their theories and beliefs about the nature of leadership and the purpose of schooling. These expectations can cause them to feel a sense of loss in terms of both their own identity as a leader (which they have developed over time) and the ways they have worked (which they have long believed were right). Risk involves perceptions of loss (Yates & Stone, 1992), and the work of school leadership is considered to be a risk for leaders when they perceive that they may potentially lose something they value. Such losses might include, for example, a sense of losing control over time or the possibility of losing available resources. A sense of vulnerability and self-threat, for example, can occur when one feels a challenge to one's self-view and favorable self perceptions are challenged (DeMatthews & Serafini, 2021). This sense of loss can be experienced at a very personal level and has also been referred to as a loss of ontological security. Ontological security represents the feelings of confidence and security we gain from having a degree of continuity in our self-identity and from the constancy of our immediate social and material environments (Giddens, 1991). Change and uncertainty can challenge this sense of ontological security and can cause people to feel a profound sense of loss.

Sometimes, people may appear reluctant to adopt new ways of thinking and working. This can be viewed by their leaders as resistance to, disinterest in, or even disdain for what is being suggested. Importantly, however, this reluctance may actually be in response to people's perceptions of risk (Twyford et al., 2017). In other words, they have a sense that they might lose something that they value if they embrace the proposed changes (Aven & Renn, 2009). People's perceptions of risk can be complex when they are involved in changes purported to bring about improvement. These perceptions should not be ignored, because they can paralyze people from taking action and cause them to turn to self-protective behaviors that are commonly mistaken for acts of resistance. Leaders need to understand that what looks like resistance may actually be the result of a person's fear of failure and their perception that they might lose their sense of competence. When leaders have a depth of understanding about what people are feeling, they are more likely to create ways to support them (Le Fevre et al., 2020).

Engaging in leadership for change is emotionally laden work, and people respond to change in different ways. Leading in uncertain contexts for uncertain futures is likely to increase perceptions of risk; so now more than ever, it is important to pay attention to the role of emotion in educational leadership. Educational leaders have a responsibility to understand the role of emotion in leadership, learning, and educational change. Being aware of their own feelings as a leader, as well as the feelings of those they lead, is a powerful tool and an important part of the narrative of what it means to lead. Narratives are a central part of leadership. Narratives help us make sense of our experiences and guide decision-making; however, sometimes the narratives that guide leadership decisions can be problematic.

The Challenge of Interrupting Problematic Narratives

Problematic narratives can exist at personal, organizational, and societal levels; they inhibit establishing and sustaining school improvements that can address issues of inequity. These are the narratives that, for example, create low expectations for certain groups of people or that assign blame to families for student achievement issues. They are also the narratives held by schools who view themselves as highly successful in their performance, even though there are students within the school community whose needs are not being met. These narratives continue to exist in part because of confirmation bias, wherein humans are hardwired to see what they want or expect to see. People interact with the world and make assumptions and choices in ways that confirm what they already believe (Hart et al., 2009). This means that educators can easily become immersed in faulty narratives, leading them to hold a false sense of security about their schools and their leadership, as well as about the nature of improvement. These problematic narratives are challenging to overcome because confirmation bias directs attention away from what is *actually* happening (Hart et al., 2009).

The negative impact of confirmation bias is also exacerbated by the way that cultural positioning influences what people see, what they prioritize, and what they act on. Cultural positioning refers to the way people experience the world through the specific cultural lenses they have grown up with unless these are intentionally interrupted (Le Fevre et al., 2020). Interrupting problematic narratives demands first being aware of the narratives we hold and value – noticing where these no longer serve education well – and changing the narrative to one that empowers leaders and educators to make the necessary changes for improvement.

Problematic narratives also exist in relation to the nature, purpose, and direction of schooling. For example, many of the fundamental values and practices of education and schooling that are currently embraced across the international stage have been established throughout histories of colonization. Schools are too often "spaces and structures that are uncontestably occupied and representative of colonizing practices that neglect indigenous peoples' worldview and ways of knowing and living" (Shizha, 2019, p. 195). In this current status quo, schools are limited in their abilities to address systemic racism in new and important ways. Changing problematic narratives takes intentional interruption (Katz & Dack, 2013), and school leadership must therefore take up the critical role of interrupting the subtle cognitive and affective supports that preserve these narratives and scaffold the status quo. For leadership to be able to respond in new ways, leaders need to be able to think, feel, and act from a place of open-mindedness. Open-mindedness demands that people hold a general epistemological outlook of fallibilism; in other words, they must recognize that they will sometimes be mistaken (Hare, 2009). To be open-minded requires a willingness to reconsider our personal theories and beliefs in the face of new information (Hare, 2009). This, in turn, requires a willingness to acknowledge that what we believe could be incorrect or misinformed. Holding a stance of open-mindedness does not mean we need to agree with other perspectives and disregard our own views (Hare, 2009); what it does mean, however, is that we should carefully examine our views, being aware of the potential impact of confirmation bias and the role that cultural positioning has in influencing how we think, feel, and act (Le Fevre et al., 2020).

Reimagining school leadership thus requires being open-minded and willing to reconsider and revise one's own and others' views in the face of new information (Blank et al., 2016). It also requires that leaders use strategies to understand the experiences and views of others, including the most vulnerable youth in our schools (Bourke & Loveridge, 2018).

The task of reimagining school leadership also demands that leaders are engaged in genuine inquiry. Inquiry is a concept that often appears in educational literature; however, empirical research undertaken in schools reveals that much of the inquiry that happens in schools is not, in fact, genuine inquiry (Le Fevre et al., 2015). Genuine inquiry can only happen when people are open-minded and when they seek to understand other perspectives. This requires holding a stance of curiosity and wonderment rather than being driven to come up with an explanation for existing beliefs. While the attributes of genuine inquiry are considered desirable by most people, they are in fact difficult to do. Research carried out in Aotearoa New Zealand reveals that educational leaders engage in minimal genuine inquiry to better understand other perspectives; instead, they spend most of their time explaining their existing point of view to others (Le Fevre et al., 2015). This is perhaps unsurprising given a large-scale research project undertaken with tens of thousands of people working across a range of sectors revealed that none were good at inquiring and being open-minded even though they espoused these attributes (Argyris & Schon, 1974). Instead, like the school leaders in the more recent research (Le Fevre et al., 2015), the participants in Argyris and Schon's studies (1975) continued to advocate for their existing viewpoints and to ignore evidence that contradicted them.

Engaging in genuine inquiry might sound simple, but it will take intentional and focused attention. For example, leaders might intentionally explore the views of stakeholders whose perspectives do not typically shape decision-making. Being willing to consider ways of working and approaches to problems that differ from those we hold is an important leadership skill. One of the key communities whose perspectives are not typically used to inform high level leadership decisions are the voices of our young people, the voices of youth. Given the complexity of education and the uncertainty and ambiguity already discussed, engaging the voices of youth is not a straightforward task however it is a critically important one.

The Challenge of Engaging the Voices of Youth

Education is about young people; however, these are the very people who often have the least voice in decisions about their future. A major challenge is the fact that students are usually the targets of initiatives for improvement rather than being engaged with in processes of leadership and change; this is despite the fact that "children and young people are 'expert witnesses' to their lives and can provide unique perspectives on and reasons for, and modes of, educational change" (Thomson, 2010, p. 810). Yet rarely are youth considered as partners in change whose voices must be sought, listened to, valued, and acted upon.

Engaging young people in decision-making should not be perceived as a nice addition; rather, it is actually a legal imperative which is the right of the child. Article 12 of the United Nations Convention on the Rights of the Child (UNCROC) legislates that a child shall have the right to express their views in matters that affect them (United Nations, 1989). Educational leadership needs to prioritize engaging the views of young people, as these views are "integral to making good decisions" (Thomson, 2010, p. 810). There is significant evidence of positive outcomes when leaders engage with student voices; for example, curriculum initiatives in health and well-being have been shown to be more effective and successful when schools listen to their students' voices (Quinlan & Hone, 2020). School leaders have an important role in terms of understanding how to engage with the lived experiences, views, and goals of the young people whose education they are entrusted with.

Engaging the voices of youth in ways that support strong school leadership is, however, challenging for many reasons, including the concern that not all voices are equal. Thomson (2010) notes how the term "voice" can imply that all young people have a collective view, but this is not the reality. There is a common assumption that the "student voice" will express a unified and cohesive view; this means that the views of many young people are not heard. In addition, there is a tendency to engage with students for whom school is perceived to be successful, thereby only accessing a small cross-section of the views, experiences, priorities, and values held by young people. The views that are traditionally accessed have been referred to as the "palatable voices of good students" (Charteris & Smardon, 2019) and these are often used in arguments to support the continuation of existing schooling practices. Postcolonial theories emphasize the importance of doing more than just listening to students and collecting data on what they say; instead, what is needed to address schooling issues is actual engagement with all students, their families, and their communities and the proactive inclusion of students whose voices often go unheard (Hynds et al., 2016).

A further challenge to engaging the voices of youth is the tendency for schools to create student voice initiatives with good intentions but to then use these as a mechanism to inform the improvement of student outcomes within the existing frameworks and understandings of effectiveness rather than to question the frameworks themselves (Mayes & Finneran, 2021). Involving youth in educational improvement is "integral to making good decisions and sustainable change" (Thomson, 2010, p. 810). Listening to the voices of youth involves more than letting students have a say; voice is a complex construct – it is about identity, emotion, the subtleties of expression, perceptions, and the context we are in (Thomson, 2010). Engaging with the voices of youth in ways that can have a fundamental impact on how young people experience schooling is an ambitious, important, and essential role of school leadership.

Engaging with the voices of youth on an extensive, meaningful, and potentially transformational level will no doubt demand much challenging and emotional work for educational leaders. For example, being open to genuine inquiry into the very purposes and processes of schooling can leave leaders feeling vulnerable and uncertain about both what they have been doing and where they are heading. The courage to explore these spaces is however integral to reimagining school leadership. An example of this is evident in the Te Kotahitanga project in New Zealand, wherein the voices of Māori students were central to researching how young people perceived success as Māori in education in New Zealand and what they needed as support from their teachers. The views of young people were then integrated into a professional learning initiative for teachers (Bishop et al., 2014).

Implications for School Leadership

This chapter now turns to a discussion of some promising approaches for leadership, which can support capability in responding to these complex challenges. Given understandings of complexity in school leadership, these approaches overlap and are connected – they are not intended to be considered in isolation from each other.

Sustaining improvement through and beyond uncertainty means leaders need to be open-minded and engage in genuine inquiry if they are to understand what improvement and success means for different communities and cultures. This notion becomes critical when consideration is given to key priorities, such as culturally sustaining education for indigenous youth. Writing about a vision for the future for indigenous New Zealand Māori students, Berryman et al. (2018) make the important point that:

> ...we must resist the privileging of attaining standardised credentials as the single marker of success. We must also resist unconsciously creating a hierarchy of success in which academic achievement is of most value. Instead, we must broaden our thinking to encompass the cultural, spiritual, and physical wellbeing of our Māori students as potential future leaders in our bicultural nation. (p. 9)

These researchers discuss the uncertainty of what it means to achieve "as Māori" in terms of Mātauranga Māori (a Māori world view). Rather than holding traditional notions of student achievement that have been constructed by dominant cultures and serve to continue inequities, school leadership needs to be open to uncertainty, including the uncertainty of what success means, how it is measured, and what it might look like in specific contexts. Indeed, the work of indigenous researchers points to the significant role of school leaders in working toward creating markers of success that are not currently defined.

Engaging students and their communities in school leadership is central to engaging the voices of youth; however, school communities are uncertain and changing entities. It can be tempting to define school communities as homogenous and static entities, yet they are always multilayered, dynamic, and changing, and they have their own hierarchies and power relations (Shizha, 2019). Recognizing this complexity is essential when being open to new ways of involving youth and school communities in leadership. It will not be simple, straightforward work;

rather, it will be complex, sometimes messy, and inherently uncertain work, which is nonetheless essential to creating connections between school leaders and the communities they serve. Being aware of the level of involvement is also important. For example, are students and their communities merely being informed or consulted, or are they actually making decisions that affect their educational experiences? There are times when different levels of involvement will make sense; however, it is important to have a continual awareness of the level of participation, how it is perceived by students and their communities, and whether it is appropriate. Adults in school do not always hold the same views as students about this. For example, Jones and Bubb (2021) found that the adults in schools had a much more positive view of the impact of student voices than the students themselves; the students "felt frustration, believing that they have a great deal to offer to improve schools, given the opportunity" (p. 243). An important aspect of school leadership is therefore to continually ask the following questions: How are we going? Are we making progress? Whose perspective have we checked? What might we need to do differently?

Engaging with diverse perspectives is key to effective leadership. For leadership to be reimagined, it will require changing views, beliefs, and ways of working. Such change will mean leaders need to be comfortable working with contested ideas and disagreement. Earlier in this chapter, I discussed the role of emotions and feelings in leadership. Working with disagreement can be uncomfortable for leaders and those they lead. It is common for people to perceive risk during periods of change and also when confronted with difficult conversations. These are situations that leadership may need support to navigate. Identifying, contesting, and changing problematic dominant narratives takes courage, collective action, and the voices of those who are currently underserved.

Leading through and beyond uncertainty in ways that develop and sustain improvement is not an easy task, but it is a key role of school leadership. While those in senior leadership positions play a critical role in supporting this, the webs of leadership and influence within and across school communities are also key. Indeed, Maake et al. (2019) state that

> ...leadership, whether good or bad, may be seen as a phenomenon of cause and effect. Like a spider's web, every strand of leadership is inextricably connected, touching one part of a web sets off a series of vibrations that reverberate throughout the whole. (p. 238)

Understanding the complexity of these relationships and influence is crucial.

Prioritizing relational practice is an important focus for school leaders if they are to be in a position to address the challenges raised in this chapter. Strong relational practice underpins all aspects of leadership presented in this chapter. As Maake et al. (2019) argue,

> Well-executed leadership is not a product, but a process. It is not contingent upon the acquisition and application of a set of leadership

skills and abilities, rather, it is contingent upon the relationship among those who lead and those who are lead (p. 239).

Creating trust in schools (Bryk et al., 2015) is not a new idea but one that remains as pertinent and relevant as when it was first introduced. Recent research on curriculum leaders in schools (Sinnema et al., 2023) focused on the importance of the relational approaches that are integral to all that leaders do. Sinnema et al. (2023) posed some key questions that leaders might ask to ensure they are focusing on relational practice:

> How are we collectively maximising the interconnections amongst those within and beyond our network?; how easy is it for our people to reach the resources of others?; are we working in ways that foster reciprocity in the ties between people?; are we thinking about and actively working to connect with those who might be marginalized in our networks? What are the problematic patterns in terms of relationships in our network, and what causes of those patterns should be reflected in the solutions we try? (pp. 169–170)

This focus on the relational nature of schools and the networks within and across them is essential. Although relational trust has been discussed in the research for some time, it has not yet been fully realized in our schools. Continually seeking to identify ways to connect and develop trust is core to the future focus of educational leadership.

Supporting communities and networks is a further priority. School leaders work in unique contexts and communities, and they work within and across multiple networks and embedded systems. According to Shizha (2019), "Community, peoplehood, and personhood are interconnected and inseparable synergies that are deeply rooted in indigenous peoples' world views and lived-experiences" (p. 195). It is vital to increase the focus on the importance and centrality of the collective (peoplehood), the importance of the individual (personhood), and ways the individual understands their expectations and responsibilities to others. As Shizha (2019) continues, "When individuals act independent of the community, their voices are not likely to be heard nor are they likely to be effective" (p. 197). School leadership has a key role in creating community and creating space for all voices to be heard. Effective leadership is about creating spaces to allow the development of leadership by and for both students and communities who have not traditionally been represented in leadership. Education has too often served to reproduce existing inequities in societies (Strom et al., 2021); however, school leadership has the potential to address this.

Leaders will face many challenges that they must navigate, but fortunately there is also evidence of some powerful ways of thinking, feeling, and acting that can support them to be effective. Leading improvement in education demands "keeping students at the center of all improvement efforts particularly those students whose educational needs are not well served by current approaches to education" (Le Fevre et al., 2020, p. 121). This will require asking difficult questions: What are we currently doing or not doing that is creating inequity? Whose voices are being listened to and acted on and who is silent? How are we creating ways for silenced voices to be represented, heard, and acted on in our leadership? Being willing to ask and respond to these difficult questions is important.

Leadership needs to continually be informed by research and evidence; however, the nature of this research and evidence must broaden. For example, key indigenous understandings of leadership frame leadership in important and different ways to colonial notions of what it means to lead and be influential. Embedding these worldviews into what it means to lead schools into the future will be important if we are to create new and more inclusive ways of educating our young people. Deep conceptual knowledge that enables people to interpret and understand new information distinguishes experts from novices. As I have argued elsewhere, "Deep knowledge allows people to work flexibly and responsively in complex and challenging settings" (Le Fevre et al., 2020). This chapter has surfaced some of the key challenges faced by educational leadership, but clearly there are many more. The types of conceptual knowledge that educational leaders need to navigate these challenges are developing. Being more aware of the role of emotion during this change is also important. The absence of a blueprint of how to lead successfully into the future will demand what Heifetz et al. (2009) call "thinking experimentally." This kind of thinking requires that leaders are open-minded, that they engage in genuine inquiry in ways that help them to manage ambiguity, and that we [or they] can work within contexts of uncertainty.

Understanding the role of emotion in leadership is an important focus for today's leaders. Uncertainty and change can evoke the self-questioning of one's legitimacy as a leader and one's capacity to fulfill new roles (Pashiardis & Brauckmann-Sajkiewicz, 2022). Being aware of this can be empowering to leaders as they begin to realize this is a norm of leadership and not a personal inadequacy. Indeed, research in New Zealand where educators were intentionally engaged in work that drew their attention to the role of emotion in their learning, change, and leadership empowered the educators to learn to live with the uncertainty and changing roles and spaces they needed to inhabit (Timperley, 2023).

School leadership is complex, demanding, emotional, and important work. Placing the full responsibility for such difficult work on positional leaders alone is neither reasonable nor likely to be effective. For this reason, creating way to support leaders as they navigate these ongoing challenges is crucial. Reimagining school leadership for the diverse, uncertain, and contested contexts of the future will require more than simply learning to do things differently; it will require questioning, challenging, and changing one's fundamental beliefs, feelings, and practices as educational leaders.

References

Argyris, C., & Schon, D. (1974). *Theory in practice: Increasing professional effectiveness.* Jossey-Bass.

Aven, T., & Renn, O. (2009). On risk defined as an event where the outcome is uncertain. *Journal of Risk Research, 12*(1), 1–11. https://doi.org/10.1080/13669870802488883

Berkovich, I., & Eyal, O. (2015). Educational leaders and emotions: An international review of empirical evidence 1992–2012. *Review of Educational Research, 85*(1), 129–167.

Berryman, M., Lawrence, D., & Lamont, R. (2018). Cultural relationships for responsive pedagogy: A bicultural mana ōrite perspective. *Set: Research Information for Teachers, 1,* 3–10. https://doi.org/10.18296/set.0096

Bishop, R., Berryman, M., & Wearmouth, J. (2014). *Te Kotahitanga: Towards effective education reform for indigenous and other minoritized students.* NZCER.

Blackmore, J. (2010). Preparing leaders to work with emotions in culturally diverse educational communities. *Journal of Educational Administration, 48,* 642–658.

Blank, A., Houkamau, C., & Kingi, H. (2016). *Unconscious bias and education: A comparative study of Māori and African American students.* Analysis & Policy Observatory: Oranui Diversity Leadership.

Boekaerts, M. (2010). The crucial role of motivation and emotion in classroom learning. In H. Dumont, D. Istance, & F. Benavides (Eds.), *The nature of learning: Using research to inspire practice* (pp. 91–112). OECD Publishing. https://doi.org/10.1787/9789264086487-en

Bourke, R., & Loveridge, J. (2018). *Radical collegiality through student voice: Educational experience, policy and practice.* Springer.

Bryk, A. S., Gomez, L. M., Grunow, A., & LeMahieu, P. G. (2015). *Learning to improve: How America's schools can get better at getting better.* Harvard Education Press.

Cahour, B. (2013). Characteristics, emergence and circulation in interactional learning. In M. Baker, J. Andriessen, & S. Jarvela (Eds.), *Affective learning together: Social and emotional dimensions of collaborative learning* (pp. 62–80). Routledge.

Charteris, J., & Smardon, D. (2019). The politics of student voice: Unravelling the multiple discourses articulated in schools. *Cambridge Journal of Education, 49*(1), 93–110.

Collie, R. J. (2021). COVID-19 and teachers' somatic burden, stress, and emotional exhaustion: Examining the role of principal leadership and workplace buoyancy. *AERA Open, 7.* https://doi.org/10.1177/233285842098618

DeMatthews, D. E., & Serafini, A. (2021). Do good principals do bad things? Examining bounds of ethical behavior in the context of high-stakes accountability. *Leadership and Policy in Schools, 20*(3), 335–354.

Giddens, A. (1991). *Modernity and self-identity: Self and society in the late modern age.* Polity Press.

Gurr, D., Longmuir, F., & Reed, C. (2021). Creating successful and unique schools: Leadership, context and systems thinking perspectives. *Journal of Educational Administration, 59*(1), 59–76.

Hadar, L. L., Ergas, O., Alpert, B., & Ariav, T. (2020). Rethinking teacher education in a VUCA world: Student teachers' social-emotional competencies during the Covid-19 crisis. *European Journal of Teacher Education*, *43*(4), 573–586. https://doi.org/10.1080/02619768.2020.1807513

Hare, W. (2009). What open-mindedness requires. *The Skeptical Inquirer*, *33*(2), 36–39. https://skepticalinquirer.org/2009/03/what-open-mindedness-requires/

Hargreaves, A. (2005). Introduction: Pushing the boundaries of educational change. In A. Hargreaves (Ed.), *Extending educational change: International handbook of educational change* (pp. 1–14). Springer.

Hart, W., Albarracín, D., Eagly, A. H., Brechan, I., Lindberg, M. J., & Merrill, L. (2009). Feeling validated versus being correct: A meta-analysis of selective exposure to information. *Psychological Bulletin*, *135*(4), 555–588. https://doi.org/10.1037/a0015701

Heifetz, R., Grashow, A., & Linsky, M. (2009). *The practice of adaptive leadership: Tools and tactics for changing your organization and the world*. Harvard Business Press.

Hynds, A. S., Hindle, R., Savage, C., Meyer, L. H., Penetito, W., & Sleeter, C. (2016). The impact of teacher professional development to reposition pedagogy for indigenous students in mainstream schools. *The Teacher Educator*, *51*(3), 230–249.

Jones, M.-A., & Bubb, S. (2021). Student voice to improve schools: Perspectives from students, teachers and leaders in "perfect" conditions. *Improving Schools*, *24*(3), 233–244.

Katz, S., & Dack, L. (2013). *Intentional interruption: Breaking down learning barriers to transform professional practice*. Corwin.

Le Fevre, D. M. (2022). Leading through crisis: The adaptive leadership of Jacinda Ardern. In M. Raei & H. Rasmussen (Eds.), *Adaptive leadership in a global economy: Perspectives for application and scholarship* (pp. 165–179). Routledge.

Le Fevre, D. M., Robinson, V. M. J., & Sinnema, C. E. L. (2015). Genuine inquiry: Widely espoused yet rarely enacted. *Educational Management Administration & Leadership*, *43*(6), 883–899. https://doi.org/10.1177/1741143214543204

Le Fevre, D. M., Timperley, H., Twyford, K., & Ell, F. (2020). *Leading powerful professional learning: Responding to complexity with adaptive expertise*. Corwin.

Maake, M. J., Wong, K. L., Perry, W. K., & Johnson, P. M. G. (2019). Indigenous leadership: A complex consideration. In E. A. McKinley & L. T. Smith (Eds.), *Handbook of indigenous education* (pp. 229–248). Springer.

Mason, M. (2008). What is complexity theory and what are its implications for educational change? *Educational Philosophy and Theory*, *40*(1), 35–49. https://doi.org/10.1111/j.1469-5812.2007.00413.x

Mayes, R., & Finneran, R. (2021). The possibilities and problematics of student voice for teacher professional learning: Lessons from an evaluation study. *Cambridge Journal of Education*, *51*(2), 195–212.

Milojevic, I. (2005). *Educational futures: Dominant and contesting visions*. Routledge.

Pashiardis, P., & Brajckmann-Sajkiewicz, S. (2022). Unravelling the business of educational leaders in times of uncertainty. *Educational Management Administration & Leadership*, *50*(2), 307–324.

Quinlan, D. M., & Hone, L. C. (2020). *The educators' guide to whole-school wellbeing: A practical guide to getting started, best-practice process and effective implementation*. Routledge.

Safir, S., & Jamila, D. (2021). *Street data: A next-generation model for equity, pedagogy, and school transformation.* Corwin.

Samier, E., & Schmidt, M. (2009). Introduction. In E. Samier & M. Schmidt (Eds.), *The emotional dimension of educational administration and leadership* (pp. 1–17). Routledge.

Shaked, H., & Schechter, C. (2020). Systems thinking leadership: New explorations for school improvement. *Management in Education, 34*(3), 107–114.

Shizha, E. (2019). Building capacity for indigenous peoples: Engaging indigenous philosophies in school governance. In E. A. McKinley & L. T. Smith (Eds.), *Handbook of indigenous education* (pp. 187–205). Springer.

Sinnema, C., Daly, A., Rodway, J., Hannah, D., Cann, R., & Liou, Y.-H. (2023). *Improving the relational space of curriculum realisation: Social Network interventions.* Emerald Publishing.

Strom, K., Mills, T., & Abrams, L. (2021). Illuminating a continuum of complex perspectives in teacher development. *Professional Development in Education, 47*(2–3), 199–208.

Thomson, P. (2010). Involving children and young people in educational change: Possibilities and challenges. In A. Hargreaves, A. Lieberman, M. Fullan, & D. Hopkins (Eds.), *Second international handbook of educational change* (pp. 809–824). Springer.

Timperley, H. (2023). *Leading professional conversations: Adaptive expertise for schools.* Australian Council for Educational Research.

Twyford, K., Le Fevre, D., & Timperley, H. (2017). The influence of risk and uncertainty on teachers' responses to professional learning and development. *Journal of Professional Capital and Community, 2*(2), 86–100.

United Nations. (1989). *Convention on the rights of the child.* Opened for signature 20 November 1989, 1577 UNTS 3 (entered into force 2 September 1990). https://www.ohchr.org/en/instruments-mechanisms/instruments/convention-rights-child

Yates, J. F., & Stone, E. R. (1992). The risk construct. In J. F. Yates (Ed.), *Risk-taking behavior* (pp. 1–125). John Wiley & Sons.

Chapter 4

Reimagining Leadership for Symmetry: A Framework for Embedding Mutual Respect Into School Improvement Efforts

Whitney M. Hegseth

Boston College, USA

Abstract

The purpose of this chapter is to propose a framework that can assist school leaders in working toward respect that is *mutual,* and *integrated* with their other school improvement efforts. I define mutual respect as the work of intervening on those power asymmetries typically found in classrooms – both between teachers and students, and among diverse groups of students – by way of according children increased equality, autonomy, and equity. Drawing on empirical examples from an ethnographic and comparative study of four elementary schools situated across two educational systems (i.e., Montessori and International Baccalaureate (IB)) and two national contexts (i.e., the United States and Canada), I highlight the need for a framework for mutual respect. The work of embedding symmetry – particularly in schools, which reflect the racism, classism, sexism, ableism, and heterosexism that is ever-present in broader society – is anything but straightforward. This is because: (1) mutual respect is multidimensional, and these dimensions can reinforce and conflict with one another in unexpected ways; and (2) mutual respect can be operationalized via a school's instructional, organizational, and social practices, again in ways that may conflict or work synergistically. By highlighting the complexity of leading for mutual respect, this framework is a first step toward supporting such efforts in leadership preparation and practice.

Keywords: Mutual respect; student autonomy; equality and equity; school improvement; school leadership

I begin this chapter by highlighting a status quo approach to respect in schools. An approach where respect exists along the margins; where teaching and according children respect is layered onto, versus integrated within, instructional improvement efforts. The time has perhaps come to reevaluate this status quo approach because, even as research demonstrates how increased respect for students is associated with more equitable achievement (Boaler, 2006), engagement (Cothran & Ennis, 2000), and resilience (Theron et al., 2014), research has also highlighted the ways in which many of our students continue to be marginalized throughout their school day (e.g., Poza, 2016; Urick et al., 2022; von Hippel & Cañedo, 2022).

The purpose of this chapter, then, is to present a framework that can assist school leaders in working toward respect that is *mutual,* and *integrated* with their other school improvement efforts. I define mutual respect as the work of intervening on those power asymmetries typically found in classrooms – both between teachers and students, and among diverse groups of students – by way of according children increased equality, autonomy, and equity.

Throughout this chapter, I will argue that a framework for mutual respect is needed because the work of embedding symmetry – particularly in schools, which reflect the racism, classism, sexism, ableism, and heterosexism that is ever-present in broader society – is anything but straightforward. This is because: (1) mutual respect is multidimensional, and these dimensions can reinforce and conflict with one another in unexpected ways; and (2) mutual respect can be operationalized via a school's instructional, organizational, and social practices, again in ways that may conflict or work synergistically.

But before I present this framework for mutual respect – a framework informed by my ethnographic and comparative study of four elementary schools situated across two educational systems (i.e., Montessori and International Baccalaureate (IB)) and two national contexts (i.e., the United States and Canada) – I must first illustrate the problems that can arise when respect exists along the margins of teaching and learning. I do so using data from this study's pilot, which involved, among other things, interviews and observations in a traditional and high-performing public school.[1] And so, we begin our journey with Mrs. Hayes.

The Problem: Respect on the Margins

Mrs. Hayes is a beloved teacher. In 2016, she had been teaching at her public elementary school in the suburbs of a Midwestern metropolitan area for over 15 years. She taught fourth grade for all save one of those years.

Mrs. Hayes reported that, as time passed, she began to worry that social-emotional learning was being squeezed out of the increasingly demanding curriculum at Fair Oaks Elementary School. Without such an education, she feared children would not learn how to take ownership over their behavior and learning; they would not learn how to be "one of the good guys." And so, motivated by student misbehavior at Fair Oaks, and the staff's desire to explicitly teach children to be better students, Mrs. Hayes worked with colleagues to fold social-emotional learning into the curriculum. They drew inspiration from the *Leader in Me* framework, which is based off of Stephen Covey's book, *The 7 Habits of Highly Effective People,* and works to transform schools to empower students with leadership and life skills.

How, exactly, did Mrs. Hayes adapt and build up *Leader in Me* at her school? She and a colleague came up with the idea to have "Groves" every other week, where each teacher would have a multiage group of students who would remain in that teacher's Grove throughout their elementary career. Students would spend those roughly 40 minutes every other week learning a common lesson related to one of the *7 Habits* (e.g., "Be proactive," "Seek first to understand, then to be understood"). Mrs. Hayes created most of these lessons for the first few years; however, she was quick to acknowledge Groves were a labor of love for the whole staff. The specialist teachers sacrificed their prep time every other week to make Groves possible, as this was the only time all students are available. Groves were followed by brief school assemblies, where each class took turns presenting something related to one of the *7 Habits*, and where students were recognized for being leaders: helping a peer with math, or organizing a classroom material without being asked.

In 2016, more than five years after the work had begun, these Groves and assemblies were still in place. Not only that, a few years after it began at Fair Oaks, other elementary schools in the district decided they, too, wanted to have Groves. And so, *Leader in Me*, and Fair Oaks' approach to implementing it, was adopted by the broader educational system. The superintendent reported *Leader in Me* to be part of the district's social justice pillar, and said it was pursued alongside the district's academic initiatives. One could find references to being a leader in student work posted along school hallways, and "YET" posters in every classroom. Teachers reported that students used *7 Habits* language daily; kindergarteners imploring their peers to "synergize," fifth graders sharing how they "sharpen the saw" on weekends. The *Leader in Me* mindset was a part of these children.

In many ways, Mrs. Hayes helped to build something that was a resounding success at her school and in her district, something that helped teachers when attempting to bolster respect in classrooms. And yet.

Though one could argue efforts to cultivate respect in Mrs. Hayes' classroom and school were being systemically supported, such support was fragile for at least two reasons. First, even as Mrs. Hayes' district adopted *Leader in Me* and the practice of Groves, this approach to respect continued to exist along the margins of teaching and learning. Second, though *Leader in Me* became a system-wide priority in Mrs. Hayes' district, a few key individuals determined whether and how it was enacted and sustained. And, because the initiative was attached at the margins, rather than being embedded into the instructional core (Cohen & Ball, 1999), changes for any of these individuals could result in *Leader in Me* becoming detached from the school and/or district.

Keeping the tenuous nature of this approach to respect in mind, I will now devote the rest of this chapter to proposing a new framework, one where respect is *mutual,* and where it is *integrated* into other school improvement efforts. I first present a framework for mutual respect, which is informed by both previous literature and my own empirical research. I then animate the framework with two empirical examples, which highlight the complexities of this improvement work. Finally, I conclude with implications for educational leaders.

Presenting a Framework for Mutual Respect

In this section, I briefly describe how previous literature and my own empirical data informed this framework for mutual respect, which I depict in Fig. 4.1. By putting literature and data in conversation with one another, I arrived at the following definition: mutual respect is the work of intervening on those power asymmetries typically found in classrooms – both between teachers and students, and among diverse groups of students – by way of according children increased equality, autonomy, and equity.

From Fig. 4.1, one understands there to be three dimensions of mutual respect: equality, autonomy, and equity. I offer definitions of these three dimensions as well as examples of how they may be observed in practice in Table 4.1. From Fig. 4.1 one also understands that mutual respect can be accorded to students via instruction, organization, and social relations. Finally, the work of mutually respecting students in classrooms is nested within, in constant interaction with, the broader school, educational system, and social and political environment. In

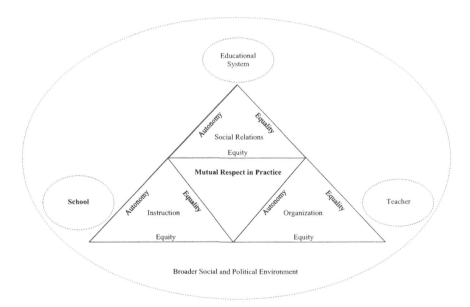

Fig. 4.1. A Framework for Examining Interactions Between Schools and Mutual Respect in Classrooms.

Table 4.1. Definitions and Examples of Mutual Respect in Practice.

Dimension	Definition	Instructional Example	Organizational Example	Social Example
Equality	To intervene on power asymmetries typically found in classrooms by ensuring all students receive: Equal exposure to learning experiences, content, and/or resources; equal expectations; equal treatment.	All students are expected to facilitate a classroom discussion once during the school year	All students get an equal amount of time in specials and with specialist teachers (e.g., art, music)	Every student gets an opportunity to eat lunch with his/her teacher twice during the school year
Autonomy	To intervene on power asymmetries typically found in classrooms by permitting students increased self-direction.	Students select a topic they want to research, and/or determine the final product they will produce to demonstrate what they have learned	Students determine how long they work on a given activity/ in a given subject area, before moving on to the next one	If there is a conflict, students help to come up with a solution, ensuring everyone moves forward peacefully
Equity	To intervene on power asymmetries typically found in classrooms by: providing differentiated supports; ensuring all students – regardless of background – are prepared for later life and school; including and amplifying voices and perspectives of minoritized students; ensuring all students – regardless of background – see themselves represented in the curriculum.	During lessons, students have frequent and easy access to resources that will provide them with extra support and/ or enrichment as needed	Students frequently work in groups where other group members are different from them, to learn the value of diverse experiences, skills, and perspectives	In class meetings, teachers and/or students work to solicit and include those voices that are less represented in the room, and/or in society

other writing, I have discussed mutual respect at the level of the classroom (e.g., Hegseth, 2023a; Hegseth, 2024). In this chapter, I focus in particular on mutual respect at the level of the school.

From the Literature: Respect as Mutual and Integrated

As I have described elsewhere (Hegseth, 2024), I rely on philosophical literature when highlighting how respect can be conceived of as *mutual*, whereas literature regarding instructional improvement illustrates ways in which respect might be *integrated* into the technical core of schooling.

Respect as Mutual

One way to define respect is to agree to abide by, or respect-as-deference. The act of respect, then, does not necessarily require one to intervene on longstanding power asymmetries. In fact, respecting someone may reinforce such asymmetries, particularly between two parties who are vastly different in age or ability. The work of *mutual* respect, on the other hand, involves creating symmetry in unlikely places, like classrooms. In her writings on respect, Lawrence-Lightfoot (2000) endeavors to shape a new view of the concept by focusing on "the way respect creates symmetry, empathy, and connection in all kinds of relationships, even those, such as teacher and student, doctor and patient, commonly seen as unequal" (pp. 9–10).

Goodman (2009) is similarly concerned with respect in the historically unequal relationship between teacher and student. She juxtaposes the philosophical stances of Kant, Mill, and Rawls to those of Dewey and Piaget as she considers what makes respect mutual, and what may make children deserving of mutual respect. In her view, to respect – as theorized by Kant, Mill, and Rawls – is to appreciate and accord dignity, equality, and autonomy. However, because children lack full capacity to reason, they are "undeserving of mutual respect," and so should only be accorded dignity even as they demonstrate "unilateral respect" to those with more perspective and reasoning capability (Goodman, 2009, p. 3). Goodman goes on to describe how Dewey and Piaget argue for more equality and autonomy for children, thus approaching the full, more mutual form of respect.

The framework discussed in this chapter conceptualizes *mutual* respect. As such, I exclude dignity, and take forward equality and autonomy; those strands of respect that Goodman (2009) described as controversial. That is, I include those dimensions that can be difficult to accord students, in light of the power asymmetries typically found between adults and children. And, in recognizing power asymmetries exist among students, as well as between adults and children, I include a third dimension of mutual respect: equity. Though equality and equity are often used interchangeably, similar to previous scholars (e.g., Caldwell et al., 2007; Gutiérrez, 2008, 2013; Souto-Manning et al., 2019), I argue the distinctions between respect-as-equality (e.g., giving students equal voice in a class discussion) and respect-as-equity (e.g., ensuring voices of minoritized students, which have been historically sidelined, are protected and amplified in a class discussion) are as important as any intentions they may hold in common.

Respect as Integrated

The instructional improvement literature offers examples of how teachers and schools integrate respect into instructional practice and organization, as opposed to thinking about respect solely in terms of social relations, and as something to layer onto the instructional core. For example, within a classroom or school, open forum discussions may be an integral part of instructional practice, where students help to create the rules and to direct the discourse (i.e., respect-as-autonomy). Similarly, a teacher or school may organize for heterogenous grouping and then ensure all students see themselves as responsible for their peers' learning (i.e., respect-as-equity). By embedding respect into daily instructional and organizational practice, the sustainability of that respect can become less reliant on a given teacher or school leader.

Based on the instructional improvement literature, I consider the work of mutual respect to involve disrupting commonplace beliefs (Alim, 2007; Ball, 2018; Ghiso, 2016; Lee, 2006), structures (Boaler, 2006), resources (Baskerville, 2011; Campano, 2007; Ghiso, 2016; Wilson et al., 2019), practices (Hess & McAvoy, 2015; Smyth, 2005), and interactions (Lampert, 2001) in schools, in efforts to intervene on power asymmetries between teachers and students, and among students. It was this literature that guided this framework's consideration of how mutual respect might be operationalized via instruction, organization, and social relations.

From the Data: Mutual Respect as Dilemma-Fraught

As previously mentioned, my empirical data also informed my conceptualization of mutual respect. As I will illustrate further in the next section, my time in the field highlighted how the work of creating and maintaining symmetry is dilemma-fraught. Indeed, this framework is built upon the premise that to teach is to manage ongoing dilemmas; for example, when one aim conflicts with another, or when prioritizing the needs of one group of students – at least temporarily – constrains supporting the needs of another group (Anagnostopoulos et al., 2020; Ball & Wilson, 1996; Goodman & Rabinowitz, 2019; Lampert, 1985, 2001). The work of mutual respect is similarly dilemma-fraught, because: (1) the three dimensions (i.e., equality, autonomy, equity) can reinforce and conflict with one another in unexpected ways; and (2) mutual respect can be operationalized via a school's instructional, organizational, and social practices, again in ways that may conflict or work synergistically.

Research Methods

The empirical examples that I draw on for the remainder of this chapter stem from my ethnographic and comparative study of four elementary schools, which were situated across two educational systems (i.e., Montessori and IB) and two national contexts (i.e., the United States and Canada). In 2017–2018, I collected data using four techniques: (1) participant observation, where I volunteered as a classroom assistant two days per week for five months at each of the four schools;

(2) semistructured interviews with the focal teachers as well as school leaders; (3) a review of system and school documents; and (4) video-cued multivocal ethnography (Tobin et al., 2009), in which I videotaped a typical day in one classroom per school, and then showed these edited 20-minute videos during focus groups with students, teachers, and school and system leaders. I analyzed the data in three phases using both inductive and deductive approaches: (1) open coding to identify emerging themes while initially processing the data (Emerson et al., 2011); (2) axial coding to identify relationships between codes within each case (Corbin & Strauss, 2007); and (3) theoretical and comparative coding across the cases using NVivo's classification and query functions (Charmaz, 2014).

With these methods and this cross-system, cross-national research design, I am better able to discern whether and how educational leaders challenge the status quo approach to respect in their broader environments, potentially offering new ways of according children more mutual respect in the classroom.

Animating the Framework

In this section, I animate this framework for mutual respect with empirical examples. In discussing the work of leaders (i.e., heads of school, directors of instruction, and teacher leaders) who are situated across different contexts and different educational systems, I highlight a central argument of this chapter: a framework for mutual respect is a necessary tool for school leaders because it helps them to see and understand why leading for symmetry is so challenging. The work of disrupting pervasive power asymmetries in classrooms and schools is both ever-changing and fraught with dilemma.

I offer below two examples: one from Montessori school leaders in east-central Canada, and one from IB school leaders in the Mid-Atlantic region of the United States. The Montessori example is an extended fieldnote, whereas the IB example is a compilation of interview and participant observation data. Within both examples, however, I discuss: (1) the part of students' multifaceted identities that leaders were aiming to mutually respect in that given moment; (2) how the dimensions of mutual respect (i.e., equality, autonomy, equity) interacted; and (3) how these dimensions interacted with one another across classroom instruction, organization, and social relations. By highlighting the complexity of leading schools for mutual respect, this framework is a first step toward supporting such practice.

Leading for Symmetry Across Languages: The Case of Montessori

I offer below fieldnotes from a professional development day in May of 2018, which was organized by the Canadian Council of Montessori Administrators (CCMA). At the start of the day, the CCMA director reported that this was the largest Canadian Montessori gathering to date; both teachers and leaders from the Canadian Montessori school where I conducted research were present. I present an excerpt from that afternoon, in which I observed elementary teachers and leaders grappling with managing high-fidelity Montessori alongside respect for children's multiple languages and literacies.

After presenting these fieldnotes, with a particular focus on comments made by heads of school and directors of instruction, I offer an analysis of the dilemma informed by the mutual respect framework. As Montessori school leaders aimed for symmetry across students' multiple languages and literacies, they needed to manage instances where respect-as-equity conflicted with respect-as-autonomy. What is more, as they managed these conflicts between the different dimensions of mutual respect, school leaders encountered different implications for classroom instruction and organization, which also then needed managing. Put simply, in aiming for symmetry, these school leaders encountered dilemmas with no simple or static solution.

Fieldnotes

The time had come for breakout groups. Elementary teachers and school leaders gathered upstairs in the café of a large Korean church located on the outskirts of a large city in east-central Canada. For 45 minutes, two Montessori practitioners – one man, one woman, both white – facilitated a conversation around a question someone had posed during that morning's presentation: how to maintain an authentic Montessori school or classroom while supporting children with high needs? What is essential, and what can be adjusted to better suit the learners at hand?

Halfway through the breakout session, the conversation turned toward specials (e.g., art, music, physical education). In standards for authentic Montessori classrooms, elementary-aged children are to have 3-hour uninterrupted work periods each morning, and 2- or 3-hour uninterrupted work periods each afternoon.[2] Only one session per week may be interrupted to accommodate special subjects, such as music or language (AMI/USA, 2022). The rationale behind this is that if children are afforded long uninterrupted blocks of time, they will cultivate the autonomy needed to direct their own learning. As such, Montessori teachers are trained to be generalists who can expose students to myriad subjects without needing to rely on specialist teachers.

In addition to the above criteria for a high-fidelity Montessori environment, Montessori practitioners were also managing the needs and requirements present within their broader context. That is, they were managing the different languages and literacies of their diverse student communities even as these leaders also managed the normative practice of offering French language instruction. Along with English, French is an official language in Canada. As such, public schools in this region of Canada are required to offer various streams of French language education starting in elementary school. Though private elementary schools are not regulated in this same way, the private school leaders I spoke with in the region reported pressure from families to offer students everything that was being offered in public schools. These pressures were felt by IB and Montessori school leaders alike; for example, in a focus group with IB school leaders in Canada, one leader said, "the parent community [has] that expectation that we would cover anything that a public school would cover and have enhancements to our program."

With the above standards and context in mind, Montessori school leaders were active participants in the conversation around different ways to manage specials, particularly language learning. One leader offered that, at his school, there are specials only one afternoon a week, which is in keeping with Montessori standards. However, in adhering to this one Montessori standard, they are violating another in order to accord students French language education: there is an extra, French-speaking teacher in the classroom. Another standard for authentic Montessori classrooms is that there is to be one trained teacher per class. Though assistants are permitted, their function is to assist the teacher with tasks like material preparation; they are not to assist the children (AMI/USA, 2022). Again, this standard is designed to foster autonomy in the children; with fewer adults in the room, children learn to regulate themselves and their peers. Thus, in working toward respect for multiple literacies, this leader reported that another problem was created around offering children enough opportunities for independence.

A couple of other leaders discussed how they managed specials and language needs by hiring bilingual teachers. There was one teacher present who taught her students in both English and Punjabi. Another school had a teacher who was bilingual in French and English, and she did her best to support the teachers in other classrooms who only taught in English. The training process for Montessori teachers is extensive and requires one year of their full-time effort. Indeed, in an interview with a Montessori teacher trainer, she described the intensive and lengthy training process as the biggest hindrance to the growth of Montessori schools: "we can't do mass production...so I would say my biggest limiting thing in terms of the work that we're doing would be attracting people, finding people who want to come take the training." Thus, leaders encountered difficulties with finding teachers who were both Montessori-trained and had the necessary language capabilities.

A final solution that was offered in this breakout session was to have a French assistant for every English-speaking teacher. In some schools, these assistants made French materials corresponding to all of the English materials in the classroom. Again, however, this solution created another dilemma: in Montessori classrooms, assistants are not to play an active role in teaching and learning. Given this, the conversation concluded with a general discussion around disconnects between the training that specialist teachers have received versus the Montessori teacher training. Such a disconnect was validated in an earlier focus group with Montessori teachers in Canada, when one teacher stated, "why is someone else who's not Montessori-trained – no offense to anyone who's not in the room – but who's not Montessori trained, bringing in their set of skills, but it's so contrary to what we do?" Montessori practitioners at the professional development similarly reported that these specialist teachers often come into the classroom with the pedagogical approach of the moment, which is ever-changing, even as it is almost constantly in conflict with the Montessori approach to teaching and learning.

As the conversation moved on to students' work journals, I got the impression that, though teachers and leaders learned different strategies from each other, there was no perfect solution for cultivating children's autonomy and literacy in multiple languages. Far from it.

Analysis of the Dilemma

With the help of the mutual respect framework, let us now take stock of the dilemma at hand. I summarize this dilemma in Table 4.2. One way to frame this dilemma is that there are three layers of interconnected conflict, and addressing any given conflict has implications for the others.

First, at this given moment, Montessori teachers and leaders alike were focused upon respecting children's multiple languages and literacies. This is aligned to the diversity present within the broader context of this large city in east-central Canada; over 120 languages are spoken by students and their families in the public school district. In my conversations with educational practitioners and scholars alike, they observed that, in Canada, rather than aiming for a melting pot, they aspire to a mosaic. That is, diverse cultures and languages should be celebrated alongside people's Canadian heritage.

There were, however, other facets of children's identities that were in focus at the time of fieldwork. For example, while I was conducting research in Canada, the teachers and students celebrated Canada amending its national anthem to be more gender neutral.[3] Another example: in a tour of public schools that was facilitated by the province's Ministry of Education, I observed rainbow flags on display outside

Table 4.2. Interrelated Priorities When Leading for Symmetry.

Potential Conflict Between...	Canada Montessori Case	US International Baccalaureate Case
Students' multifaceted identities	Focus on children's languages and literacies versus focus on their gender identities and family compositions.	Focus on students' socioeconomic status versus focus on their race and ethnicity.
Dimensions of mutual respect	Respect-as-equity (i.e., multiple languages of instruction) versus respect-as-autonomy (i.e., fewer adults in the room).	Respect-as-equity (i.e., international-mindedness) versus respect-as-autonomy (i.e., inquiry-based instruction).
Processes of mutual respect	Instructing for equity versus organizing for autonomy.	Organizing for equity versus instructing for autonomy.

schools, and bulletin boards next to school bathrooms that discussed gender-based violence. When I asked about these displays, educational leaders informed me that the district was actively challenging assumptions around heteronormative nuclear families, trying to "grow our normal" around the families surrounding students. In foregrounding such concern for children's languages and literacies, might Montessori school leaders risk allocating resources and attention away from also respecting students' diverse gender identities and family compositions?

A second potential conflict is between two dimensions of mutual respect that I outlined in the previous section: respect-as-equity and respect-as-autonomy. The decisions these leaders are making – such as having an extra French-speaking adult in the room – could be viewed as an equity move. That is, these leaders are working to ensure that students' many literacies and languages are recognized, valued, and amplified within the classroom. Research supports the need for and benefits of this respect (e.g., Ghiso, 2016; Poza, 2016).

However, as I alluded to within the fieldnotes, Montessori school leaders were encountering the dilemma that, by foregrounding respect-as-equity, their ability to respect children's autonomy was being constrained. As I have argued elsewhere (Hegseth, 2021), my review of Montessori system-level documents suggests that, above all, this system prioritizes respecting children's autonomy. Further, both observation and video-cued focus group data suggest that Montessori teachers in both Canada and the United States attempted equity by driving with autonomy (Hegseth, 2023a): in ceding some of their own power in the classroom (i.e., according children more autonomy), Montessori teachers scaffolded children's opportunities to uphold equity themselves. What happens to the Montessori approach, to the system's theory of action, when school leaders lead with equity instead of leading with autonomy?

The third layer of conflict as Montessori school leaders attempt symmetry is that, depending on how they manage the above two conflicts, there are different implications for respecting students via instruction and classroom organization. In the framework outlined in the previous section, I stated that educators can respect students via instructional and organizational moves, as much as via social relations. However, these different ways of operationalizing mutual respect can also conflict with one another, similar to conflicts between the different dimensions of mutual respect. As seen in the fieldnotes, by changing the organization of Montessori classrooms to support multiple languages (e.g., adding more adults to the room), Montessori leaders were then creating a different dilemma, in that this constrained teachers' abilities to give students the space needed to direct their own learning. As one school leader in Canada discussed the misalignment between the Montessori method and regulations around student-teacher ratios in the broader environment, he concluded with, "in the general scheme of things, [people assume] more adults is better, and [Montessorians] just don't believe that. Adults ruin everything."

Throughout this section, I have posed a few questions. For both the Montessori school leaders and me, there is no degree of certainty when responding to these questions. Taken together, these fieldnotes and the analysis thereof demonstrate that the only constant in working toward symmetry is the dilemma, and the exact nature of that dilemma is ever-changing.

Leading for Symmetry Across Socioeconomic Status: The Case of IB

In the following section, I present empirical data from my time as a participant observer in an urban IB school situated in the Mid-Atlantic region of the United States. Along with fieldnotes, I include below related conversations, interviews, and member checks with teachers and leaders at the school, which provide additional context around the school's dilemma. Put simply, leaders at this school were grappling with managing high-fidelity IB alongside respect for the diverse socioeconomic backgrounds of students and their families.

After presenting these data, I offer an analysis of this school-level dilemma that is informed by the mutual respect framework. As the IB school leaders worked to disrupt power asymmetries related to socioeconomic status, they focused on respect-as-equity both in creating a dual-language immersion program, and in supporting their students to be successful within that program. However, as time passed, teachers and leaders alike recognized that the forms of respect they had foregrounded were compromising opportunities to respect children's autonomy, which is another key tenet of respect in the IB system. In working toward one form of symmetry, these leaders were then faced with another sort of dilemma.

From the Field

One priority within IB's approach to teaching and learning is to cultivate international-mindedness in IB students. And, one way to cultivate such international-mindedness is via language learning. The IB system offers guidance to IB elementary schools around language learning, "The school ensures that students learn a language in addition to the language of instruction (at least from the age of seven)" (International Baccalaureate Organization [IBO] 2020, p. 11). In response to this system-level standard, the IB school in the United States created an English/Mandarin dual-immersion learning environment for students. Pre-K 3 and Pre-K 4 students are fully immersed in Mandarin. Then, from kindergarten onward, students alternate days with an English and Chinese teacher who collaborate closely to teach all content areas to their shared students.

Practitioners at this public charter IB school frequently described how organizing for dual-immersion was an equity move. Only three percent of the students at this school speak Mandarin at home, and the school is recognized as one of the most diverse elementary schools in the country. For these students, then, the school's teachers and leaders reported that fluency in these two languages could open more doors in today's globalized society. When describing the appeal of the school's English/Mandarin program, the Head of School alluded to such equitable preparation in stating, "brown boys speaking Chinese, you can write your ticket."

Equity was at the forefront of leaders' minds when creating the dual-immersion program; equity remained at the forefront as leaders continuously worked to better support students from diverse socioeconomic backgrounds in succeeding with the program. Such supports evolved over time. In her interview, the Head of School described creating texts and corresponding recordings so students could practice reading Mandarin at home, regardless of whether their parents could support. She explained:

> None of us were linguists, none of us had language training, but this is just what we thought the right thing to do was. The other thing we did was kids learn to read by reading, right? And nobody – I have a 3% heritage population – nobody speaks Chinese at home, they're all Black or white, but not native-speaking Chinese people. We said, 'let's go ahead and create this take-home reading system.' So we had our team write these Chinese books and then put the audio on this parent protected portal so that the kids would have the books to read, and they could listen, and as you pass levels, you got new books. So we literally have 1000 paper books upstairs that we wrote to make sure that the kids were reading.

Such efforts were aligned with what teachers and leaders reported in conversations. One focal teacher with whom I worked at this school explained that, with all their adjustments, the school was aiming for students to be supported internally, ensuring that they could thrive in the dual-immersion program even if their family didn't have the resources to support their literacy in one or both of the languages. In an interview with this fourth grade and intervention teacher, I asked her how she supported struggling students. She stated:

> The two biggest things that we see impacted here...one is the Chinese and two is socioeconomic status. And so, a lot of the kids that excel at Chinese, it's not that you're excelling in your Chinese class, it's that you can afford a Chinese tutor or an English tutor or a math tutor...but for a kid who's struggling, if you don't have the outside resources, really until two years ago there was no support for you here.... we had to switch our model and so now you've seen [a team of intervention teachers] come in, and then my position was created and [another teacher's] position was created for us to address all of that internally, because the expectation can't be that you just get a tutor.

Efforts at equity were thus wide-reaching and extensive at this IB school. However, because of this dual-language instruction and organization, students had half the time with a given teacher each school year. Across interviews, focus groups, and member check conversations, teachers reported time being a major constraint. From their perspectives, this lack of time produced another dilemma: there was less time to cultivate students' independence via inquiry-based instruction, which is another form of respect within the IB system.

As time passed, leaders at this school increasingly recognized how inquiry-based instruction, and the forms of respect associated with it (e.g., respect-as-autonomy), could be constrained given the time devoted to instructing and organizing for dual-language immersion. In member check conversations after fieldwork, I learned of the school's ongoing attempts to balance respect for students' autonomy alongside respect-as-equity. For example, during her member check, a teacher leader reported a few changes since the time of fieldwork. The IB system had released new expectations for their Primary Years Programme (PYP, for students aged 3–12), which involved folding in more opportunities for student agency. In light of this, this teacher leader reported that her school was pushing itself to find even more ways for students to exercise their independence. She offered an example of how the school had changed its after-school clubs (e.g., math club) so students could now elect into these equitable supports:

> To go along with the idea of giving kids more choice... we also offer a morning club, which we call ATL. So it's like IB's Approaches to Learning, and so originally it was going to be for kids that we felt needed extra executive functioning help. And [then] we realized that even though Johnny might need executive functioning help, if Johnny doesn't want to be there getting that help, it's not going to be useful, so we also give it to the students as a choice... it was interesting, too, because some parents contacted us and were like 'why isn't my child getting organization help?' and [we explained] 'it's because your child didn't choose it.'... It's helping the parents to see that we want the kids to learn to be their own advocates.

Despite parent resistance, the school engaged with this tension as they implemented guidance from the IB system, according increased autonomy for students over their equitable supports.

As I worked with teachers and leaders at this IB school, I observed, more than anything, evolution. I watched and heard about ongoing attempts to better support both international-mindedness and inquiry, all while attempting symmetry across the diverse socioeconomic backgrounds of students and families. Amid this evolution, it seemed that the only constant was this: every solution to one problem gave rise to yet another dilemma.

Analysis of the Dilemma

It is again time to take stock of the dilemma with the assistance of the mutual respect framework. In doing so, one must keep track of three interrelated priorities for the leaders at this IB school, which are summarized in Table 4.2: (1) respecting and supporting the socioeconomic diversity of students and families; (2) upholding the IB system's tenets of inquiry-based instruction (i.e., according students respect-as-autonomy) and cultivating international-mindedness in students (i.e., according students respect-as-equity); and (3) respecting children via both instructional and organizational moves.

At the time of fieldwork, teachers and leaders at this urban IB school were focused on disrupting the asymmetry that often exists between more and less financially privileged students. These practitioners mentioned time and again that a student's success at this school should not be contingent upon having a tutor support them at home. What is more, the actions of these leaders and teachers aligned to their espoused view that students from all socioeconomic backgrounds deserve to excel in their dual-immersion program.

In addition to socioeconomic status, however, the school was focused on disrupting other pervasive asymmetries. For example, I have described elsewhere (Hegseth, 2023b) how a teacher at this school drew on Teaching Tolerance (now Learning for Justice) resources when addressing the racial slur "boy," which she had overheard on the basketball courts during recess. The racial and ethnic diversity within this IB school was a source of pride, and the school worked to create symmetry in a range of ways: through the curriculum to which students were exposed, through the professional development teachers undergo, and through hiring a racially and ethnically diverse teaching staff and leadership team. In light of this, how were leaders at this school to balance ongoing concern for symmetry across class *and* across race and ethnicity? Do such efforts always work in synergy, or are they sometimes in conflict with one another?

As I have argued elsewhere (Hegseth, 2021), my review of IB system-level documents suggests the IB system designs instructional supports that offer relatively balanced attention to ensuring equality, autonomy, and equity for students. One can perhaps see such balance in two central priorities within IB's approach to teaching and learning: international-mindedness and inquiry-based instruction. Participants in this IB school frequently discussed their dual-immersion program as an equity move, one that fostered international-mindedness in students. Alongside this priority, IB teachers and leaders described inquiry-based instruction as a form of instruction that accords children ample autonomy over the questions they ask and answer in the classroom. Thus, any conflicts between supporting international-mindedness and supporting inquiry at this school might also be framed as a conflict between respect-as-equity and respect-as-autonomy.

Another way to frame the dilemma is in terms of how respect is operationalized. At this IB school, leaders designed elaborate instructional and organizational supports to facilitate immersion in both English and Mandarin. Respect-as-equity was apparent in what students learned, but also in how they were organized to learn. However, such robust organizing for equity served to constrain inquiry-based instruction, and thus respect-as-autonomy. Teachers and leaders at this IB school recognized that, in organizing for dual-immersion, the school had to create an elaborate timetable. This timetable offered teachers limited flexibility; time was ever their "kryptonite." In watching a video of a classroom in this school, IB teachers from a different national context noticed the same conflict. A fourth grade teacher at an IB school in Canada commented:

> IB is supposed to be a freer flowing block of time where you can follow the direction of the student interest and inquiry (Teacher: [The US IB video] was very teacher-directed). Yeah, it felt very

'the teacher says we do this, and then we do this, and then we do this.' And as much as I think it is so incredibly fantastic to have the English/Mandarin ... that takes away a little, maybe, from the IB, the flow of it.

Put simply, the organizing for equity was conflicting with teachers' ability to instruct for autonomy.

Taken together, the data presented above tells a story of IB school leaders who were ever-mindful of equity as they designed a dual-immersion program, and then supported students from diverse socioeconomic backgrounds in thriving within said program. These leaders developed robust organizational and instructional supports for this equity, and for cultivating this international-mindedness. However, such organizing for equity constrained the time needed to accord students autonomy with inquiry-based instruction. By working toward symmetry in one way, teachers and leaders at this school became increasingly aware of the need to address symmetry in other ways.

Conclusion

This chapter began with Mrs. Hayes and a description of a more status quo approach to respect in schools. I then presented a framework intended for school leaders who seek to accord students a respect that is more *mutual*, and more *integrated* within the technical core of schooling. Such a framework has potential to help school improvement efforts related to disrupting power asymmetries between adults and children, and among diverse groups of children.

After presenting this framework for mutual respect, in which I detailed its different dimensions (i.e., equality, autonomy, equity) and the different ways it can be operationalized (i.e., via instruction, organization, social relations), I animated the framework with empirical examples from two educational systems and two national contexts. With these examples, I demonstrate how the work of creating symmetry in schools is ever-changing; the only constant is the dilemma. As educators and leaders work to respect the many facets of students' identities, the different dimensions of mutual respect can reinforce or conflict with one another in unpredictable ways. So, too, can mutual respect interact in surprising ways when it's being operationalized across classroom instruction, organization, and social relations.

By describing some of the dilemmas Montessori and IB school leaders encountered, I highlight the use of a framework for mutual respect. Such a framework can first prompt leaders to become better aware of the many forms of asymmetry at play (e.g., across class, gender, race). This framework can then offer leaders various options for according (e.g., respect-as-equity, as-autonomy) and operationalizing (e.g., via instruction, organization) symmetry. Finally, by providing a frame for understanding how efforts at symmetry can reinforce and conflict with one another in unpredictable ways, this framework can help leaders to better anticipate ongoing dilemmas related to mutual respect. Anticipating such dilemmas is a first step toward managing for more symmetry within a leader's school context.

Before discussing implications, I must highlight a few more complexities of leading for mutual respect, which were not discussed in this chapter. First, though I did not discuss respect-as-equality or respect via social relations within this chapter, these forms and processes of respect are ever-present in schools, and integral to leaders' efforts when leading for symmetry. Second, it is important to acknowledge that the aim may not always be symmetry. In my other writing (Hegseth, 2021), I discuss how this framework rests on the premise that increased mutual respect in classrooms is a desired goal for all families, teachers, and schools. There are many reasons why symmetry may not be possible; for example, leaders must juggle multiple priorities alongside symmetry, and are only in partial control of all that transpires within their schools. There are also many reasons why symmetry may not be desirable; for example, families may encourage children to act in deference toward adults because of their cultural tradition or the view that more symmetrical interactions could endanger children – particularly minoritized children – in broader society (Bankston & Hidalgo, 2006). Finally, while this chapter is focused on mutual respect at the level of the school, these Montessori and IB school leaders were informed by their broader educational systems. I discuss the implications of this final point below.

Implications for Leadership Preparation and Practice

The framework proposed in this chapter – a framework for embedding mutual respect into school improvement efforts – is one that helps us to reimagine the work of school leaders. When the aim is symmetry, educational leaders must consider how to locate respect within the very fabric of teaching and learning, as opposed to simply invoking the term in school mottos and mission statements, or discussing it in a stand-alone training. Indeed, when the aim is to scale symmetry, there are implications for both leadership preparation and practice.

When reimagining school leadership for symmetry, the first step is to introduce and discuss this framework in leadership preparation programs. This is because this mutual respect framework can help aspiring leaders to make the complex work of symmetry more explicit. By acknowledging that myriad facets of students' identities deserve respect *while also* illustrating that there are multiple ways to accord and operationalize respect, this framework functions as a tool that can help aspiring leaders to better understand the ongoing dilemmas they will manage in their daily work to disrupt power asymmetries.

A second implication is around leadership practice. The three dimensions of mutual respect outlined in this framework are far from exhaustive. What is more, there may be other ways to operationalize mutual respect, beyond instruction, organization, and social relations. Given this, the framework sketched in this chapter might serve as a useful starting point for practicing school leaders, to then be expanded upon in conversations with youth and the communities surrounding their school. Together with these stakeholders, school leaders might elaborate on how to accord mutual respect to diverse student groups. For example, perhaps connection surfaces as another important dimension of mutual respect, and entails outreach within, but also beyond the school community. Previous scholars have discussed the imperative of building respect and understanding across institutional boundaries and roles (e.g., Bang et al., 2016; Galloway & Ishimaru, 2019; Penuel et al., 2015). This framework and the respect that it supports would necessarily evolve from such collaborations.

A third and final implication of the framework discussed in this chapter stems from the following observation: school leaders do not have total control over their school's organizational and instructional priorities, much like teachers do not have total control over instruction and organization within their classrooms. If one were again to refer to Fig. 4.1, one would observe that the work of mutual respect is nested; within classrooms, schools, systems, and the broader social and political environment. The educational system in which a school is situated can matter for the mutual respect at that school. Indeed, in my other writings (e.g., Hegseth, 2023a, 2023b), I demonstrate how a system's educational infrastructure can have implications for the mutual respect that teachers practice and that students experience in school.

A next step in reimagining leadership for symmetry is thus further exploration of how mutual respect might be supported at the level of the system. Research around mutual respect at the meso-level of leadership is a step toward understanding how to disrupt power asymmetries not only across classrooms, but also across schools.

Notes

1. The scenario with Mrs. Hayes is from this study's pilot, in which I examined the relationship between system designs and classroom practice across four educational systems (Aspire Charter Management Organization, high-functioning public, International Baccalaureate (IB), and Montessori) and three states (in Western, Eastern, and Midwestern United States). I conducted interviews and observations, and I collected documents for analysis. I then selected two systems from the pilot for further study: IB and Montessori.
2. While there are various forms of accreditation Montessori schools can seek to signal their fidelity of implementation, when discussing the supports of the Montessori system, I imply Association Montessori Internationale (AMI). I do so because this is the system as it was originally designed, and AMI guidelines are those to which many teachers and schools aim to adhere.
3. The Canadian Senate passed a bill in early 2018 to change the second line of "O Canada" from "in all thy sons" to "in all of us."

References

Alim, H. S. (2007). Critical hip-hop language pedagogies: Combat, consciousness, and the cultural politics of communication. *Journal of Language, Identity and Education*, 6(2), 161–176.

Anagnostopoulos, D., Cavanna, J., & Charles-Harris, S. (2020). Managing to teacher ambitiously in the first year? *The Elementary School Journal, 120*(4), 667–691.

Association Montessori International/USA. (2022). https://amiusa.org/schools/standards-for-ami-montessori-classrooms/. Accessed on March 1, 2022.

Ball, D. L. (2018, April). *Just dreams and imperatives: The power of teaching in the struggle for public education*. Presidential Address at the meeting of the American Educational Research Association, New York, NY.

Ball, D. L., & Wilson, S. M. (1996). Integrity in teaching: Recognizing the fusion of the moral and intellectual. *American Educational Research Journal, 33*(1), 155–192.

Bang, M., Faber, L., Gurneau, J., Marin, A., & Soto, C. (2016). Community-based design research: Learning across generations and strategic transformations of institutional relations toward axiological innovations. *Mind, Culture and Activity, 23*(1), 28–41. https://doi.org/10.1080/10749039.2015.1087572

Bankston, C. L., III, & Hidalgo, D. A. (2006). Respect in Southeast Asian American children and adolescents: Cultural and contextual influences. *New Directions for Child and Adolescent Development, 114*. https://doi.org/10.1002/cad.173

Baskerville, D. (2011). Developing cohesion and building positive relationships through storytelling in a culturally diverse New Zealand classroom. *Teaching and Teacher Education, 27*(1), 107–115. https://doi.org/10.1016/j.tate.2010.07.007

Boaler, J. (2006). How a detracked mathematics approach promoted respect, responsibility, and high achievement. *Theory Into Practice, 45*(1), 40–46.

Caldwell, C., Shapiro, J. P., & Gross, S. J. (2007). Ethical leadership in higher education admission: Equality vs. equity. *Journal of College Admission*, 14–19.

Campano, G. (2007). Honoring student stories. *Educational Leadership*, 48–54.

Charmaz, K. (2014). *Constructing grounded theory* (2nd ed.). Sage.

Cohen, D. K., & Ball, D. L. (1999). *Instruction, capacity, and improvement* (CPRE Research Report Series). Consortium for Policy Research in Education, University of Pennsylvania, Graduate School of Education, Philadelphia, PA.

Corbin, J., & Strauss, A. L. (2007). *Basics of qualitative research: Techniques and procedures for developing grounded theory*. Sage.

Cothran, D. J., & Ennis, C. D. (2000). Building bridges to student engagement: Communicating respect and care for students in urban high schools. *Journal of Research & Development in Education, 33*(2), 106–117.

Emerson, R. M., Fretz, R. I., & Shaw, L. L. (2011). *Writing ethnographic fieldnotes*. University of Chicago Press.

Galloway, M. K., & Ishimaru, A. M. (2019). Leading equity teams: The role of formal leaders in building organizational capacity for equity. *Journal of Education for Students Placed at Risk*. https://doi.org/10.1080/10824669.2019.1699413

Ghiso, M. (2016). The laundromat as the transnational local: Young children's literacies of interdependence. *Teachers College Record, 118*(1), 1–46.

Goodman, J. F. (2009). Respect-due and respect-earned: Negotiating student–teacher relationships. *Ethics and Education, 4*(1), 3–17.

Goodman, J. F., & Rabinowitz, M. (2019). It's not fair, I don't want to share: When child development and teacher expectations clash. *Phi Delta Kappan, 101*(1), 6–11.

Gutiérrez, R. (2008). A "gap gazing" fetish in mathematics education? Problematizing research on the achievement gap. *Journal for Research in Mathematics Education, 39*(4), 357–364.

Gutiérrez, R. (2013). The sociopolitical turn in mathematics education. *Journal for Research in Mathematics Education, 44*(1), 37–68.

Hegseth, W. M. (2021). *Respect by design: How different educational systems interact with mutual respect in classrooms* (Doctoral dissertation). https://doi.org/10.7302/1364

Hegseth, W. M. (2023a). Attempting equity in classroom practice: A debate across educational systems. *The Elementary School Journal, 124*(1), 129–156.

Hegseth, W. M. (2023b). Systemic supports for anti-racist practice in Montessori classrooms. In G. Noblit (Ed.), *Oxford research encyclopedia of education*. Oxford University Press.

Hegseth, W. M. (2024). Teaching and learning for mutual respect: A framework for disrupting pervasive power asymmetries. *Educational Researcher, 53*(3), 175–183.

Hess, D. E., & McAvoy, P. (2015). *The political classroom: Evidence and ethics in democratic education*. Routledge.

International Baccalaureate Organization. (2020, April). *Programme standards and practices*. Author.

Lampert, M. (1985). How do teachers manage to teach?: Perspectives on problems in practice. *Harvard Educational Review, 55*(2), 178–195.

Lampert, M. (2001). *Teaching problems and the problems of teaching*. Yale University Press.

Lawrence-Lightfoot, S. (2000). *Respect: An exploration*. Perseus.

Lee, C. D. (2006). 'Every good-bye ain't gone': Analyzing the cultural underpinnings of classroom talk. *International Journal of Qualitative Studies in Education, 19*(3), 305–327. https://doi.org/10.1080/09518390600696729

Penuel, W. R., Allen, A. R., Coburn, C. E., & Farrell, C. (2015). Conceptualizing research–practice partnerships as joint work at boundaries. *Journal of Education for Students Placed at Risk, 20*(1–2), 182–197. https://doi.org/10.1080/10824669.2014.988334

Poza, L. E. (2016). "Puro spelling and grammar": Conceptualizations of language and the marginalization of emergent bilinguals. *Perspectives on Urban Education, 13*(1), 20–41.

Smyth, T. S. (2005). Gateways to experience: Respect, reciprocity, and reflection in the classroom. *Kappa Delta Pi Record, 42*(1), 38–41.

Souto-Manning, M., Rabadi-Raol, A., Robinson, D., & Perez, A. (2019). What stories do my classroom and its materials tell? Preparing early childhood teachers to engage in equitable and inclusive teaching. *Young Exceptional Children, 22*(2), 62–73.

Theron, L., Liebenberg, L., & Malindi, M. (2014). When schooling experiences are respectful of children's rights: A pathway to resilience. *School Psychology International, 35*(3), 253–265.

Tobin, J., Hsueh, Y., & Karasawa, M. (2009). *Preschool in three cultures revisited: China, Japan, and the United States*. University of Chicago Press.

Urick, A. M., Ford, T. G., Page Wilson, A. S., & Consuegra, E. (2022). How does instructional leadership influence opportunity to learn in mathematics? A comparative study of pathways for grade 4 students in the U.S. and Belgium. *Research in Comparative and International Education, 17*(3), 372–398. https://doi.org/10.1177/17454999221086360

von Hippel, P. T., & Cañedo, A. P. (2022). Is kindergarten ability group placement biased? New data, new methods, new answers. *American Educational Research Journal, 59*(4), 820–857. https://doi.org/10.3102/00028312211061410

Wilson, C. M., Hanna, M. O., & Li, M. (2019). Imagining and enacting liberatory pedagogical praxis in a politically divisive era. *Equity & Excellence in Education, 53*(2–3), 346–363.

Chapter 5

Critically Reflexive School Leadership and the Racial-Discipline Gap: Leading for Racial Justice

Conor L. Scott[a] and Melinda M. Mangin[b]

[a]Bridgewater-Raritan School District, USA
[b]Rutgers University, USA

Abstract

In recent decades, school discipline has become increasingly characterized by zero-tolerance policies that mandate predetermined punitive consequences for specific offenses. Zero-tolerance policies have not been shown to improve student behavioral outcomes or school climate. Further, these disciplinary policies are applied unevenly across schools and student populations. Despite the well-documented research base that demonstrates that these practices are ineffective, they remain commonplace in K-12 school across the United States. Transformative and culturally responsive educational leadership requires school leaders to examine the historical, societal, and institutional factors that contribute to the racial-discipline gap within their particular schools. This process requires committing to leading for racial justice, self-reflexive practice, and having the courage to boldly name and dismantle practices that do not create equitable outcomes for students on the margins. Drawing on tenets of Critical Race Theory and Culturally Responsive School Leadership to situate the history and proliferation of harmful disciplinary practices, this chapter discusses how critically reflexive school leaders can mobilize restorative practices to dismantle the systems, structures, and practices that reproduce inequities in schools. The chapter provides aspiring and practicing school leaders with the knowledge needed to reform existing school discipline policies and implement practices that support racial justice.

Keywords: Exclusionary discipline; restorative practices; critical reflexivity; inequity in schools; racial-discipline gap

Introduction

In recent decades, school discipline has become increasingly characterized by zero-tolerance policies that mandate predetermined punitive consequences for specific offenses (Findlay, 2015; Heilburn et al., 2015; Skiba et al., 2014). Zero-tolerance policies frequently include exclusionary practices, such as in- or out-of-school suspension, expulsion, and arrest, which have numerous harmful consequences for students (Wun, 2018). When children are excluded from school, they are more likely to engage in negative behaviors, drop out of school, engage in criminal behavior, and enter the criminal justice system (APA, 2008; Payne & Welch, 2018). Moreover, these disciplinary policies are applied unevenly across schools and student populations. Black, Latinx, Indigenous, queer, and disabled students experience disproportionate rates of school discipline (Palmer & Greytak, 2017; Payne & Welch, 2018) creating a "racial-discipline gap" (Curran, 2016; Gregory et al., 2010).

Culturally responsive school leadership demands that school administrators critically evaluate disciplinary policies and practices (Khalifa, 2018; Rivera-McCutchen, 2021). The US Departments of Justice and Education have called on states to adopt restorative practices, including mediation, peer counseling, restorative circles and conferences, and other preventative measures to reduce schools' overreliance on exclusionary consequences. Restorative practices are an alternative to punitive and exclusionary discipline and focus on accepting responsibility, restoring harmony, and repairing the social contract (Gregory et al., 2014; Martinez et al., 2022; Payne & Welch, 2018). Greater reliance on restorative practices has the potential for improved school climate, increased academic achievement, and reduced rates of suspension and arrest in schools (Ortega et al., 2016; Rainbolt et al., 2019).

This chapter examines the historical, societal, and institutional factors that contribute to the racial-discipline gap in schools. The authors discuss how critically reflexive school leaders can mobilize restorative practices to dismantle the systems, structures, and practices that reproduce inequities in schools. The chapter provides aspiring and practicing school leaders with the knowledge needed to reform existing school discipline policies and implement practices that support racial justice.

School Discipline: Shifting Locus of Control

Throughout the first 100 years of American public education, teachers had authority to discipline children in the absence of their parents based on the principle *in loco parentis* (Stuart, 2010). During the 19th century, the predominantly male teaching force emphasized strict adherence to classroom rules and violators were often subjected to corporal punishment (i.e., hitting misbehaving children), which was widely accepted as educative (Kafka, 2011; Warnick & Scribner, 2020). Later, during the Progressive Era, the teaching force became increasingly female and reformers advocated for more humanistic discipline, prompting a decline in the use of corporal punishment (Kafka, 2011; Warnick & Scribner, 2020). Social workers and counselors were consulted to help "treat" unruly behavior and students deemed "low intelligence" were placed in classes with reduced expectations for behavior and learning (Reese, 2005; Warnick & Scribner, 2020). During the late 1930s and early 1940s, beliefs about school discipline were tied to America's war efforts and the desire for future soldiers capable of following orders (Kafka, 2011).

It wasn't until the Cold War period that teaching and discipline became increasingly separate processes with separate professionals responsible for each. In the 1950s and 1960s, Cold War politicians fiercely critiqued progressive educational reforms as communist endeavors. During those uneasy years, the *Brown* decision nominally ended students' racial segregation in America's public schools; the Supreme Court reaffirmed students' rights to due process; and the Sputnik landing increased political, social, and economic pressure on teachers, administrators, and boards of education (Kafka, 2011; Tyack & Cuban, 1995). At the same time, politicians portrayed youth as being increasingly violent, unruly, and deviant (Hinton, 2015). In response to the increase in work demands and the increased "threat" of student misbehavior, teachers demanded that their roles and disciplinary responsibilities be redefined (Kafka, 2011).

Beginning in the 1960s, teachers' unions in Los Angeles were among the first to advocate for administrators, rather than teachers, to oversee disciplinary policies (Rubel, 1977). Teachers argued that a centralized set of disciplinary practices managed by school administrators would protect them from liability from parents (due to increased racial tension between white teachers and Black and Mexican parents and students), would allow teachers to focus on meeting students' academic needs, and would convey dignity and increased teacher professionalism (Kafka, 2011). In response to teachers' demands, Los Angeles Unified School District (LAUSD), with the support of administrators and white parents, codified the nation's first comprehensive system of zero tolerance policies in the mid-1970s (Kafka, 2011). In theory, the reforms created a uniform discipline system that allowed for a more democratic, centralized system of punishment (Kafka, 2011). However, by shifting discipline away from teachers to administrators, discipline lost its educative connection to teaching and learning and, instead, became focused on punishment (Garcia, 2008).

School Collaboration With Law Enforcement

The shift in school discipline practice toward administrator oversight and punishment evolved further to include increased collaboration with law enforcement. Following the racial unrest of the 1960s in predominantly Black areas such as Newark, New Jersey, Watts, California, and Detroit, Michigan, the Johnson Administration labeled Black youth as threats to national security and convinced policymakers to pass the Juvenile Justice and Delinquency Prevention Act of 1974. Ostensibly meant to create social, educational, and employment programs for minoritized youth, the Juvenile Justice and Delinquency Prevention Act codified a symbiotic working relationship between youth social services and policing and led to the modern carceral state (Hinton, 2016). Public schools were required to partner with criminal justice organizations, including the police and juvenile correctional facilities, in order to be eligible for government funding needed to create youth social services programs (Hinton, 2015). The Act also included a "potentiality clause," which labeled any youth who was abandoned, neglected, or dependent on state-run social welfare programs as potential criminals, and thus subject to inclusion in a juvenile delinquency prevention program (Hinton, 2015).

Throughout the 1970s and 1980s, a climate of punishment spread throughout the country and the public schools. School officials collaborated with criminal justice agencies to enact school-based policies that resulted in criminal sanctions for students who violated these rules. LAUSD took the lead, working with the Los Angeles Police Department to increase police and security presence in Los Angeles schools (Hinton, 2015, 2016). Many other urban school districts followed suit, including New York, Chicago, Detroit, and Miami, creating new programs with law enforcement agencies to introduce policing in schools in the name of safety (Hinton, 2016). For example, in 2004, the Los Angeles County Schools partnered with the Los Angeles County Prosecutor to establish the Abolish Chronic Truancy (ACT) program, which subjected students and their guardians to court sanctions, fines of $250-$900 for each offense, and suspension of their driver's license for nonpayment. Of the 47,000 ACT tickets issued between 2004 and 2008, 88% of them were issued to Black and Latinx students. Programs like ACT were seen as a "necessary savior" to help "clean up schools;" however, partnerships with the criminal justice system forced students to attend schools that are more focused on controlling and punishing student behavior than on being educative spaces (Sojoyner, 2016).

Increased connections between schools and the criminal justice system positioned educational leaders as an extension of law enforcement. Instead of working with individual students, teachers, student support services, and families to address the root causes of undesirable behaviors, principals and other school administrators focused on reactionary and punitive responses to these behaviors. Rather than positively shaping student behavioral outcomes, these approaches led to increased rates of suspension and expulsion from school, increased arrests of students, and increased racial disparities in student disciplinary outcomes. Further, school administrators' collaboration with law enforcement led to a leadership paradigm that focused on compliance, rather than a critically reflexive leadership paradigm where school leaders evaluated how they could improve school climate, student sense of belonging, and students' abilities to make positive behavioral choices.

School Discipline and the Legal Codification of Zero-Tolerance Policies

Although collaborations with law enforcement and punitive disciplinary practice spread throughout public schools in the 1970s and 1980s, zero-tolerance practices were first codified into law with the 1994 amendment of the Elementary and

Secondary Education Act to include the Gun-Free Schools Act (Giroux, 2003). Motivated by a fear of youth violence and in response to school shootings in primarily white schools, the Gun-Free Schools Act mandated that schools expel students in possession of a firearm, knife, or other weapon for a minimum of 1 year and states that did not comply with the mandate risked losing federal funding (Simson, 2014). The legislation also provided funding for the training of school security personnel and for states and school districts to purchase surveillance equipment such as metal detectors (Gun-Free Schools Act, 1994). Within a year of the passage of the Gun-Free Schools Act, all 50 states enacted legislation that put into place zero-tolerance policies for possession of a weapon (Irby, 2014). In 1997, the Elementary and Secondary Education Act was once again amended to include the Safe Schools Act (Casella, 2003). The Safe Schools Act extended the Gun-Free Schools Act's mandate of expelling students for possession of weapons to also expelling students for a minimum of 1 year for possession of drugs and drug paraphernalia on school premises.

The term "zero tolerance" is used to describe a policy with strict, pre-determined penalties that affords no discretion, leniency, or "tolerance" that could result in a reduced punishment. Both the 1994 Gun-Free Schools Act and the Safe Schools act of 1997 established "zero-tolerance" for the possession of weapons or illicit drug and mandated harsh, immutable punishment: expulsion for a minimum of 1 year. Arguably, the federal government's involvement in school disciplinary policy has been limited to what could be considered "the most serious offenses," the possession of weapons and illicit drugs. However, state and local governments have expanded the use of zero-tolerance policies beyond the most serious offenses to include less serious, subjective offenses that do not pose a risk to school safety (Wun, 2018). For example, 26 states permit suspension and/or expulsion as an appropriate punishment for "willful defiance," an offense that is subjective and difficult to define (Temple University Policy Surveillance Program, 2018). As such, students can be removed from school for vague offenses that are construed as "willful defiance," which may actually reflect a cultural mismatch between the student and teacher or administrator. Although disciplinary policies are considered to be "race neutral," implicit biases impact the ways in which school staff view student behavior (Anyon et al., 2017; DeMatthews et al., 2017). For example, when Black girls advocate for their needs in schools, raced and gendered tropes often lead educators to view them as "loud," "aggressive," and "defiant," and subject them to disciplinary consequences for challenging authority (Carter Andrews et al., 2019; Morris, 2016).

As a result of the enactment of zero-tolerance policies in schools, punitive practices such as suspension and expulsion are the dominant disciplinary model in schools across the country. During the 2017–2018 school year, approximately 2.5 million public school students received at least one out-of-school suspension. These suspensions have resulted in over 11 million missed instructional days for students. Analysis of the national disciplinary data reveals that there were only 95,000 "mandatory violations," or violations that require suspension or expulsion under federal law (i.e., violent offenses, sexual assault, possession of weapons, etc.) (U.S. Department of Education Office of Civil Rights, 2021). Therefore, the vast majority of suspensions throughout the United States are for "discretionary violations" (i.e., defiance, disrespectful behavior, etc.).

As a result of the proliferation of zero-tolerance policies, schools across the country now provide local education agencies and school administrators with a great deal of latitude to interpret and punish student misbehavior. This has resulted in school administrators disproportionately disciplining students for nonviolent, subject offenses and has helped to create a culture of punishment within public schools.

Adverse Impacts of Zero-Tolerance Policies and Practices

Research on zero-tolerance policies and practices consistently demonstrates a lack of positive effects and numerous adverse impacts. In 2008, the American Psychological Association's Zero Tolerance Task Force released the results of a 10-year study that found no scientific evidence to support the claim that zero tolerance policies improved school safety or school climate. A study of 10,000 Virginia teachers found that teachers in schools with the highest level of support for zero-tolerance policies reported feeling less safe in school when compared to teachers in schools with reduced support for zero-tolerance policies (Huang & Cornell, 2021). Similarly, both large-scale quantitative and small-scale qualitative studies of students who either attended schools with high rates of exclusionary discipline or who themselves received an exclusionary consequence found that the use of exclusionary consequences was associated with poorer perceptions of school climate (Anyon et al., 2016; Huang & Anyon, 2020; Kupchick, 2016).

Zero-tolerance policies are also ineffective in positively shaping student behavior and engagement in school. When students are suspended from school, they lose out on essential instructional time and academic opportunities, which increases the likelihood that students will fail a class or need to repeat a grade, reducing on-time graduation rates and increasing the likelihood of students dropping out (Fabelo et al., 2011; Girvan et al., 2021; Gregory et al., 2010; Skiba et al., 2014). Students who experience exclusionary discipline are more likely to feel disconnected from school, become distrustful of authority, display chronic absenteeism, and engage in future maladaptive behaviors (APA, 2008; Gregory et al., 2021; Payne & Welch, 2018). Punitive approaches to discipline remove students from school without teaching students a replacement behavior, which limits students' opportunities to build and practice self-regulation skills within the classroom (Gregory et al., 2021). Moreover, each time a student is suspended from high school, their chance of dropping out increases 20% (Gregory et al., 2010). In turn, students who drop out of high school are more likely to live in poverty, engage in criminal behavior, and encounter the criminal justice system (APA, 2008).

Overall, zero-tolerance and exclusionary discipline policies have failed to prove effective in their intended purpose of creating safer school environments. Due to the significant adverse impact that these policies have on students' well-being, the American Academy of Pediatrician's Council on School Health (2013) referred to the use of exclusionary disciplinary practices as "increasingly questionable" (p. 1000). Additionally, in response to the growing evidence of the lack of efficacy of zero-tolerance policies, in a joint "Dear Colleague" letter, the United States Department of Education and Department of Justice (2014) have called on schools to examine alternatives to exclusionary discipline. Despite this call to action, zero-tolerance policies and exclusionary discipline remain common practices in schools and among school administrators. For example, in the 10-year period between 2008 and 2018, just three states (Georgia, Maine, and Massachusetts) passed new legislation mandating that administrators use alternatives to exclusionary discipline such as positive behavior support or referrals to counseling programs prior to suspending or expelling a student (Temple University Policy Surveillance Program, 2018).

Zero-tolerance and exclusionary discipline policies rely upon educational enforcing ineffective and reactionary rules and policies that drive students away from education, rather than creating welcoming and affirming school cultures where students can grow from their mistakes and develop the skills that they need to be well-adjusted citizens. If zero-tolerance policies and exclusionary discipline practices were effective deterrents of maladaptive behavior, schools would see a decrease rather than an increase in disciplinary sanctions issued.

The Racial Discipline Gap

The prevalence of racial disproportionality in exclusionary discipline is well documented. According to the U.S. Department of Education (2014), racial disproportionality occurs when so-called "race neutral" policies produce disparate outcomes for different racial or ethnic groups. In the case of school discipline, racial disproportionality exists when children of color are overrepresented in being issued exclusionary consequences. Nearly 50 years ago, the first national study of school suspensions found that Black students were between two and three times more likely to be suspended than their white peers (Children's Defense Fund, 1975). Since that time, education scholars have invested significant efforts into exploring the prevalence and causes of racial disproportionality in rates of exclusionary discipline (Mizel et al., 2016).

Not only do Black and Latinx students continue to be disproportionally represented in exclusionary discipline, but the racial-discipline gap has continued to grow. Specifically, between 1972 and 2010, exclusionary discipline rates for Black students increased from 11.8% to 24.3% and from 6.1% to 12% for Latinx students, while rates of exclusionary discipline among white students rose from 6% to 7.1% (Losen & Martinez, 2013). The U.S. Department of Education's Office of Civil Rights (2019) found that despite the fact that Black students account for 16% of the school population, they account for 40% of all out-of-school suspensions and 30% of all expulsions. While much of the literature on racial disproportionality among Black children has focused on boys, Black girls also bear the burden of disproportionality. Black girls account for 34% of school-based arrests (Morris, 2016) and 46% of Black girls receive multiple exclusionary consequences (Esposito & Edwards, 2018). According to data collected by the U.S. Department of Education Office for Civil Rights (2018), approximately 22.5% of schools across the country have racial disparities in school discipline for Black and Latinx students.

Across the literature, there is evidence that race-specific factors contribute to disproportionate punitive consequences for Black children (Welch & Payne, 2010). Efforts to identify factors unrelated to race that could explain the racial discipline gap have been unsuccessful. Even when controlling for socioeconomic status (Rausch & Skiba, 2004; Skiba et al., 2002), student achievement (Gregory et al., 2010; Rocque, 2010), and rates of behavior (Bradshaw et al., 2010; Skiba et al., 2002), race remains the leading cause of disproportionate rates of exclusionary discipline. Although Black students and white students self-report similar levels of unsafe behavior in schools, Black students are more likely to receive disciplinary consequences that result in school exclusion (Blake et al., 2020; Dinks et al., 2007; Pena-Shaff et al., 2019). Racial disproportionality is explained best by differential processing and differential treatment theories, meaning that Black students are held to different standards than white students and Black students receive more punitive sanctions than white students (Gregory et al., 2010; U.S. Department of Education, 2014).

Black students also experience disproportionate exclusionary practices. Disciplinary data show that exclusion is not restricted to violent offenses as intended; rather, Black students are excluded from school for non-violent and subjective offenses such as tardiness, truancy, disrespectful behavior, and willful defiance (Girvan et al., 2017; Skiba et al., 2014; Smolkowski et al., 2016). Black students receive a disproportionate number of sanctions for subjective offenses, such as disrespectful behavior (Fabelo et al., 2011; Forsyth et al., 2015). Schools with higher rates of Black enrollment rely more heavily on punitive practices and are less likely to use milder punishments such as warnings and referrals to counseling services (Rocha & Hawes, 2009; Welch & Payne, 2010). In response to the alarming disproportionate rates of school discipline by student race, critically reflexive school leaders must examine and challenge the systems and practices within their schools that continue to promote equitable outcomes in student discipline.

Restorative Practices as an Alternative to Punitive and Exclusionary Discipline

In response to the overwhelming evidence demonstrating the adverse effects of exclusionary discipline, especially for marginalized students, government agencies, scholars, and practitioners have called on schools to implement alternative practices to punitive and exclusionary discipline. The use of restorative practices in schools could be an alternative way to improve student behavior and reduce the need for exclusionary discipline.

Restorative practices draw from the concept of "restorative justice," which originated in the criminal justice system as a way for offenders to take responsibility for their actions and repair harm inflicted upon the victim. Over the past

15 years, restorative practices have entered schools as an alternative to punitive and exclusionary discipline (Ortega et al., 2016). The goal of restorative justices is "to build positive emotions, such as empathy and excitement, and rid the community of negative emotions, such as anger and humiliation. This is in contrast to a more punitive orientation, in which the goal is fact building and punishment" (Payne & Welch, 2018, p. 226). In many ways, restorative practices are the antithesis to zero-tolerance policies and punitive discipline (Ortega et al., 2016; Weaver & Swank, 2020). Zero-tolerance policies rely on a third party administering an arbitrary punishment. In a restorative model, the focus is on restoring harmony, repairing the social contract, and getting offenders to reflect upon and accept responsibility for their offense (Ortega et al., 2016; Rainbolt et al., 2019; Weaver & Swank, 2020).

Several restorative justice practices have been researched in school settings. Restorative circles are among the most widely utilized practices and the "most essential" component of restorative justice in schools (Gregory et al., 2014). Circles can be used either proactively or responsively (Payne & Welch, 2018). In proactive circles, students have the opportunity to discuss academic, emotional, or classroom-specific topics. This sharing of experiences and goals helps students to learn about each other and build community. When restorative circles are used proactively, "students gain understanding of the complexity of human motivations and develop empathy for those around them" (High, 2018, p. 531). Restorative circles can also be utilized by staff and students as a responsive strategy when someone has caused harm to another member of the community. Responsive restorative circles are meant to engage students in a collaborative problem-solving approach where students discuss their feelings, identify who has been harmed, develop a plan to repair the damage, and discuss how the conflict can be prevented in the future (Gregory et al., 2014). Rather than excluding or removing an offender for committing an offense, responsive circles seek to hold students accountable in a way that encourages them to see how they harmed someone else and evaluate how they can repair the harm (Mansfield et al., 2018; Payne & Welch, 2018). In contrast, exclusionary disciplinary practices deprive students of opportunities to learn how to resolve interpersonal conflict and reduce bias (Snapp & Licona, 2017).

Restorative conferences may be another effective alternative to punitive discipline in schools (Anyon et al., 2016; Jain et al., 2014; Morrison & Vaandering, 2012; Rainbolt et al., 2019). Unlike restorative circles, which are used in the classroom to address minor issues, restorative conferences are used to address major behavioral infractions. Restorative conferences are highly formalized meetings that seek to identify the problem, understand why it happened, and identify a solution. In these conferences, the victim and offender's voices are central, and there is an attempt to repair harm rather than use punitive or exclusionary discipline (Anyon et al., 2016). These conferences can also provide students with wraparound support, such as counseling, to help facilitate student success (Jain et al., 2014).

Numerous researchers have explored the efficacy of restorative practices in schools. Studies have found that the use of restorative justice practices in schools significantly reduces disciplinary referrals (Gregory & Clawson, 2016; Rainbolt et al., 2019), significantly reduces the use of out-of-school suspensions

(Jain et al., 2014; Mansfield et al., 2018; Rainbolt et al., 2019), and reduces police citations in schools (Ortega et al., 2016) for Black and Latino students. Restorative practices in schools have also been shown to improve school climate. For example, students report that teachers who use restorative practices are more respectful (Gregory et al., 2018). Students and staff report improved relationships following the implementation of restorative practices (Ortega et al., 2016; Rainbolt et al., 2019; Weaver & Swank, 2020). A qualitative study conducted in Denver with 35 students and teachers (Ortega et al., 2016) and quantitative research with 17,650 students in Oakland (Jain et al., 2014) have also found that restorative practices result in improved academic achievement. Additional positive outcomes include reduced truancy and drop-out rates (Jain et al., 2014). These studies suggest that, the implementation of restorative justice in schools may reduce the harmful effects of exclusionary discipline, foster more positive school climate, and improve students' academic achievement. Despite these benefits, punitive disciplinary practices remain the dominant practice among school leaders.

Implications for School Leaders, Leadership Preparation, and Research

Given what is known about the adverse effects of zero-tolerance policies and exclusionary discipline, especially for Black, Latinx, Indigenous, queer, and disabled students, it is incumbent upon our educational leaders to take proactive steps to address and correct inequitable school discipline systems. Administrators often view discipline policies as being "race neutral" policies that promote safety and accountability when, in reality, racial bias plays a significant role in how students' behaviors are evaluated and addressed (Simson, 2014). To challenge and correct misconceptions of racial neutrality, school leaders must be critically self-reflexive. Critically self-reflexive practice involves school leaders "involves the interrogation of, and planning for, educational reforms situated within social and cultural context of schooling that are rife with inequity" (Pak & Ravitch, 2021, p. 3). In other words, school leaders must question their schools' disciplinary philosophies, practices, outcomes, and organizational decision-making to determine the (un)intended effects that current practices have on various groups of students. Critical self-reflexivity goes beyond self-reflection, wherein leaders are asked to think about their own individual biases or roles in reproducing injustice, and instead, calls upon leaders to examine, name, and disrupt the systems of power and collective actions that maintain and reproduce injustice (Pak & Ravitch, 2021).

School leaders who critically evaluated their beliefs about the role and function of school discipline can begin the work of dismantling inequity in school discipline. Specifically, leaders must reflect on the purpose of discipline in schools, who or what behaviors deserve to be disciplined, and how implicit biases may impact these beliefs. Critically reflective school leaders also question how these beliefs have been learned and reinforced and are also challenged to think about what evidence they have that supports the belief that punitive and reactionary disciplinary practices are effective, equitable, and just for all learners. Once leaders begin to address their own biases and deeply held beliefs about the perceived value of discipline, they will likely see the inadequacy of our current punitive system for improving student outcomes or making schools safer for all learners. By understanding and addressing their own biases, school leaders can begin to engage in self-reflexivity – where they work with their school communities to name and dismantle inequitable practices and systems – which will help drive organizational change within their schools.

At the school level, critically reflexive leaders evaluate their school's current practices and procedures and begin to imagine new and innovative responses to typical student disciplinary issues. To that end, school leaders can start by assembling a team of stakeholders, including administrators, teachers, counselors, support staff, parents, and community members who are committed to challenging culturally biased disciplinary practices. To make its work meaningful, the school-based team must examine their school's disciplinary data to identify trends in terms of disproportionality by racial and ethnic group (i.e., Latinx students' rate of enrollment compared to rate of disciplinary consequence) and by infraction type (i.e., subjective offenses such as insubordination compared to objective offenses such as use of illicit substances). Naming disparate outcomes in discipline as a problem allows teams to begin developing solutions. Sharing disciplinary data with the whole school can also lead to solution finding. Situating the data within a broader conversation about racial discipline, systemic racism, and how seemingly "race-neutral" policies can lead to disparate outcomes for groups of students.

The data can be used to drive small-group conversations among staff members about what inequities might exist in school discipline, why these equities may exist, how these equities conflict (or support) the school's mission and values, and what are some potential solutions that the school can take in addressing these issues. When school leaders engage all staff members in these critical conversations, there is a clear message that all staff members play a role in naming and dismantling inequitable practices.

A critical next step is to collaboratively identify responsive practices that will help students build skills and repair harm for the code of conduct violations that occur most frequently. The school-based team can help to turnkey and model what restorative practices look like in action to help build a shared understanding for all staff members. For example, proactive and preventative restorative circles in homerooms or classrooms can be used to help build community, teach communication skills, reduce conflict, and ultimately, reduce instances of physical altercations. This approach allows staff members to think holistically about students' needs and to teach them the positive interpersonal skills that can be used in times of conflict to repair harmony within the school community.

The transition from traditional disciplinary methods to nonpunitive, restorative practices may be met with speculation and doubt rather than hope and curiosity by certain stakeholders. Therefore, it is essential that paradigm shift is supported by central office leadership. District-level leaders have an ethical and professional obligation to ensure racial equity within schools. To support their students, teachers, and principals, district-level officials can provide access to external professional development and training for school-based teams tasked with shifting their school's disciplinary paradigm from punitive to restorative. District-level leaders are also charged with working with principals to evaluate current resource allocations to ensure alignment with district and school goals. Rather than utilizing limited funds to hire school resource officers or security personnel who do not have formal training in child and adolescent development, trauma-informed practices, or counseling skills, critically reflexive leaders assist in the hiring of additional school counselors, social workers, and psychologists to help create culture focused on student social-emotional development and well-being rather than accountability and consequences.

Critically reflexive leaders also ensure that there is clarity regarding staff members' roles and responsibilities within the discipline process. School counselors, school psychologists, and school social workers are often asked to assist with disciplinary investigations or are consulted about student consequences. To protect counselors' roles as mental health support professionals, their roles must be distinct and separate from the school discipline process. Rather, counselors should be tasked with teaching conflict resolution skills, addressing trauma, addressing racial bias, and developing students' coping skills through individual counseling sessions, targeted counseling groups, and whole-school lessons and programming. By providing these staff members with a clear, nonpunitive focus, leaders can ensure that their school counselors can focus on preventative and proactive supports for all students.

Conclusion

Graduate schools of education that adopt a racial justice approach can actively work to facilitate the development and implementation of non-punitive school discipline practices and, simultaneously, reduce the overreliance on zero-tolerance policies. Both theoretical and practical coursework can be leveraged to facilitate widespread change. Helping teacher candidates develop culturally responsive classroom practices will help aspiring educators begin to think about their approaches to teaching, learning, and management. When students are placed in classrooms where teachers consider their unique gifts, cultures, and interests, students are less likely to engage in "problematic" behaviors (Paris & Alim, 2017). Additionally, teacher preparation programs have a responsibility to introduce aspiring teachers to restorative classroom practices, including restorative circles and conferences. To ensure that each student-teacher has the opportunity to practice implementing restorative practices during their internships, standards for competency in restorative practices can be included as part of the student-teacher's evaluation. By purposefully including implementation of restorative practices as a student-teaching requirement, university programs demonstrate their commitment to racial justice and nonpunitive approaches to student discipline. To help cooperating teachers and schools in supporting student-teachers' implementation of restorative practices, graduate schools of education can also provide each school with information and training on these practices at the beginning of the school year.

Administrator preparation programs also have an obligation to facilitate the implementation of non-punitive discipline practices. Close reading of current research about the adverse impacts that punitive disciplinary practices have on students' academic and interpersonal development can help aspiring leaders understand the need for new approaches to school discipline. Specific attention should be given to how students with multiple intersecting marginalized identities are impacted by punitive practices. Administrator preparation programs can also task aspiring leaders to confront their biases and examine how negative beliefs about students' identities impact leaders' perceptions of "wrong-doing." At the practical level, aspiring leaders must be prepared for the day-to-day realities of administering school discipline. Often, school administrators rely on punitive practices because they have not been taught or experienced alternatives such as restorative practices. Principal preparation programs can provide explicit instruction, modeling, role play, and case study discussions so that aspiring administrators can begin to plan how to employ alternatives to punitive discipline before they assume a leadership role.

Finally, the findings from this review of the extant literature also have implications for future research. Broadly speaking, we need research that identifies how to create the conditions needed to implement culturally sustaining, non-punitive approaches to discipline. This includes investigations into the root causes of racial disciplinary disparities, which remain under-researched and under-theorized (Welsh & Little, 2018). New lines of research, aimed at understanding school leaders' role in the design and implementation of school discipline policies can provide insights into the factors that sustain punitive discipline practices in schools. Case studies that examine the effective implementation of restorative practices in a range of school settings can provide educators with practical knowledge needed to successfully change existing disciplinary policies. Longitudinal studies that examine the positive impacts of restorative justice on schools and students over time may provide further evidence of the potential benefits of non-punitive discipline and justification for change. Relatedly, federal funding and state education budgets should include financial incentives for districts to implement and evaluate nonpunitive disciplinary practices.

References

American Academy of Pediatrics. (2013). Policy statement: Out-of-school suspension and expulsion. *Pediatrics*, *131*(3), 1000–1007. https://doi.org/10.1542/peds.2012-3932

American Psychological Association. (2008). Are zero tolerance policies effective in the schools?: An evidentiary review and recommendations. *American Psychologist*, *63*(9), 852–862. https://doi.org/10.1037/0003-066x.63.9.852

Anyon, Y., Gregory, A., Stone, S., Farrar, J., Jenson, J. M., McQueen, J., Downing, B., Greer, E., & Simmons, J. (2016). Restorative interventions and school discipline sanctions in a large urban school district. *American Educational Research Journal*, *53*(6), 1663–1697. https://doi.org/10.3102/0002831216675719

Anyon, Y., Lechuga, C., Ortega, D., Downing, B., Greer, E., & Simmons, J. (2017). An exploration of the relationships between student racial background and the school sub-contexts of office discipline referrals: A critical race theory analysis. *Race, Ethnicity, and Education, 21*(3), 390–406. https://doi.org/10.1080/13613324.2017.1328594

Blake, J. J., Smith, D. M., Unni, A., Marchbanks III, M. P., Wood, S., & Eason, J. M. (2020). Behind the eight ball: The effects of race and number of infractions on the severity of exclusionary discipline sanctions issued in secondary school. *Journal of Emotional and Behavioral Disorders, 28*(3), 131–143. https://doi.org/10.1177/1063426620937698

Bradshaw, C. P., Mitchell, M. M., O'Brennan, L. M., & Leaf, P. J. (2010). Multilevel exploration of factors contributing to the overrepresentation of black students in office disciplinary referrals. *Journal of Educational Psychology, 102*(2), 508–520. https://doi.org/10.1037/a0018450

Carter Andrews, D. J., Brown, T., Castro, E., & Id-Deen, E. (2019). The impossibility of being "perfect and white": Black girls' racialized and gendered schooling experiences. *American Educational Research Journal, 56*(6), 2531–2572. https://doi.org/10.3102/0002831219849392

Casella, R. (2003). Zero tolerance policy in schools: Rationale, consequences, and alternatives. *Teachers College Record, 105*(5), 872–892. https://doi.org/10.1111/1467-9620.00271

Children's Defense Fund. (1975). *School suspensions: Are they helping children?* U.S. Department of Health, Education, and Welfare.

Curran, F. C. (2016). Estimating the effect of state zero tolerance laws on exclusionary discipline, racial discipline gaps, and study behavior. *Educational Evaluation and Policy Analysis, 38*(4), 647–668. https://doi.org/10.3102/0162373716652728

DeMatthews, D. E., Carey, R. L., Olivarez, A., & Saeedi, K. M. (2017). Guilty as charged? Principals' perspectives on disciplinary practices and the racial discipline gap. *Educational Administration Quarterly, 53*(4), 519–555. https://doi-org.proxy.libraries.rutgers.edu/10.1177%2F0013161X17714844

Dinks, R., Cartaldi, E. F., & Lin-Kelly, W. (2007). *Indicators of school crime and safety*. National Center for Educational Statistics. https://nces.ed.gov/pubs2008/2008021.pdf

Esposito, E., & Edwards, E. B. (2018). When Black girls fight: Interrogating and (re)imagining dangerous scripts of femininity in urban classrooms. *Education and Urban Society, 50*(1), 87–107. https://doi.org/10.1177/0013124517729206

Fabelo, T., Thompson, M. D., Plotkin, M., Carmichael, D., Marchbanks III, M. P., & Booth, E. (2011). *Breaking schools' rules: A statewide study of how school discipline relates to students' success and juvenile justice involvement*. Council of State Governments Justice Center; Public Policy Research Institute at Texas A&M University. http://justicecenter.csg.org/resources/juveniles

Findlay, N. M. (2015). Discretion in student discipline: Insight into elementary principals' decision making. *Educational Administration Quarterly, 51*(3), 472–507. https://doi-org.proxy.libraries.rutgers.edu/10.1177%2F0013161X14523617

Forsyth, C. J., Biggar, R. W., Forsyth, Y. A., & Howat, H. (2015). The punishment gap: Racial/ethnic comparisons in school infractions by objective and subjective definitions. *Deviant Behavior, 36*(4), 276–287. https://doi.org/10.1080/01639625.2014.935623

Garcia, M. (2008, March 8). '68 to '08: We're not finished. *Los Angeles Times.* https://www.latimes.com/archives/la-xpm-2008-mar-08-oe-garcia8-story.html

Giroux, H. (2003). Racial injustice and disposable youth in the age of zero tolerance. *International Journal of Qualitative Studies in Education, 16*(4), 553–565. https://doi.org/10.1080/0951839032000099543

Girvan, E. J., Gion, C., McIntosh, K., & Smolkowski, K. (2017). The relative contribution of subjective office referrals to racial disproportionality in school discipline. *School Psychology Quarterly, 32*(3), 392–404. https://doi.org/10.1037/spq0000178

Girvan, E. J., McIntosh, K., & Santiago-Rosario, M. R. (2021). Associations between community-level racial biases, office discipline referrals, and out-of-school suspensions. *School Psychology Review, 50*(2–3), 288–302. https://doi.org/10.1080/2372966X.2020.1838232

Gregory, A., & Clawson, K. (2016). The potential of restorative approaches to discipline for narrowing racial and gender disparities. In Skiba, R. J., Mediratta, K., & Rausch, M. K. (Eds), *Inequality in school discipline: Research and practice to reduce disparities* (pp. 153–170). Macmillan.

Gregory, A., Clawson, K., Davis, A., & Gerewitz, J. (2014). The promise of restorative practices to transform teacher-student relationships and achieve equity in school discipline. *Journal of Educational and Psychological Consultation, 26*(4), 325–353. https://doi.org/10.1080/10474412.2014.929950

Gregory, A., Huang, F. L., Anyon, Y., Greer, E., Downing, B., & Bradshaw, C. (2018). An examination of restorative interventions and racial equity in out-of-school suspensions. *School Psychology Review, 47*(2), 167–182. https://doi.org/10.17105/SPR-2017-0073.V47-2

Gregory, A., Osher, D., Bear, G. G., Jagers, R. J., & Sprague, J. R. (2021). Good intentions are not enough: Centering equity in school discipline reform. *School Psychology Review, 50*(2–3), 206–220. https://doi.org/10.1080/2372966X.2020.186191

Gregory, A., Skiba, R. J., & Noguera, P. A. (2010). The achievement gap and the discipline gap: Two sides of the same coin? *Educational Researcher, 39*(1), 59–68. https://jstor.org/stable/27764554

Gun-Free Schools Act of 1994, 20 USC § 7961. (1994). https://uscode.house.gov/view.xhtml?req=granuleid:USC-prelim-title20-section7961&num=0&edition=prelim

Heilburn, A., Cornella, D., & Lovegrove, P. (2015). Principal attitudes regarding zero tolerance and racial disparities in school suspensions. *Psychology in the Schools, 52*(5), 489–499. https://doi.org/10.1002/pits.21838

High, A. J. (2018). Using restorative practices to teach and uphold dignity in an American school district. *Notes from the Field, 52*(2), 525–534. https://doi.org/10.7202/1044479ar

Hinton, E. K. (2015). *From the war on poverty to the war on crime: The making of mass incarceration in America.* Harvard University Press.

Hinton, E. K. (2016). Creating crime: The rise and impact of national juvenile delinquency programs in Black urban neighborhoods. *Journal of Urban History, 41*(5), 800–824. https://doi.org/10.1177/0096144215589946

Huang, F., & Anyon, Y. (2020). The relationship between school disciplinary resolutions with school climate and attitudes toward school. *Preventing School Failure, 64*(3), 212–222. https://doi.org/10.1080/1045988X.2020.1722940

Huang, F. L., & Cornell, D. G. (2021). Teacher support for zero tolerance is associated with higher suspension rates and lower feelings of safety. *School Psychology Review*, *50*(2–3), 388–405. https://doi.org/10.1080/2372966X.2020.1832865

Irby, D. J. (2014). Trouble at school: Understanding school discipline systems as nets of social control. *Equity & Excellence in Education*, *47*(4), 513–530. https://doi.org/10.1080/10665684.2014.958963

Jain, S., Bassey, H., Brown, M., & Kalra, P. (2014). *Restorative justice in Oakland schools: Implementation and impacts*. Oakland Public Schools.

Kafka, J. (2011). The history of "zero tolerance". In *American public schools*. Palgrave MacMillan.

Khalifa, M. A. (2018). *Culturally responsive school leadership*. Harvard Education Press.

Kupchik, A. (2016). *The real school safety problem: The long-term consequences of harsh school punishment*. University of California Press.

Losen, D. J. & Martinez, T. E. (2013). Out of school and off track: The overuse of suspensions in American middle and high schools. *The Center for Civil Rights Remedies*. https://escholarship.org/uc/item/8pd0s08z

Mansfield, K. G., Rainbolt, S., & Sutton Fowler, E. (2018). Implementing restorative justice as a step toward racial equity in school discipline. *Teachers College Record*, *120*, 1–24. https://www.tcrecord.org/Content.asp?ContentId=22385

Martinez, A., Villegas, L., Ayoub, L. H., Jensen, E., & Miller, M. (2022). Restorative justice and school-wide transformation: Identifying drivers of implementation and system change. *Journal of School Violence*, *21*(2), 190–205. https://doi.org/10.1080/15388220.2022.2039682

Mizel, M. L., Miles, J., Pedersen, E. R., Tucker, J. S., Ewing, B. A., & D'Amico, E. J. (2016). To educate or to incarcerate: Factors in disproportionality in school discipline. *Children and Youth Services Review*, *70*, 102–111. https://doi.org/10.1016/j.childyouth.2016.09.009

Morris, M. (2016). *Pushout: The criminalization of Black girls in schools*. The New Press.

Morrison, B. E., & Vaandering, D. (2012). Restorative justice: Pedagogy, praxis, and discipline. *Journal of School Violence*, *11*(2), 138–155. https://doi.org/10.1080/15388220.2011.653322

Ortega, L., Lyubansky, M., Nettles, S., & Espelage, D. L. (2016). Outcomes of a restorative circles program in a high school setting. *Psychology of Violence*, *6*(3), 459–468. https://doi.org/10.1037/vio0000048

Pak, K., & Ravitch, S. M. (2021). *Critical leadership praxis for educational and social change*. Teachers College Press.

Palmer, N. A., & Greytak, E. A. (2017). LGBTQ student victimization and its relationship to school discipline and justice system involvement. *Criminal Justice Review*, *42*(2), 163–187. https://doi.org/10.1177/0734016817704698

Paris, D. & Alim, H. S. (Eds.). (2017). *Culturally sustaining pedagogies: Teaching and learning for justice in a changing world*. Teachers College Press.

Payne, A. A., & Welch, K. (2018). The effect of school conditions on the use of restorative justice in schools. *Youth Violence and Juvenile Justice*, *16*(2), 224–240. https://doi.org/10.1177/1541204016681414

Pena-Shaff, J. B., Bessette-Symons, B., Tate, M., & Fingerhut, J. (2018). Racial and ethnic differences in high school students' perceptions of school climate and disciplinary practices. *Race Ethnicity and Education, 22*(2), 269–284. https://doi.org/10.1080/13613324.2018.1468747

Rainbolt, S., Fowler, E. S., & Mansfield, K. C. (2019). High school teachers' perceptions of restorative discipline practices. *NASSP Bulletin, 103*(2), 158–182. https://doi.org/10.1177/0192636519853018

Rausch, M. K., & Skiba, R. J. (2004). Unplanned outcomes: Suspensions and expulsions in Indiana. *Education Policy Briefs, 2*, 1–7.

Reese, W. J. (2005). *America's public schools: From the common school to "No child left behind"*. The Johns Hopkins University Press.

Rivera-McCutchen, R. L. (2021). "We don't got time for grumbling": Toward an ethic of radical care in urban leadership. *Educational Administration Quarterly, 57*(2), 257–289. https://doi.org/10.1177/0013161X20925892

Rocha, R., & Hawes, D. (2009). Racial diversity, representative bureaucracy, and equity in multicultural districts. *School Science Quarterly, 90*(2), 326–344. https://doi.org/10.1111/j.1540-6237.2009.00620.x

Rocque, M. (2010). Office discipline and student behavior: Does race matter? *American Journal of Education, 116*(4), 557–581. https://doi.org/10.1086/653629

Rubel, A. J. (1977). "Limited good" and "social comparison:" Two theories, one problem. *Ethos: Journal of the Society for Psychological Anthropology*, 224–238. https://doi.org/10.1525/eth.1977.5.2.02a00070

Simson, D. (2014). Exclusion, punishment, racism, and our schools: A critical race theory perspective on school discipline. *UCLA Law Review, 61*(2), 508–562. https://ssrn.com/abstract=2129117

Skiba, R. J., Arredondo, M. I., & Williams, N. T. (2014). More than a metaphor: The contribution of exclusionary discipline to a school-to-prison pipeline. *Equity & Excellence in Education, 47*(4), 546–564. https://doi.org/10.1080/10665684.2014.958965

Skiba, R. J., Michael, R. S., Nardo, A. C., & Peterson, R. L. (2002) The color of discipline: Sources of racial and gender disproportionality in school punishment. *The Urban Review, 34*, 317–342. https://doi.org/10.1023/A:1021320817372

Smolkowski, K., Girvan, E. J., McIntosh, K., Nese, R. N. T., & Horner, R. H. (2016). Vulnerable decision points for disproportionate office discipline referrals: Comparisons of discipline for African American and white elementary school students. *Behavioral Disorders, 41*(4), 178–195. https://doi.org/10.17988/bedi-41-04-178-195.1

Snapp, S. D., & Licona, A. C. (2017). The school-to-prison pipeline and the pipeline population: The patterns and practices of its production and dismantling possibilities. In S. T. Russell & S. S. Horn (Eds.), *Sexual orientation, gender identity, and schooling: The nexus of research, practice, and policy*. Oxford University Press.

Sojoyner, D. M. (2016). *First strike: Educational enclosures in Black Los Angeles*. University of Minnesota Press.

Stuart, S. (2010). In loco parentis in the public schools: Abused, confused, and in need of change. *Valparaiso University Legal Studies Research, 10*(3), 1–47. https://scholarship.law.uc.edu/uclr/vol78/iss3/4

Temple University Policy Surveillance Program. (2018). School discipline laws. https://lawatlas.org/datasets/school-discipline-policies

Tyack, D. B., & Cuban, L. (1995). *Tinkering toward utopia: A century of public school reform*. Harvard University Press.

U.S. Commission on Civil Rights. (2019). Beyond suspensions: Examining the school discipline policies and connections to the school-to-prison pipeline for students of color with disabilities. https://www.usccr.gov/files/pubs/2019/07-23-Beyond-Suspensions.pdf

U.S. Department of Education Office of Civil Rights (2018). *2015–2016 civil rights data collection: School climate and safety*. https://www2.ed.gov/about/offices/list/ocr/docs/school-climate-and-safety.pdf

U.S. Department of Education Office of Civil Rights. (2021). *Civil rights data collection (CRDC) for the 2017–2018 school year*. https://www2.ed.gov/about/offices/list/ocr/docs/crdc-2017-18.html

U.S. Department of Justice & U.S. Department of Education. (2014). Joint "Dear Colleague" letter. https://www2.ed.gov/about/offices/list/ocr/letters/colleague-201401-title-vi.html

Warnick, B. R., & Scribner, C. F. (2020). Discipline, punishment, and the moral community of schools. *Theory and Research in Education*, *18*(1), 98–116. https://doi.org/10.1177/1477878520904943

Weaver, J. L., & Swank, J. M. (2020). A case study of the implementation of restorative justice in a middle school. *RMLE Online*, *43*(4), 1–9. https://doi.org/10.1080/19404476.2020.1733912

Welsh, R. O., & Little, S. (2018). The school discipline dilemma: A comprehensive review of disparities and alternative approaches. *Review of Educational Research*, *88*(5), 752–794. https://doi.org/10.3102/0034654318791582

Welch, K., & Payne, A. A. (2010). Racial threat and punitive school discipline. *Social Problems*, *57*(1), 25–48. https://doi.org/10.1525/sp.2010.57.1.25

Wun, C. (2018). Schools as carceral sites: A unidirectional war against girls of color. In A. I. Ali & T. L. Buenavista (Eds.), *Education at war: The fight for students of color in America's public schools*. Fordham University Press.

Chapter 6

"But How Will This Improve Outcomes?" Tensions and Lessons of Improvement During a Racial Equity Transformation at Copley Public Schools

Patricia M. Virella

Montclair State University, USA

Abstract

The chapter delves into the transformative journey of Copley Public Schools (CPS) toward creating a more inclusive and just learning environment, mainly focusing on racial equity. The district's history of state control due to academic underperformance led to a shift toward antiracist and equitable practices under former superintendent Danielle Crane. In this chapter, I emphasize the importance of achieving racial equity in schools, highlighting how one large urban school district engaged in a multiyear transformational process toward racial equity. The partnership between CPS and a university's educational leadership department was designed to address racial equity through a multiyear plan involving school and district leaders. The approach centered around Vygotsky's Zone of Proximal Development, emphasizing support for professional growth and equitable student outcomes. I outline a detailed plan grounded in research and best practices, focusing on leadership roles in shaping school culture and driving transformation. Lessons learned from the district's racial equity transformation highlight positive outcomes while addressing challenges such as historical practices influencing policies and systemic barriers to improvement. Leaders worked toward forming coalitions of progress, emphasizing the importance of understanding past influences on present environments and the need for informed decision-making to foster racially equitable educational settings.

Keywords: Inclusive practices; systemic barriers; racial equity; Vygotsky's Zone of Proximal Development; school leadership

Introduction

Copley Public Schools (CPS) is a school district in an urban emergent city serving a diverse student population primarily composed of LatinX and Black students, with a small number of Arabic students. The district has a checkered history of state control due to its underwhelming academic performance. State control entailed limited autonomy over critical district-level and school-level decisions such as curricula, policies, and other organizational routines. CPS navigated those difficulties, but unfortunately, the anticipated progress was not seen, resulting in their transfer of authority back to the local district from state control. After struggling with state control due to underwhelming academic performance, CPS took a bold step toward creating a more inclusive and just learning environment in 2021. Recognizing the systemic issues highlighted by the protests following George Floyd's murder and the inequalities that arose due to the COVID-19 pandemic, the former superintendent, Danielle Crane, embarked on a transformative journey to become an antiracist and equitable school district.

Achieving racial equity in education is crucial to creating a fair and just learning environment that provides equal opportunities for all students. Unfortunately, the systematic denial of equal education to students of color has resulted in racial inequities in student performance, perpetuating disparities in academic success. Students of color often attend schools with fewer resources, are more likely to be exposed to exclusionary discipline, and are less likely to be tracked into advanced classes, creating a significant education debt. To address this issue, it is essential to implement school-based strategies that embed racial and ethnic equity and acknowledge the impact of racial inequity and injustice on students of color. However, the decentralization of race in educational policy has led to the dilution of racial equity. Policies that fail to address racial equity issues openly are ineffective in addressing the needs.

In this chapter, I offer critical insights and reflections on a 3-year transformative initiative in a school district. The focus is on the strategies and approaches employed by the district to enhance academic performance through an equity-oriented, antiracist transformation. I provide an abbreviated review of the theoretical literature that informs the partnership, followed by lessons learned from school principals and how they propelled the transformation forward. The chapter also explores barriers encountered and strategies used to overcome them. Through in-depth analysis, this chapter aims to explicate the strategies and approaches that the district employed to foster transformational change. It provides valuable insights into the complex process of district transformation, highlighting the challenges and opportunities that arise during this period. The chapter underscores the importance of adopting a collaborative approach that involves all stakeholders, such as school leaders, teachers, students, families, and community members. Overall, this chapter comprehensively analyzes the district's journey toward equity-minded transformation and provides practical recommendations for other school districts seeking to promote equity, antiracism, and academic excellence.

Partnering With Copley Public Schools

Years of smaller initiatives with the university led to the partnership between CPS and the university's educational leadership department. As a result, CPS approached the department to explore how they could collaborate on a district-wide initiative to address racial equity. In 2021, after conversing with district leadership, the author had the opportunity to meet with the school leaders to discuss their initial thoughts on a multileveled and multiyear plan for CPS. The district and university's goal was to initiate an effort to bring about transformational change across the district and address the different mindsets of school and district leaders that were creating barriers for some students while providing opportunities for others.

To achieve this, the initiative focused on the school and district leaders, including district supervisors, assistant principals, principals, assistant superintendents, and the superintendent. The initiative's aim was chosen because of the recent leadership that recognized the critical role of leaders in shaping the school culture, climate, and conditions and their ability to drive transformation. The professional learning approach centered around Vygotsky's Zone of Proximal Development (ZPD), which emphasizes providing the right level of support to individuals to help them achieve their full potential.

I selected this theoretical approach to situate professional learning because Vygotsky's sociocultural theory emphasizes the significance of social interactions, cultural influences, and the role of language in cognitive development. By applying this theory to the context of racial equity, leaders can foster inclusive and equitable learning environments that empower students to engage critically with issues of race and culture. The partnership recognized the importance of adult learning principles that require learner-centered methods and a cooperative learning environment.

To ensure that the plan was sustainable and aligned with district priorities, such as creating a student-centered learning environment, challenging students' learning, empowering and motivating families, and increasing partnerships with institutions to support the students, the partnership worked closely with district leadership to create a highly detailed, coherent, and organized plan grounded in research and informed by best practices. The partnership recognized that during times of change, particularly when engaging in difficult conversations about race, individuals may have a hard time engaging in these conversations. Therefore, the plan must be well-supported and aligned with district priorities to ensure its success.

Year one was focused on understanding the leaders' racial equity literacy, level of commitment to the transformation, and rate of change at their schools. The first year was learning for the leaders and change agents, setting goals to transform their schools into an equity orientation, and understanding how data can help create more equitable opportunities and outcomes. Year two was focused on making more substantive changes at the district and school levels, looping in teachers, and making organizational changes such as grading and discipline policies; the second year also included school walk-throughs to understand how schools were enacting an equity-oriented and antiracist instructional delivery, school culture, and climate.

At the culmination of the second year, a wealth of knowledge was gained regarding the infusion and diffusion of professional learning throughout the schools. The end of year two served as a platform for internalizing the principles of transformational efforts, ultimately spurring positive outcomes.

Principals and Their Impact on Student Achievement

School principals are often called the head teachers of the school. Scholarship has shown that instructional leadership is paramount in principals' jobs. Grissom et al. (2021) found causal evidence that principals have a substantial impact, more so than we initially thought of as a field. Moreover, research has shown that principals are at the helm of making critical decisions that can influence positive or negative student outcomes, depending on their decisions (Cruickshank, 2017). The impact of school leaders on student outcomes, particularly in infusing equity into their decision-making and leadership processes, has been supported by scholarly research. According to Butterfoss (2021), leaders who prioritize equity seek out the voices of traditionally underrepresented groups in decision-making bodies, which can lead to transformational results for the student learning experience. A study by Day et al. (2016) emphasizes the significant influence of school leadership on the quality of teaching and learning, which in turn affects student outcomes. The study discusses the importance of transformational and shared instructional leadership in improving school performance and student achievement. It highlights that when these forms of leadership are integrated, they substantially influence student outcomes (Day et al., 2016). Furthermore, Virella and Cobb (2021) discuss how school leaders responded to the COVID-19 crisis as an opportunity to provide more equitable education for all students, highlighting the positive outcomes of their efforts to focus on equity. These studies demonstrate that leaders who infuse equity in their decision-making and leadership processes have spurred more academic achievement than those without.

Importance of Promoting Inclusion, Equity, and Excellence for Every Student

Promoting inclusion, equity, and excellence for every student is crucial for creating a fair and effective education system. Research has emphasized the importance of including all children in schools and ensuring that efforts to promote inclusion and equity are based on an analysis of particular contexts (Ainscow, 2020; Ainscow et al., 2019). Inclusive and equitable principles should inform all national education policies, including the curriculum, assessment, supervision, school evaluation, teacher education, and budgets, across all stages of education, from early years to higher education (Ainscow, 2020). Addressing discriminatory institutional barriers and fostering creativity, equity, and inclusion through social justice praxis is essential to ensure that diverse student populations have the resources and support they need (Olzman, 2022; Ramlackhan & Catania, 2022).

Furthermore, there is a necessity for the coexistence of equity and excellence in inclusive and special education. A focus on equity should be combined with measures to promote excellence for all learners to optimize overall outcomes (Hornby, 2020). Ensuring diversity through equity and inclusion requires all stakeholders to acknowledge, listen, educate, and act to create an inclusive environment in educational institutions. This holistic approach is supported by the idea that special education and inclusive education should be seen as equally essential components of effective education systems, and a balance of both is necessary to provide an equitable and excellent education for all learners, including those with special educational needs and disabilities. Therefore, promoting inclusion, equity, and excellence for every student is a moral imperative and a fundamental requirement for developing a truly effective and fair education system. By incorporating the insights from the scholarly articles, it is evident that promoting inclusion, equity, and excellence in education is a multifaceted endeavor that requires a comprehensive and context-specific approach to policy and practice. It is essential to integrate inclusive and equitable principles into all aspects of education and address institutional barriers to provide all students with the opportunity to thrive and succeed.

Equity Leadership as a Theoretical Lens for Transformation

The concept of equity leadership plays a critical role in school districts, as emphasized by Galloway and Ishimaru (2015). Ishimaru's research, in particular, highlights the significance of equity leaders in addressing long-standing educational inequities and reshaping district practices toward equity for all students. The research also highlights how equity leaders contribute to improving schools by implementing new approaches, seeding equity ideas, and developing policies that reshape district practices. This underscores the importance of investing in equity leadership within districts to enhance educational opportunities for marginalized students. Equity directors play an essential role in fostering transformative agency for educational justice. Bartlett (2023) advocates for collaborative efforts between families, communities, and schools to codesign justice-based initiatives that promote equity, social justice, and transformational learning. This partnership is viewed through a theoretical lens to excavate further how transformations occurred in CPS. Focusing on leadership is a critical aspect of district transformation efforts grounded in this theoretical framework.

Methodology

Content analysis examines and analyzes a collection of communications. It is often used for its reliability and replicability in empirical studies (Krippendorff, 1989; Neuendorf & Kumar, 2015). Krippendorff (1989) explained that analyzing communicative practices within data allows one to understand an issue's meanings in a particular context. Content analysis is a research method used to examine and analyze a collection of communications, such as texts, to determine the presence of certain words, themes, or concepts within the data. It can be applied to various text forms, field research notes, and conversations (Neuendorf & Kumar, 2015). Researchers use content analysis to identify patterns in communication, find correlations and patterns in how concepts are communicated, understand the intentions of an individual, group, or institution, and identify propaganda and bias in communication. One of the key advantages of content analysis is its noninvasive nature, as it does not require simulating social experiences or collecting survey answers (Krippendorff, 1989).

Data were obtained through an institutional agreement with the district. Qualitative data were drawn from professional development sessions, including school principals and district-level supervisors. The data used are from seven professional development sessions conducted in June 2022 and June 2023, where the leaders were asked to fill in a Padlet using the TQE (Thoughts, Questions, Epiphanies) protocol method designed by Cult of Pedagogy (Gonzalez, 2018). I chose this particular protocol because the author significantly emphasizes incorporating critical pedagogical practices in schools. For adult learning, I included protocols that educational leaders could impart to their teachers and use themselves. This approach effectively embeds modeling through experiential learning. Padlet was used as a data collection tool because research has shown that Padlet increases thinking skills and writing descriptive text (Taufikurohman, 2018). The protocol was used as a guide to elicit responses, reflecting on the year of professional development conducted by the researcher. Hammond (2020) offers protocols to help facilitate discussions about equity through structured and distributed deep conversations. The protocol asks participants to respond to their thoughts, questions, and epiphanies about the progress of the antiracist district transformation. As a result, the six Padlets were gathered from June 2021 to June 2023. The sample contains 74 responses from 50 principals (elementary, middle, high, and alternative schools) and 28 district leaders. Comments ranged from 3 to 65 words in length.

I used ATLAS.ti qualitative software to store and analyze the data. I analyzed the data set together in five steps. First, I read over the Padlets to get a global understanding of what the participants wrote, enabling immersion in the data. Secondly, I applied Braun and Clarke's (2006) and Lochmiller's (2021) approach to thematic analysis by framing the data through a constructionist orientation. Braun and Clarke (2006) explain that thematic analysis can be a "constructionist method, which examines how events, realities, meanings, experiences and so on are the effects of a range of discourses operating within society" (p. 81). I used the constructionist orientation to apply my interpretation of the data, rooted in the research question: How, if at all, do leaders tether the racial equity transformation to improved academic outcomes? As such, my research moved from simply describing what participants reported to offering an interpretation of our observed patterns. I coded the Padlets in Atlas.ti. Individual codes produced a sense of the data, which informed how I assigned value to different perspectives, experiences, or recollections. Finally, I codified findings, discussing where the preponderance of evidence lay and how to present these findings through a social justice-oriented lens (Huffman & Tracy, 2018).

Oscillations Between Dissonance and Consonance

Many leaders expressed a disconnect between a transformation toward racial equity and academic achievement. For example, one leader explained, "I am wondering what impacts this will have on student outcomes." While another leader stated, "It can be very challenging to quantify goals about belief systems." The literature clearly shows that focusing on equity and culturally relevant pedagogy spurs our academic outcomes across the school population. Moreover, we know from empirical research that an equity and culturally relevant focus on schools benefits all students. However, school leaders needed help determining how they are learning about equity, which would improve their academic outcomes.

At the end of the year, school leaders and district leaders participated in the same activity, writing their thoughts, questions, and epiphanies regarding the racial equity transformation efforts on a Padlet. Unlike the first year, more leaders expressed that they could see how focusing on racial equity transformation would spur outcomes. Moreover, while the school and district leaders were candid in the resistance of some teachers and district leaders regarding the racial equity transformation year, it appears that year allowed the leaders to be more critical and vocal and present evidence of racial equity initiatives that indeed spurred outcomes.

Lessons Learned From Copley Public School District

Over 2 years, an ardent focus on racial equity transformation has yielded several noteworthy lessons. Among these lessons, there were positive outcomes that enabled the school district to leverage the catalyzing energy of this new initiative. One key finding was the shift in mindset among the principals keen on advancing racial equity. They effectively transitioned from operating in silos of progress to forming coalitions of progress while simultaneously dismantling some of the coalitions of resistance across the district. Another positive outcome of the racial equity transformation was the enhanced agency and voice of the students.

Additionally, specific systemic barriers to improving outcomes were removed. However, some lessons were learned that impeded the progress of the racial equity transformation. One of the main reasons for this hindrance was the need to recognize historical practices that have influenced how specific policies, procedures, and organizational routines have been created in the district. As previously mentioned, several leaders questioned how the district would respond within their embedded policies to improve racial equity, which has yet to be seen. For instance, discipline, attendance, and uniform policies have remained the same despite growing concerns about the lack of racial equity embedded in those policies. Another significant lesson learned that could jeopardize progress is the high turnover rate and constant personnel switching across buildings, needing to be united under the racial equity transformation front. District leaders made assumptions that the leaders could quickly move from building to building and still be able to create racially equitable schools without understanding that leaders who were relocated had to restart the process of learning about their faculty and staff, as well as how policies were being enacted in their new school context. In summary, four overarching lessons have been learned due to the racial equity transformation. These lessons include the positive outcomes of forming coalitions of progress, improving and enhancing student agency and voice, the need to acknowledge historical practices that influence policies and routines, and removing systemic barriers to improve outcomes, which I describe in more detail below.

Forming Coalitions of Progress

At the beginning of year one, many leaders began to express how they felt they were left alone when they wanted to do racial equity work. It became clear that one of the significant barriers to understanding how to discuss racial equity was the prohibition of a connection to the district goals and the feeling that the district leaders needed to support a racial equity approach. By the end of year two, it was evident from the data that leaders started to connect to find problems and solutions at the organizational level to spur outcomes further. For example, one leader wrote, "I enjoyed hearing from various people throughout the district. As someone relatively new to the district, it was invaluable to hear how people connected to problems and solutions."

Similarly, another leader shared, "While we discuss sensitive topics, we need to be open-minded to various perspectives and experiences from others. Our district represents so many ethnicities that we must combine these aesthetics to enhance teaching and learning. Furthermore, we must model the behaviors and concepts we expect others to follow." For some leaders who began expressing discomfort with the sensitive topics being discussed, such as racial equity and inequities, the data suggest that they made incremental changes to align with the new district initiatives. One principal shared, "Racism is not a topic of comfort for me. I typically do not engage in conversations about it. These sessions have required me to self-reflect to be aware of my biases. I am thankful for the breakout rooms as they have forced me to speak/share my thoughts and learn from the leaders on the calls." At the beginning of year one, many district leaders felt unsupported in their efforts to promote racial equity. However, by the end of year two, it was evident that their efforts had paid off. Leaders had begun to connect and were discussing problems and solutions at the organizational level. The positive feedback from leaders demonstrated that they had become more open-minded and willing to discuss sensitive topics such as racial equity and biases. The district's diverse ethnic makeup was considered an asset to enhance education and learning. The incremental changes made by some leaders who initially struggled with discussing racial equity reflected a growing understanding of the importance of self-reflection and awareness of one's biases. The district's ongoing commitment to racial equity will continue to foster a supportive and inclusive environment for all.

Finally, the data suggest that leaders were beginning to find a coalition of progress by leaning into their discomfort and tethering the racial equity transformation to actions. A leader shared, "Everyone needs to be onboard. This is a team effort, and we must keep working toward the goal." Ishimaru and Galloway (2021) express or found in their study that one central barrier to improving racial equity and improving outcomes was a focus on a "hearts and minds approach," which maintains that the only way to get toward an equity-oriented center is to focus on how people connect to racial inequities through their heartstrings and their mindset. Instead, the data suggest from this study that leaders were working in tandem to understand how their hearts and mindsets were changing, but also buying large tethering their actions to the racial equity transformation. This demonstrates that leaders can also work in these tandem ways during transformational efforts, ultimately expediting improvement across the district in specific ways. In all of the Padlet boards, over 20 comments across the 2 years demonstrated that leaders were working on expanding their own racial literacy and abiding by and elaborating on racial equity and transformational efforts. The following quote from a leader demonstrates an illustrative quote that captures what several leaders wrote on the Padlet boards. "To move forward, we must have uncomfortable conversations that allow us to reflect on our thoughts, words, and actions."

On the other hand, there was evidence of leaders who expressed that the heart and mind approach was the only necessary approach to reaching the desired goals and staying away from the notion that the organization itself has to change. One leader wrote, "Everyone, regardless of race/ethnicity, must be willing to learn about everyone else. Mindsets and hearts must change for us to achieve what we seek."

The leaders' efforts to address racial equity were more comprehensive than merely discussions and conversations. Instead, they were taking concrete actions to address racial inequities within their organization. This included implementing new policies and procedures that ensured a more inclusive and welcoming environment for people from diverse backgrounds. Additionally, they conducted training sessions to sensitize their staff members about the importance of diversity and inclusion and how to be more sensitive to the needs of people from different cultures. Notably, the leaders' focus was not just on addressing racial equity within their organization but were also committed to the broader community. They collaborated with other organizations and community groups to create a more equitable and just society, thus working toward social and economic justice. For instance, some leaders worked toward increasing access to quality education for children from marginalized communities, while others advocated for policies that promoted social and economic justice. The leaders demonstrated a solid commitment to creating a more equitable and just school environment and were willing to invest the requisite effort and time to achieve their goals. They recognized that addressing racial equity is not just a matter of changing policies and procedures but also requires a shift in mindset and attitudes toward people from different backgrounds. By working together and taking action, the leaders made significant progress toward their goals, creating a more inclusive and welcoming environment for everyone involved.

It is important to note that the leaders' efforts toward addressing racial equity did not just result in a more inclusive and welcoming environment but also led to improved outcomes. For instance, by reevaluating policies such as grading, the leaders enhanced the quality of inclusivity in their school district. This increased student and parent satisfaction and loyalty, leading to better outcomes for the school district. Moreover, the leaders' efforts toward creating a more equitable and just school district also positively impacted the broader community. By collaborating with other organizations to increase access to quality education for children from marginalized communities, they created a more level playing field for their students. This led to improved educational outcomes and increased opportunities for their students, potentially in the long term. Overall, the leaders' efforts toward addressing racial equity resulted in a more inclusive and welcoming environment and led to tangible improvements in outcomes. By creating policies and procedures that ensured equitable treatment of people from diverse backgrounds and by working toward creating a more equitable and just school district, the leaders were able to make a meaningful impact on the lives of those around them.

Challenging Historical Practices That Influence Organizational Routines and Policies

Virella (2024) explain that leaders need to be aware of the past to ground decision-making in reality to cultivate critical hope. Further, Virella (2024) explain that educators and leaders must have a solid understanding of the events, policies, and instructional issues that manifest as a result of today's struggles and embedded practices that influence schools and communities that are also influenced by leadership for social change. The data from the study suggest that the leaders across the schools in the district were highly aware of the past and how it influenced their present school environment. For example, a leader commented that they "have a historic opportunity to continue to promote equitable education by supporting teachers who are in line with the district goals or supporting them as they learn to align to the district goals. There is an urgency to what we do here." The awareness of school leaders regarding past events holds a significant influence over their endeavors to foster racially equitable environments. Some leaders showed an awareness of the influence of historical context on their school environment, sharing, "There is an overuse of references to 'police,' 'prison,' 'not graduating' from school adults to young children of color (across our district and school)." School leaders' awareness of past events significantly impacts their efforts to create racially equitable environments. Some leaders demonstrated an understanding of the influence of historical context on their school environment, as evidenced by their observation of the overuse of specific negative references to young children of color. By acknowledging the impact of historical context, leaders are taking the first step toward creating more inclusive and equitable learning environments for all students.

Informed decision-making necessitates a comprehensive understanding of the historical context of systemic racism and its impact on education. According to Gorski and Swalwell (n.d.), school leaders must undertake the task of "normalizing the naming of inequity, taking responsibility, and modeling for staff how to do this without being defensive" (p. 1) to recognize and respond to inequity. Additionally, Ngounou and Gutierrez (2017) stress the need for school leaders to study, honor, and comprehend the intricacies of both individual experiences and the long-standing history to lead for racial equity. Consequently, awareness of the past is an indispensable element for school leaders to effectively address and dismantle racial inequities in educational settings.

Removing Systemic Barriers to Improve Outcomes

The process of organizational transformation entails removing barriers that hinder attaining desired outcomes (Jansson, 2013). In the context of schools, removing systemic barriers paves the way for new opportunities. In CPS, district and school administrators engaged in discussions aimed at dismantling systemic barriers that had been entrenched for decades. For instance, homework and attendance policies and the dress code policy surfaced as areas requiring more equitable approaches for racial equity transformation. Scholarly literature has established that policies such as discipline, attendance, and homework exacerbate inequitable opportunities for children, particularly those of color (Gregory et al., 2017). The racial equity transformation in CPS underscores the significance of removing systemic barriers to enhance outcomes. District leaders realized that their policies, practices, and routines needed to be more connected to the desired outcomes, consequently marginalizing students and impeding academic achievement. Lack of planning time and focus initiatives that relied on interdependence and connection were among the systemic barriers impeding progress. Another lesson learned was the importance of district leaders working collaboratively with school principals to ensure equitable instruction that enhances academic achievement. The district leaders engaged in practices aimed at evaluating policies that served as systemic barriers. Equitable grading emerged as a policy that required transformational efforts to dismantle systemic barriers.

Conclusion

The CPS District underwent a comprehensive racial equity transformation over 2 years, resulting in several positive outcomes. One key finding was the shift in mindset among leaders who effectively transitioned from operating in silos of progress to forming coalitions of progress. This shift was critical in promoting every student's inclusivity, equity, and excellence, regardless of their racial backgrounds. Furthermore, the transformation led to enhanced agency and voice of the students, empowering them to contribute meaningfully to their education. By removing systemic barriers to improving outcomes, the district created a more inclusive and equitable learning environment that supported the success of all students. However, some lessons were learned that impeded progress, such as the need for recognition of historical practices that have influenced specific policies and routines, the high turnover rate, and the constant switching of personnel across buildings. These challenges highlighted the need for a more comprehensive understanding of the district's unique historical context and the importance of promoting stability in leadership positions.

In summary, four overarching lessons were learned, including the positive outcomes of forming coalitions of progress, improving and enhancing student agency and voice, the need to acknowledge historical practices that influence policies and routines, and removing systemic barriers to improve outcomes. This chapter provides critical insights, lessons learned, and reflections on the transformative initiatives that spanned 3 years. It effectively ties together the various elements discussed, emphasizing the lessons learned and the positive outcomes of the district's racial equity transformation. By acknowledging the challenges and the progress made, the chapter offers a comprehensive understanding of the district's journey toward becoming an anti-racist and equitable school district.

Implications for Future Research and Practice

The CPS District's racial equity transformation offers valuable lessons for both research and practice. Firstly, it highlights the importance of forming coalitions of progress while dismantling resistance coalitions. This suggests that a collaborative approach to addressing racial equity is more effective than working alone. Research can explore different strategies for forming coalitions of progress and overcoming resistance to change. Secondly, acknowledging the impact of historical practices on policies and routines is essential to creating inclusive and equitable learning environments for all students. Educators and leaders can be sensitized to the importance of historical context and how to address it in their schools. Research can investigate the impact of historical context on educational policies and practices and identify effective ways to address it. Thirdly, removing systemic barriers is crucial to improving outcomes for marginalized students. This requires a comprehensive understanding of how policies and routines impact these students and how they can be transformed to create more equitable opportunities. Practice can involve evaluating policies and practices that serve as systemic barriers and transforming them to create more inclusive and equitable learning environments. Research can explore the impact of systemic barriers on marginalized students and how they can be dismantled. Finally, enhancing student agency and voice is vital to creating a more equitable and just school district. This means giving students a say in policies and practices that affect them. Practice can involve creating opportunities for students to voice their opinions and involve them in decision-making. Research can explore different approaches to enhancing student agency and voice and their impact on educational outcomes.

It is imperative to prioritize racial equity in education to improve our society. Research has consistently shown that addressing racial and educational disparities can bring significant benefits, including increased social mobility and economic growth. A focus on racial equity in education is not only a matter of justice but also has practical importance. Therefore, prioritizing racial equity in education is not just a moral obligation but also a means to foster economic growth and social mobility and create a more inclusive society.

References

Ainscow, M. (2020). Promoting inclusion and equity in education: Lessons from international experiences. *Nordic Journal of Studies in Educational Policy*, 6(1), 7–16.

Ainscow, M., Chapman, C., & Hadfield, M. (2019). *Changing education systems: A research-based approach*. Routledge.

Bartlett, T. (2023). Review of just schools: Building equitable collaborations with families and communities by Ann Ishimaru. *Journal of Educational Research and Practice*, 13(1), 307–313. https://doi.org/10.5590/JERAP.2023.13.1.21

Braun, V., & Clarke, V. (2006). Using thematic analysis in psychology. *Qualitative Research in Psychology*, 3(2), 77–101.

Butterfoss, J. (2021). *Catalyzing leadership for equity*. Urban Institute. https://www.urban.org/sites/default/files/2022-12/Catalyzing%20Leadership%20for%20Equity.pdf

Cruickshank, V. (2017). *The influence of school leadership on student outcomes*.

Day, C., Gu, Q., & Sammons, P. (2016). The impact of leadership on student outcomes: How successful leaders use transformational leadership to improve student learning. *Educational Management Administration & Leadership*, 44(5), 682–701. https://doi.org/10.1177/1741143215590787

Galloway, M. K., & Ishimaru, A. M. (2015). Radical recentering: Equity in educational leadership standards. *Educational Administration Quarterly*, 51(3), 372–408.

Gonzalez, J. (2018). *Cult of Pedagogy. The TQE Method*. https://www.cultofpedagogy.com/tqe-method/. Accessed on March 28, 2024.

Gorski, P., & Swalwell, K. (n.d.). *Moving from equity awareness to action*. ASCD. https://www.ascd.org/el/articles/moving-from-equity-awareness-to-action

Gregory, A., Skiba, R. J., & Mediratta, K. (2017). Eliminating disparities in school discipline: A framework for intervention. *Review of Research in Education*, 41(1), 253–278.

Grissom, J. A., Egalite, A. J., & Lindsay, C. A. (2021). How principals affect students and schools. *Wallace Foundation*, 2(1), 30–41.

Hammond, Z. (2020). The power of protocols for equity. *Educational Leadership*, 77(7), 45–50.

Hornby, G. (2020). The necessity for coexistence of equity and excellence in inclusive and special education. In *Encyclopedia of inclusive and special education*. Oxford University Press.

Huffman, T., & Tracy, S. J. (2018). Making claims that matter: Heuristics for theoretical and social impact in qualitative research. *Qualitative Inquiry*, 24(8), 558–570.

Ishimaru, A. M., & Galloway, M. K. (2021). Hearts and minds first: Institutional logics in pursuit of educational equity. *Educational Administration Quarterly*, 57(3), 470–502.

Jansson, J. (2013). From movement to organization: Constructing identity in Swedish trade unions. *Labor History*, *54*(3), 301–320.

Krippendorff, K. (1989). Content analysis. *International Encyclopedia of Communication*, *1*(1), 403–407.

Lochmiller, C. R. (2021). Conducting thematic analysis with qualitative data. *Qualitative Report*, *26*(6), 2029–2044.

Neuendorf, K. A., & Kumar, A. (2015). Content analysis. In *The international encyclopedia of political communication* (pp. 1–10). John Wiley & Sons, Inc.

Ngounou, G., & Gutierrez, N. (2017). Learning to lead for racial equity. *Phi Delta Kappan*, *99*(3), 37–41.

Olzman, M. D. (2022). Collaging educational orientations: A whitening of mindfulness. *Western Journal of Communication*, *86*(2), 241–249.

Ramlackhan, K., & Catania, N. (2022). Fostering creativity, equity, and inclusion through social justice praxis. *Power and Education*, *14*(3), 282–295.

Taufikurohman, I. S. (2018). The effectiveness of using Padlet in teaching writing descriptive text. *Journal of Applied Linguistics and Literacy*, *2*(2), 71–88.

Virella, P. M. (2024). Cultivating critical hope while leading during crisis: A qualitative cross-comparative analysis. *American Journal of Education*, *130*(2), 275–300.

Virella, P. M., & Cobb, C. (2021, April). Leveraging the crisis for equity and access in the long term: A brief research report. In *Frontiers in education* (Vol. 6, p. 618051). Frontiers Media SA.

Chapter 7

Leading Through Climate Disasters and Environmental Injustice: Past, Present, and Future

Megan Rauch Griffard[a], Diamond Ebanks[b] and Jacob D. Skousen[a]

[a]University of Nevada Las Vegas, USA
[b]University of North Carolina at Chapel Hill, USA

Abstract

This chapter discusses the role of school leadership in the face of climate disasters and environmental injustices. These disruptions to schooling are emblematic of an increasing global uncertainty. School leaders play a pivotal role mitigating uncertainty following an environmental crisis or disaster through leadership activities that support their communities. However, preparing school leaders for unexpected disruptions to schooling has often been overlooked by preparation programs and professional development. The goal of this chapter is to equip school leaders with an essential understanding of both the influence of environmental injustice on schools and the tools to respond effectively to these events. First, the chapter contextualizes environmental injustice and inequality as a factor that influences school and student performance, especially for students living below the poverty line and students of color. Next, it synthesizes how school leaders have responded to prior instances of climate disasters and environmental injustices. Finally, it presents key considerations for school leaders confronting future occurrences.

Keywords: Environmental justice; crisis leadership; climate disasters; school leadership; mitigating uncertainty

Introduction: Leading Through Disasters and Environmental Injustice

This chapter discusses the role of school leadership in the face of climate disasters and environmental injustice. School leaders play a pivotal role mitigating uncertainty following an environmental crisis or disaster through leadership activities that support their communities (O'Connor, 2013; Potter et al., 2021; Sherrieb et al., 2012). However, preparing school leaders for unexpected disruptions to schooling has been overlooked by preparation programs and professional development (Grissom & Condon, 2021; Urick et al., 2021).

When evaluating the panoply of factors that can impede educational progress in schools, a key consideration is the physical environment in which school-age children live. Local context is strongly tied to opportunities and outcomes in education (Acevedo-Garcia et al., 2020). Community and neighborhood quality are highly predictive of school quality and student achievement, both in the near- and long-term (Ainsworth, 2002; Chetty et al., 2016; Hayes & Taylor, 1996; Ruiz et al., 2018). For example, Acevedo-Garcia and colleagues (2020) described how the physical environment in which children live, such as their access to green spaces and housing vacancy rates, are tied to learning opportunities and school quality. Chetty and colleagues (2016) found that young children in families that moved from higher poverty to lower poverty neighborhoods increased their college-going rates.

Geography and weather are also components of the physical environment in which school-age children live. These components become increasingly important in light of global climate change, which has brought a major increase in the frequency and intensity of climate disasters (Changon, 2010; Dettinger, 2011; Gardiner, 2006). Although commonly referred to as climate disasters because they originate in nature, climate disasters are closely tied to politics, economics, and social capital (Slettebak, 2012; Straub, 2021; Tierney, 2019). Climate disasters, which include phenomena like earthquakes, hurricanes, mudslides, tsunamis, and volcanic eruptions, are defined as "extreme events of nature that surpass the capacity of the [human] system to reflect, absorb, or buffer" (Kates, 1971, p. 438). Because they intersect with the built human environment, disasters can hinder the well-being and resilience of both individuals and communities (NOAA, 2018; Tschakert et al., 2020). Climate disasters cost the US more than $802 billion and claimed more than 5,000 lives between 2010 and 2019 (Smith, 2020).

Disasters and environmental injustice are emblematic of increasing global uncertainty. Exposure to climate disasters exacerbates preexisting socioeconomic and political challenges and results in adverse outcomes for affected communities, such as heightened levels of poverty, unemployment, and violence (Tierney, 2019). Importantly, climate disasters disproportionately have adverse impacts on historically and socially marginalized communities, such as people of color, people experiencing poverty, and people living in rural areas (Davis et al., 2021; Howell & Elliot, 2019). Predisaster conditions, such as poverty and social capital, are important predictors of disaster recovery for both individuals and communities (Fothergill & Peek, 2015; Tierney, 2019).

When climate disasters occur, one way that communities often cope is by leaning on local leaders for guidance and support as they navigate the emotional, physical, and psychological aspects of recovery (Leadbeater, 2013; Lin et al., 2018; Sherrieb et al., 2012). Across various disasters, school leaders – superintendents and school principals – have emerged as examples of such leaders (Brooks, 2014; Goswick et al., 2018; Kanter & Abramson, 2014; Mutch, 2015).

This chapter serves as a starting point to address the need to equip school leaders with an essential understanding of both the influence of environmental injustice on schools and the tools to respond effectively to these events. To do this, the chapter will address the past, present, and future of school leaders' role in climate disasters and environmental injustice. First, looking to the past, the chapter will contextualize environmental injustice and inequality to show how it influences school and student performance, especially for students living below the poverty line and students of color. Second, looking to the present, the chapter will synthesize how school leaders have responded to prior instances of climate disasters and environmental injustices. Finally, looking to the future, the chapter will present a portrait of a reimagined school leader, one who possesses the skills, knowledge, and disposition needed to support their communities following a disaster or environmental injustice. It will describe how school leaders can incorporate equity-focused leadership practices to advocate for their schools' needs and to build their capacity to support sustainability, learning, and inclusivity when confronted with climate disasters and environmental injustices.

The Past: Historical and Contextual Factors Influencing Climate Disasters and Environmental Injustice

This section begins by situating schools in communities. Drawing upon history, it establishes the link between the students and communities served by certain schools and their experiences of climate disasters and environmental injustice. Next, the section reviews the extant literature on disasters and schooling, focusing on how these events disproportionately affect disadvantaged schools and student populations (e.g., Fuller, 2014; Lamb et al., 2013; Ward et al., 2013).

Location and Experiences of Disasters and Environmental Injustice: Historical Context

Natural disasters have the potential to wreak havoc on large swaths of the population, but their impacts are disproportionately felt by historically marginalized groups. Specifically, the time in exposure to the natural disaster, the long-term impact of the natural disaster, and its long-standing impacts are more likely to be felt by racial and ethnic minorities, the elderly, very young, women, and those in poverty (Bathi & Das, 2016; De Silva & Kawasaki, 2018; Llorente-Marrón et al., 2020; Marino & Faas, 2020; Reid, 2013). However, these characteristics are merely proxies of marginalizing societal forces that enable us to peer into patterns of inequitable access to resources or fewer protections against disasters. Due to histories of violence and contemporary systems of oppression, such as racism, xenophobia, sexism, and agism, and the ways these systems intersect in individuals' lives, the historically marginalized groups listed above experience social, political, and economic stressors that leave them with increased risk of disaster exposure and increased likelihood suffering after a disaster (Jacobs, 2019; Marino & Faas, 2020).

Historically marginalized groups that experience systemic racism are often the same groups that are hit hardest by natural disasters, with higher rates of loss of life, injuries, property damage and loss, and other economic losses, such as increased unemployment rates and decreased economic productivity (Derakhshan et al., 2020). Scholars have argued that research on the impacts of natural disaster on historically marginalized groups tend to essentialize race. When this occurs, the burden of natural disaster subsequently becomes the responsibility of the individuals or communities. Ideally, research should draw attention to systemic racism or classism structures as problems (Jacobs, 2019).

The ability to secure resources and navigate bureaucratic processes, as indicated by social and political capital, plays a crucial role in predicting hazard recovery. This becomes especially pertinent when hazard events exacerbate socioeconomic and political disparities, posing greater challenges for communities to bounce back (Tierney, 2019). Conversely, communities with higher socioeconomic status tend to possess more substantial social and political capital, encompassing greater resources, knowledge, and network connections. As an example, Frankenberg and colleagues (2013) observed that individuals with greater educational attainment demonstrated increased resilience following a hazard. Additional research indicated that residences in lower socioeconomic regions were more prone to damage in the aftermath of a hazard (Mower, 2019; Sturgis, 2018). This, combined with prolonged wait times for insurance and FEMA assistance, resulted in extended periods of displacement for occupants, impeding their ability to recover.

Impacts of Disasters and Environmental Injustice on Student Outcomes

School leadership ought to be concerned with disasters and environmental injustice because it negatively impacts student outcomes and experiences, as well as overall school performance. In this section, we explain how natural disasters impact student cognitive (i.e., achievement and persistence) and noncognitive (i.e., attendance, behavior, and mental health) following a disaster. Importantly, the research discussed here affirms that negative outcomes disproportionately impact children of color and children experiencing poverty. Table 7.1 presents a summary of the studies cited in this section.

Experience of a climate disaster has been shown to negatively affect student achievement (Lamb et al., 2013). It also can impede the delivery of high-quality instruction (Fothergill & Peek, 2015). As Lamb et al. (2013) explained in their study of student achievement following Hurricane Katrina, disasters cause "more

Table 7.1. Scholarship on the Student Outcomes Following a Natural Disaster.

Authors	Disaster Type	Disaster Year	Disaster Location	Study Method	Brief Synopsis of Key Findings
Lamb et al. (2013)	Hurricane	2005	Gulf Coast	Quantitative	Student achievement decreased in the year after Hurricane Katrina. While more affluent schools and districts rebounded quickly in subsequent years, schools serving primarily students of color, students experiencing poverty, and rural communities continued to lag.
Fothergill and Peek (2015)	Hurricane	2005	New Orleans	Qualitative	Students and teachers both suffered emotionally following Hurricane Katrina. Black children experienced negative impacts from the hurricane for many years after the event.
Fuller (2014)	Hurricanes	1988–2000	North Carolina	Quantitative	Children whose mothers experienced a natural disaster while pregnant had lower academic achievement than their peers whose mothers had not experienced the disaster. The effect size was larger for Black children.
Ward et al. (2013)	Hurricane	2005	Mississippi	Quantitative	Students who were displaced following Hurricane Katrina were already academically behind. The gap widened in the years following the disaster.
Shorr (2006)	Hurricane	2005	Mississippi	Quantitative	Affluent school districts in Mississippi could reopen after Hurricane Katrina in less time than schools in lower socioeconomic school districts. Reopening more quickly meant that affluent families were less likely to relocate to other states, which had economic advantages for local areas.

(Continued)

Table 7.1. (Continued)

Authors	Disaster Type	Disaster Year	Disaster Location	Study Method	Brief Synopsis of Key Findings
Esnard et al. (2017)	Hurricane	2017	Texas	Quantitative	Texas school districts in more urbanized counties with higher concentrations of people of color and people living in poverty were more likely to experience longer school closures than suburban districts.
Barrett et al. (2012)	Hurricane	2005	Dallas-Fort Worth	Quantitative	Students relocated to Texas after Hurricane Katrina experienced greater mental distress than their peers in schools. More affluent schools in Dallas-Fort Worth were generally more adept at addressing the needs of displaced students who arrived there having been displaced by Hurricane Katrina.
Tian and Guan (2015)	Hurricane	2005	Louisiana	Quantitative	Students who were displaced following Hurricane Katrina were more likely have interactions with school discipline systems.
Gaffney (2006)	Multiple	2001–2005	U.S.	Qualitative	Children fare better after a natural disaster or catastrophic event when they are surrounded by supportive adults.
O'Toole (2018)	Earthquake	2011	New Zealand	Qualitative	Teachers reported emotional exhaustion and burnout following a devastating earthquake.
Pane et al. (2008)	Hurricane	2005	Louisiana	Quantitative	Students displaced by Hurricane Katrina were more likely to experience issues with attendance, academic performance, discipline, and mental health.

Study	Disaster	Year	Location	Method	Findings
Swenson et al. (1996)	Hurricane	1989	South Carolina	Quantitative	Young children who lived through Hurricane Hugo had higher anxiety and other mental health problems than their peers. Problems persisted longer for children whose mothers experienced distress in the aftermath of the storm.
Kuntz et al. (2013)	Earthquake	2011	New Zealand	Quantitative	Teachers reported greater feelings of burnout following a devastating earthquake.
Jeffers (2014)	Hurricane	2005	New Orleans	Quantitative	Black students and students with disabilities were more likely to receive discipline infractions in New Orleans charter schools after Hurricane Katrina.
Imberman et al. (2012)	Hurricane	2005	Houston	Quantitative	Schools that enrolled higher numbers of students displaced by Hurricane Katrina had higher rates of absenteeism and disciplinary issues.

Note: Studies are listed in the order in which they appear in the subsection, "Impacts of Disasters and Environmental Injustice on Student Outcomes."

than just physical damage" (p. 80). Disasters interfere with students' ability to learn when students are unable to concentrate in class, are chronically absent, or have to change or drop out of school. Disasters also interfere with teachers' ability to demonstrate care for students (Fothergill & Peek, 2015). Moreover, the negative outcomes associated with disasters have been found to be worse among students of color, students experiencing poverty, and students living in rural communities (Fuller, 2014; Lamb et al., 2013; Shorr, 2006; Ward et al., 2013).

The impact of disasters can impact children throughout their lifetime. For example, in a study of child development, Fuller (2014) found that the children of mothers who experienced a natural disaster while pregnant had an average of -0.036 standard deviations (SDs) lower achievement in elementary school math. Among the children of Black women, the effect size was larger at -0.040 SDs. One SD is equivalent to the achievement gained by the average fifth grader of the course of a single school year (Kraft, 2020). Fuller's work underscores how disasters have disproportionately negative effects on historically marginalized subgroups. At the other end of the spectrum, as Fothergill and Peek (2015) observed in their case studies of Black children in New Orleans after Hurricane Katrina, the authors observed that two of the six students whom they followed dropped out of college. Likewise, Di Pietro (2017) found that college enrollment, persistence, and on-time graduation was lower among university students in L'Aquila, Italy, after a major earthquake in 2009 compared to students in other Italian provinces.

At the K-12 level, Lamb et al. (2013) found that student achievement in math was lower for third, fifth, and eighth graders in Mississippi schools in the school years following Hurricane Katrina in 2005. The researchers noted that the decrease in achievement was highest among students attending school closest to the epicenter of the hurricane and students attending rural schools. Lamb et al. (2013) suggested that the effect observed for students near the initial impact zone of Hurricane Katrina could be attributed to more severe consequences stemming from the disaster, such as displacement, home damage, or parental job loss. They also suggested that the decrease in achievement observed for students in rural schools may be due to a lack of access to resources. Although math achievement scores eventually rebounded back to the levels prior to the disaster, the researchers noted a faster rebound in more populous and affluent school districts.

Importantly, Ward and colleagues (2013) found that students in Mississippi who had to change schools due to damaged or destroyed homes were already academically behind their peers before Hurricane Katrina, and the gap widened in the post-Katrina years. The researchers proposed that the decline in performance among displaced students resulted from "the compounding effects of trauma and displacement upon what is already weaker academic performance" (p. 315).

Further highlighting the gaps between advantaged and disadvantaged student groups, Shorr (2006) found that affluent school districts in Mississippi could reopen after Hurricane Katrina in less time than schools in lower socioeconomic school districts. Reopening more quickly meant that affluent families were less likely to relocate to other states. Keeping families from moving was important in maintaining the local tax base that funded public schools in affluent districts. Although Mississippi school districts impacted by Hurricane Katrina experienced average enrollment decreases of 14%, the decreases were as high as 40% in less affluent districts. Similarly, looking at another disaster, Esnard and colleagues (2017) found that after Hurricane Ike in 2009, Texas school districts in more urbanized counties with higher concentrations of people of color and people living in poverty were more likely to experience longer school closures than suburban districts. The researchers posited that longer school closures were likely going to lead to greater learning loss.

In addition to negatively impacting student academic achievement, experience of disaster interferes with other outcomes, including discipline and attendance (Barrett et al., 2012; Tian & Guan, 2015). Increased stress, behavior challenges, and depressive symptoms are also more likely to be present among both students and teachers following a disaster (Fothergill & Peek, 2015; Gaffney, 2006; O'Toole, 2018; Pane et al., 2008; Swenson et al., 1996). Disasters are also associated with increased turnover intentions among teachers (Kuntz et al., 2013). Similar to academic outcomes, a school's capacity to attend to students' psychological and emotional needs is affected by the socioeconomic status and demographic composition of its students. Barrett et al. (2012) found that more affluent schools in Dallas-Fort Worth were generally more adept at addressing the needs of displaced students who arrived there having been displaced by Hurricane Katrina. While the authors largely attributed this difference to better-trained teachers and supportive leadership, they also noted that these schools enrolled the smallest proportion of Black students. Additionally, they pointed out that schools with fewer Black students demonstrated less consistency and fairness in their treatment of students overall. Similarly, Jeffers (2014) found that Black students and students with disabilities were more likely to receive discipline infractions in New Orleans charter schools after Hurricane Katrina.

Experience of disasters also creates a spillover effect that extends onto students who attend schools with them after an event. Imberman et al. (2012) observed that students in Houston high schools, where significant numbers of students displaced by Hurricanes Katrina and Rita were enrolled, experienced elevated rates of absenteeism and disciplinary issues following the enrollment of displaced students. Likewise, a 10-percentage point rise in displaced students correlated with a 0.2% to 0.4% increase in disciplinary infractions.

As these studies have shown, the experience of climate disaster is associated with a host of negative outcomes for students across the lifetime of their education, with impacts observed in both the near- and long-term. In the research discussed here, students of color and students experiencing poverty more often experienced more negative outcomes and negative outcomes for longer periods of time. It is important for school leaders to be aware of these disproportionate impacts from natural disaster exposure.

The Present: The Role of School Leadership in Disaster Response

Having established the influence of climate disasters and environmental injustice in schooling, the next task in this chapter is to describe the current evidence about how school leadership has responded to this reality. This section describes the roles and responsibilities school leaders assume following a disaster or environmental injustice. Table 7.2 presents a summary of the literature cited in this section that discusses these various roles and responsibilities.

To begin with, the experience of climate disaster or crisis reshapes school leaders' roles and responsibilities, thrusting them into a position as managers of the crisis for the local community (e.g. Brooks, 2014; Gouwens & Lander, 2008; O'Connor, 2013). Examples of new duties include: pushing to safely and quickly reopen schools and acting decisively, providing emotional support to students and teachers, communicating with stakeholders, brokering with outside agencies and organizations, and organizing supplies and resources to students and families in need (Bowman, 2008; Lee et al., 2008; O'Connor, 2013; Potter et al., 2021; Sherrieb et al., 2012; Ward & Shelley, 2008). Despite the efforts of school leaders, they encountered challenges along the way, especially when it came to streamlining and synthesizing their response, as is described in the final part of this section. This discussion sets the stage for our reimagined portrait of a crisis-ready school leader.

Reopening Schools

Time out of school due to a disaster is associated with greater learning loss, especially among students of color, students experiencing poverty, and students living in rural areas (Esnard et al., 2017; Lee et al., 2008). For this reason, as well as several others described below, reopening schools is a top priority for school leaders faced with climate disasters. Two examples illustrate the importance of reopening schools.

After Hurricane Katrina ravaged the U.S. Gulf Coast, Mississippi school leaders made reopening schools their preeminent goal. Schools provide "some sense of stability and familiarity for several hours a day during an otherwise chaotic existence" (Bowman, 2008, p. 720). More practically speaking, Mississippi schools impacted by Hurricane Katrina provided meals to 30% of students before the hurricane, a figure that rose to 45% afterward (Bowman, 2008; Ward & Shelley, 2008). Local school leaders worked with authorities to provide two free, hot meals to students every day, even in the weeks leading up to school reopening (Ward & Shelley, 2008). Additionally, from an economic perspective, the reopening of schools helped maintain recent economic growth in the region, marked by a rise in population, home prices, and construction (Bowman, 2008).

In the aftermath of a devastating tornado that ended the 2010–11 school year in Joplin, Missouri, the school superintendent adopted a similar approach, as highlighted by Goswick et al. (2018) and Kanter and Abramson (2014). Steeped in the commitment to reopen schools, the superintendent played a pivotal role in restoring some semblance of normalcy in the aftermath of the tornado. He placed a symbolic countdown clock in the district's central office, marking the time remaining until the commencement of the 2011–12 school year. The clock served as an emblem of the superintendent's determination for an on-time start to the

Table 7.2. Scholarship on the Role of School Leadership Following a Natural Disaster.

Authors	Disaster Type	Disaster Year	Disaster Location	Study Method	Brief Synopsis of Key Findings
Gouwens and Lander (2008)	Hurricane	2005	Mississippi	Qualitative	School superintendents assumed roles of crisis management for the broader communities following Hurricane Katrina.
O'Connor (2013)	Earthquake	2011	New Zealand	Qualitative	Principals recalled how they supported emotionally traumatized students and parents following a devastating earthquake.
Bowman (2008)	Hurricane	2005	Mississippi	Qualitative	School leaders provided essential emotional and physical (i.e., food and supplies) support to students and families following Hurricane Katrina. They also focused on reopening schools quickly to provide stability and structure to the community.
Lee et al. (2008)	Hurricane	2005	Mississippi	Quantitative	School leaders who implemented counseling and mental health support services for students and staff were perceived as favorably by stakeholders.
Potter et al. (2021)	Tornado	2019	Dallas	Qualitative	Case study coauthored by the school principal describes how he assumed a protective role toward teachers and worked to keep teachers' focus on their students by not burdening them with extraneous tasks and responsibilities.

(*Continued*)

Table 7.2. (Continued)

Authors	Disaster Type	Disaster Year	Disaster Location	Study Method	Brief Synopsis of Key Findings
Sherrieb et al. (2012)	Hurricane	2008–2009	Southeastern U.S.	Quantitative	School leaders can act as brokers between school communities and policymakers and governmental leaders, providing the former with needed aid and relief and the latter with highly relevant local knowledge to inform decision-making because they are usually among the closest leaders to a local community, and as such they are the best equipped to understand the needs and capacity their community has during a natural disaster.
Ward and Shelley (2008)	Hurricane	2005	Mississippi	Quantitative	School leaders worked to provide hot meals to students even when schools were not open following Hurricane Katrina. They also provided supplies to students and families.
Goswick et al. (2018)	Tornado	2011	Joplin, MO	Qualitative	The Joplin superintendent demonstrated commitment to students and families by working tirelessly to reopen local schools after a tornado caused an early end to the prior school year.
Kanter and Abramson (2018)	Tornado	2011	Joplin, MO	Qualitative	The Joplin superintendent also provided training for teachers and staff coping strategies

Author	Disaster Type	Year	Location	Methodology	Findings
Mutch and Gawith (2014)	Earthquake	2011	New Zealand	Qualitative	Research worked with school principals to design projects for students at three schools that were aimed at helping them navigate their trauma and grief after the Christchurch earthquake. Moreover, once school reopened, additional counselors were available at all schools, and several community mental health providers also gave assistance to struggling students and staff for anxiety and depression.
Nastasi and Jayasena (2014)	Tsunami	2004	Sri Lanka	Mixed Methods	A local educational leader worked with a research team to develop and implement a culturally aligned social and emotional program for Sri Lankan students and teachers aided in their recovery from the 2004 tsunami.
Pfefferbaum et al. (2012)	Multiple	NA	U.S	Theoretical	Schools are a key place in the system of support children need following a disaster.
Masten and Narayan (2012)	Multiple	NA	Global	Qualitative	Schools are important in children's recovery after a disaster because they offer a sense of normalcy, structure, and routines, which are crucial aspects in the role of children's recovery.
Prinstein et al. (1996)	Hurricane	1992	Florida	Quantitative	Schools provide space for children to emotionally process trauma and reestablish routines after a disaster.

(Continued)

116 *Megan Rauch Griffard et al.*

Table 7.2. (*Continued*)

Authors	Disaster Type	Disaster Year	Disaster Location	Study Method	Brief Synopsis of Key Findings
Seyle et al. (2013)	Earthquake	2004	Indonesia	Quantitative	Researchers worked with local schools to develop an intervention to reduce teacher burnout following a major earthquake.
Kuntz et al. (2013)	Earthquake	2011	New Zealand	Quantitative	Teachers reported greater experiences of emotional exhaustion, burnout, and turnover intentions following a major earthquake.
Fletcher and Nicholas (2016)	Earthquake	2011	New Zealand	Qualitative	Principals described how they supported students and communities following a major earthquake.
Akbaba-Altun (2005)	Earthquake	1999	Turkey	Qualitative	Principals in Turkey discussed how they viewed their role in supporting their schools following a major earthquake, despite receiving minimal support from governmental agencies. Study highlights the importance of including school-level leaders in policy conversations.
Anderson (2005)	Hurricane	2005	Louisiana	Theoretical	Study discusses how important school leaders are as advocates for children, who do not have the agency to voice their needs sufficiently from a policy perspective.

Note: Studies are listed in the order in which they appear in the section, "The Present: The Role of School Leadership in Disaster Response."

new academic term and as a motivational tool for his subordinates to work toward that goal. An administrator reflected on the significance of the clock, stating, "If we didn't have the mission, if we didn't have a purpose, at the time, I think I can speak for myself, I would have floundered, I would have said, 'What are we doing?'" (Goswick et al., 2018, p. 550).

Providing Emotional Support to Students and Teachers

Aside from being able to meet the physical needs of students by providing them food, school leaders have aimed to reopen schools to meet the emotional and psychological needs of students, teachers, and other stakeholders following a climate disaster (Bowman, 2008; Mutch & Gawith, 2014; Nastasi & Jayasena, 2014; O'Toole, 2018). Through leadership, schools create a place for children to navigate recovery (Pfefferbaum et al., 2012). Schools are important in children's recovery after a disaster because they offer a "rapid restoration of routines, schools, and opportunities to play or socialize with peers" are crucial aspects in the role of children's recovery (Masten & Narayan, 2012, p. 251). A study on the effects of Hurricane Andrew on children found that emotional processing and routine were the important types of support children can receive after a disaster, which largely occur in school and are facilitated by school leadership (Prinstein et al., 1996).

O'Connor (2013) elaborated on the role of school leaders in the emotional recovery process for school communities in their case study of Christchurch, New Zealand principals following the 2011 earthquake, which actually occurred during the school day and included several aftershocks in the subsequent hours when students were waiting for parents and caregivers to be able to safely pick them up. The researchers detailed how these educational leaders embraced a "pedagogy grounded in love" to support traumatized students (O'Connor, 2013, p. 431). Principals recounted their experiences with comforting tearful children and diverting their attention from their fears with games and food. In order to achieve this, they recounted setting aside their own apprehensions about the earthquake to project an image of composed authority. As one principal expressed, "It was six hours before all the children had been picked up. I was the last to leave. That's what a principal does; it's like being the captain of a ship" (O'Connor, 2013, p. 427).

Schools in Mississippi played a crucial role in helping students emotionally navigate the losses and devastation caused by Hurricane Katrina over the long-term. Both students and staff faced considerable psychological stress due to the disaster, according to a survey by Ward and Shelley (2008). Similarly, survey findings from Lee et al. (2008) showed that school leaders who implemented counseling and mental health support services for students and staff were perceived as most effective by stakeholders. They also created opportunities for students and staff to process the trauma caused by the storms. An illustrative example of this approach is evident in *The Storm: Students of Biloxi, Mississippi Remember Hurricane Katrina*, a compilation of stories and drawings by Gulf

Coast students and teachers (McGrath, 2006). Another such example involves an art class in Houston, where students crafted collages reflecting their experiences with Hurricane Katrina. In their pursuit to reopen, school leaders exemplified that "functioning schools create an unparalleled opportunity to provide mental health services to children after such a disaster" (Bowman, 2008, p. 729).

Giving students space to process their experiences of disaster was also shown to be useful in other contexts. For instance, working collaboratively with school principals, Mutch and Gawith (2014) designed projects for students at three schools that were aimed at helping them navigate their trauma and grief after the Christchurch earthquake. In the first school, the researchers and school leaders interviewed children in groups about their memories of the earthquake. In the second school, the community planted a memorial garden together on campus. In the third school, children created a documentary with interviews from community members about their experiences with the disaster. In all three cases, the schools' projects proved to be useful tools for helping students "to move to a new level of awareness, understanding and engagement" (Mutch & Gawith, 2014, p. 64). Similarly, Nastasi and Jayasena (2014) found that a culturally aligned social and emotional program for Sri Lankan students and teachers aided in their recovery from the 2004 tsunami.

Similarly, in Joplin, Missouri, the superintendent established structures that enabled students' processing of the trauma of the tornado. During the summer, the school district provided training for teachers and staff coping strategies for anxiety and depression. Moreover, once school reopened, additional counselors were available at all schools, and several community mental health providers also gave assistance to struggling students and staff (Kanter & Abramson, 2014). Importantly, the district also established new bus routes that allowed displaced students to return to their usual school, which helped "normalize" their return to school and stabilize their emotional recovery (Kanter & Abramson, 2014, p. 216). To further normalize students' experiences and support their emotional recovery, some Christchurch school leaders adopted disaster drills to help familiarize students with the process of an earthquake. Kusumasari and Alam (2011) found that leaders who did so helped ease anxiety among students and teachers in their schools.

Researchers have also identified ways that school leaders have successfully supported teachers following a disaster. For example, Seyle and colleagues (2013) developed a burnout mitigation tool that helped teachers manage their experiences of burnout following a major earthquake in rural Indonesia. Importantly, the researchers observed that teachers who suffered from burnout were less able to be supportive of their students' needs. Seyle and colleagues (2013) noted that teachers' burnout hampers recovery in the local community because teachers and schools, "particularly those working with indigenous populations and serving rural areas, are an important resource for assisting with the community's recovery" (Seyle et al., 2013, p. 399). Preventing teacher burnout was also top of mind for Philip D. Potter, a school principal in Dallas, Texas, after the area was impacted by a series of deadly tornadoes in 2019. He described assuming a protective role toward teachers and worked to keep teachers' focus on their students by not burdening them with extraneous tasks and responsibilities. As an example, Potter recalled turning down a press engagement that would not have authentically supported his school and would have wasted teachers' time and energy (Potter et al., 2021). In a study of teacher burnout following the Christchurch earthquakes, Kuntz and colleagues (2013) concluded, "The onus is therefore placed on organizations to manage their job requirements and support systems available in a disaster context" (p. 66).

Taken altogether, the body of evidence discussed here centers schools and school leaders as sites for students and teachers' emotional recovery from disasters. From the first hours immediately after the event and in the months and years that follow, school leaders play an important role in facilitating how students and teachers can process these events.

Meeting Community Needs

Beyond supporting the students and educators who are in their school buildings day in and day out, school leaders also assume responsibility for providing communication, leadership, and, when appropriate, reassurance, to community members. School leaders are called upon to shift their roles to a broader leadership role that supports the broader community during the recovery process (Fletcher & Nicholas, 2016). Often, this involves giving people what they need in the moment, whether it is emotional reassurance or resources and supplies.

Principals in O'Connor's (2013) study of the role of school principals immediately after the Christchurch earthquake described how they saw their role as leading more than just students and teachers. As one remarked, "I put on my principal's smile. Parents arrived and were standing outside. I realized then that I had an audience and my response needed to be calm and instantaneous, I had to look like I was in control" (O'Connor, 2013, p. 427). The choices made by these principals in the immediate aftermath of the earthquake underscore the crucial role of school leaders in times of disaster. Both internal and external stakeholders turned to them for decisions and guidance. Despite grappling with their own emotional turmoil, the principals acknowledged the community's needs and acted accordingly.

A practical measure that school leaders often become responsible for following a climate disaster is the organization and distribution of donations and other resources. For example, after Hurricane Katrina, Mississippi schools were overwhelmed by an influx of donations, placing the onus on school leaders to coordinate and allocate these resources. Despite the external generosity, the donated supplies frequently fell short of alleviating the difficult circumstances that locals faced, as many of the donations did not align with the most urgent needs of students and the community. As one school leader described, "Heaps of unused clothing and storage areas full of unneeded backpacks bore testimony to this disconnect" (Ward & Shelley, 2008, p. 345). To mitigate the burden of organizing donations, a Mississippi superintendent recommended designating a point person within a school district to manage donations (Lee et al., 2008). Similarly, Potter, the Texas school principal, said he encouraged donors to send gift cards to teachers to avoid extraneous donations.

Brokering With Outside Agencies and Organizations

One important reason why school communities broadly need school leaders are central to disaster recovery is because they often possess the bureaucratic capabilities and social capital to advocate on behalf of their students and families with outside organizations and agencies (Akbaba-Altun, 2005; Gouwens & Lander, 2008). School leaders can act as brokers between school communities and policymakers and governmental leaders, providing the former with needed aid and relief and the latter with highly relevant local knowledge to inform decision-making (Sherrieb et al., 2012). School leaders are usually among the closest leaders to a local community, and as such they are the best equipped to understand the needs and capacity their community has during a natural disaster (Sherrieb et al., 2012).

School leaders' capability to act in a brokering role is especially important for communities experiencing poverty. Following Hurricane Katrina, Anderson (2005) wrote that the disaster "raise[d] the issue of the degree to which poor children, even in a developed country like the U.S., are more vulnerable to disaster because their families may not have the resources to live in safe neighborhoods or the means to evacuate out of harm's way" (p. 163). Because climate disasters act as reflective mirrors for communities to recognize and tackle prevailing social issues, then children become amplified reflections of these inequities due to their limited agency and voice in postdisaster decision-making (Anderson, 2005). School leaders should always be advocates for children, and therefore, they play a central role in recovery efforts connected to them and their families and communities.

Crisis and Disaster Management as Gap in Leadership Preparation

Given the ways that climate disasters can disrupt students' educational progress, especially among students who are from historically or socially marginalized groups, it is important that school leaders are aware of and equipped to respond to these events. However, prior research has shown that this is often not the case. While the research discussed in this section provides an overview of some of the things school leaders have done that have been helpful for their students, teachers, and communities, crisis management writ large is a critical but neglected aspect of school leadership training (Grissom & Condon, 2021; Urick et al., 2021). Crisis management is typically absent from the curriculum of most principal preparation programs and in-service training. Neither is crisis management integrated into the national standards for educational leaders.

For example, Hurricane Katrina underscored that Mississippi school leaders were not sufficiently prepared to effectively manage a major crisis or disaster. According to results from a study conducted by Lee and colleagues (2008) asking stakeholders to share their perceptions of school leaders' effectiveness in managing Hurricane Katrina and future disasters, a staggering 80% of respondents expressed concern that their local school's emergency plans continued to be too vague for disasters of the magnitude the region had just experienced. In evaluating these plans,

Lee and colleagues (2008) found that less than 20% had been updated within a year of Hurricane Katrina. Despite the shortcomings of their plans, school leaders expressed an intention to use the lessons learned from Hurricane Katrina to better prepare for future disasters. As one leader shared, "All systems had plans, but they were incomplete. Now we know what to do" (Lee et al., 2008, p. 328). Similarly, following a major earthquake in Turkey, Ozmen (2006) and Konakli and Kaplan (2019) found that school administrators reported preparedness for future earthquakes and disasters were lower than recommended guidelines for such a seismically-active region. Adding to this point, Akbaba-Altun (2005) found that principals felt that federal response guidelines provided to them for earthquakes were inadequate.

Regardless of whether sufficient training has been made available, it is necessary for school leaders to be prepared to respond to disasters. As Gainey (2010) argued, schools have a public policy obligation to prepare for disasters because they are responsible for the safety and welfare of children, who are one of the most vulnerable segments of the population. The author explained, "The nature of a crisis places the ability of the school district to safeguard its mission, students, employees, and other stakeholders in jeopardy. This jeopardy makes it essential that school districts transform them-selves into crisis-ready organizations" (Gainey, 2010, p. 306).

The research discussed in this section provides an overview of some of these expectations for school leaders to help students, teachers, families, and communities navigate the process of recovery. Although extant literature highlights the emotional toll of natural disasters on non-school leaders (i.e., students and teachers), there is not yet research on the toll these events have on school leaders. Perhaps this is because school leaders are expected to have the tools and training to manage these events, as well as the tools and training to manage their own emotional experiences of disasters. However, as the COVID-19 pandemic made abundantly clear, school leadership preparation and professional development often neglects to prepare school leaders for the roles and responsibilities that communities will expect them to fill in the wake of a crisis or disaster (Grissom & Condon, 2021; Urick et al., 2021). In the section below, we describe how school leaders can become equipped to manage these crisis events.

The Future: A Portrait of the Reimagined School Leader

Climate disasters and the associated environmental injustices that precipitate them are emblematic of an increasingly uncertain global context in which school leaders must operate.

Disasters and other crisis events are an inevitable and "inherent reality of schools and school communities" (Smith & Riley, 2012, p. 53). As Tierney (2019) imagined:

> Disaster-related losses in the form of death, injury, illness, and economic costs will continue to rise. These effects will be borne disproportionately by the poor countries of the world and by the most vulnerable groups, in both developed and less developed countries... Disasters will interact with other social ills, such as

wars and civil wars to produce severe humanitarian crises. As weather extremes become more common as a consequence of climate change, floods, droughts, and other perils will increase food insecurity and will threaten livelihoods. Conflicts over resources will become more frequent (2019, 127–128).

For school leadership, the certainty of crisis necessitates that they be prepared for and respond appropriately to crises and disasters.

Following the outbreak of the COVID-19 pandemic, Grissom and Condon (2021) outlined three fundamental competencies that school leaders should employ in times of disaster and crisis. Because their framework draws on literature prior to the pandemic, we believe these competencies are also applicable to natural disasters. They are: (1) communication, (2) emotional intelligence, and (3) analysis, sensemaking, and judgment. Regarding communication, the authors stressed how important it is for leaders to provide transparent, frequent, and consistent communication to build trust and garner support during a crisis or natural disaster. Regarding emotional intelligence, school leaders must acknowledge and address the stress and trauma introduced by a crisis. Leaders who do so can contribute to better long-term outcomes and foster a more stable school community for the future. Lastly, the competency of analysis, sensemaking, and judgment requires leaders to effectively utilize available information for decision-making, even when they may have imperfect or incomplete data. Utilizing this competency empowers school leaders to take immediate action while also allowing them to refine their responses for future crisis or disaster situations.

We see evidence of these competencies in the studies described in the previous sections. For example, leaders demonstrated the competency of communication when they broker with outside agencies to garner needed supplies for their communities (e.g., Bowman, 2008; Sherrieb et al., 2012). Other leaders demonstrated emotional intelligence by providing opportunities and physical space for students, teachers and communities to emotionally process their experiences and regain a sense of normalcy (e.g., Goswick et al., 2018; Mutch & Gawith, 2014). Other leaders employed analysis, sensemaking, and judgment to guide their decision-making after a disaster occurred. For example, school leaders in Mississippi and Missouri who prioritized reopening schools recognized that it was in the best interest of their communities physically, emotionally, and economically to have schools in session (Goswick et al., 2018; Lamb et al., 2013; Shorr, 2006).

An Evolving Role for School Leaders

When a climate disaster occurs, the role of school leader inevitably changes (Gouwens & Lander, 2008). In the aftermath of such an event, school leaders' priority is to address the immediate needs of the community. School leaders must acknowledge the importance of prioritizing students' basic needs – particularly food and emotional support – understanding that effective learning hinges on meeting these requirements. In summarizing how school leaders in New Zealand responded to the earthquakes, Mutch (2015) explained that principals' focus became "dealing with an immediate crisis, managing their schools as post-disaster community hubs, rebuilding the fabric of their school communities, and all the while being sensitive to the physical, emotional, social, and psychological needs of their staff, students and families" (Mutch, 2015, p. 192).

The recovery efforts undertaken by school leaders also contribute to the development of social capital among students, staff, and school communities. In doing so, school leaders can demonstrate their commitment to fostering connections and building a sense of community. For instance, Joplin superintendent's use of a countdown clock for the school's reopening symbolized a shared goal and emphasized the importance of an on-time reopening for providing essential resources to the community's needy students. Other efforts, such as appointing a point person to manage donations, showcase the extension and connection of various social networks within and beyond schools and districts. Strategically, this approach also aligns external generosity with the unmet needs of students and families in the affected area, promoting a sense of unity and support. Additionally, school superintendents play a pivotal role as linking entities, connecting groups to centers of power and governmental influence. Their ability to navigate and advocate for schools and communities in policy spaces establishes them as essential figures in influencing broader social and political contexts (Sherrieb et al., 2012).

School leaders must also pay special attention to the toll a climate disaster places on a teacher. Kuntz and colleagues (2013) emphasized that there are far-reaching consequences of teacher stress, emotional exhaustion, and burnout after a disaster. These emotions often lead to turnover and attrition. Griffard (2022) found that schools in North Carolina had higher rates of teacher turnover following two major hurricanes, Matthew in 2016 and Florence in 2018. By supporting teachers, school leaders are lending support and stability to students and the community.

Portrait of a Reimagined School Leader

While it is important to note that "different types of crises call for different responses" (Johnson & Hackman, 2013, p. 440), regardless of the crisis, in the aftermath, effective leadership in P-12 schools is crucial to support the well-being of students, teachers, and communities. First, establishing a comprehensive crisis response plan, in preparation of a disaster, is paramount. Norris et al. (2009) emphasized the importance of predisaster planning to mitigate the impact of traumatic events on students and teachers. Key to this planning is the development of an interdisciplinary crisis team, including individuals with expertise in mental health, counseling, and community outreach (Brymer et al., 2006). Another step in predisaster planning is regularly conducting drills and simulations to test the responsiveness of the team and identify areas of improvement. Additionally, school leaders should collaborate with community stakeholders, allocate resources for crisis training, and develop communication strategies to ensure a coordinated and swift response if a disaster occurs.

After a disaster has occurred, meeting the physical and psychological needs of students, teachers, and the school community is crucial. P-12 school leaders should strive to reopen schools quickly and act decisively to ensure that supports are prepared for students, teachers, and the community. While physical needs are important, mental health supports are essential for the well-being of the school community. Greenberg et al. (2017) underscored the impact of natural disasters on mental health, particularly among children. School leaders can work to integrate trauma-informed practices into the curriculum, provide counseling services, and train teachers to recognize and address signs of trauma in students. Resources such as the agency within the US Department of Health and Human Resources called the Substance Abuse and Mental Health Services Administration (see https://www.samhsa.gov/) offers guides and toolkits specifically tailored for educators looking to incorporate trauma-sensitive approaches into their teaching methods. These resources provide evidence-based strategies to create a safe and supportive learning environment for students who may have experienced trauma. Additionally, creating a supportive and empathetic school environment can contribute to the emotional recovery of students and staff.

Third, fostering community engagement and collaboration is vital for rebuilding and recovery. Peek and Stough (2010) highlighted the importance of social capital in post-disaster contexts. School leaders should facilitate partnerships with local organizations, businesses, and government agencies to enhance support systems. This collaborative approach can extend beyond immediate relief efforts, involving the community in long-term initiatives that promote resilience and address ongoing challenges faced by students, teachers, and families.

By incorporating these practical steps (see Fig. 7.1), school leaders can play a pivotal role in not only responding to the immediate aftermath of a natural disaster but also in building a foundation for sustained recovery and growth within the P-12 educational community.

While P-12 school leaders could utilize the previously discussed practical steps, there is an additional perspective that should be addressed. The role of the P-12 school leader has evolved over time (Rousmaniere, 2013). Preparing and leading school communities through disasters is an example of this evolution. Researchers have found that the role has expanded to include so many responsibilities that it has become daunting and seemingly impossible to balance the many responsibilities simultaneously (Davis et al., 2005). Levine (2005) noted that one of the changes to the traditional role of the school leader is leading "through an era of profound social change" (p. 5). The ways in which school leaders have been able to lead, and in many cases, create socially just changes and equity within schools has been studied for many decades; however, much of this research has been conducted more recently (Skousen, 2020). In fact, scholars have posited that equity-focused and social justice oriented leaders are the P-12 school leaders that are needed (Furman, 2012; Lugg & Shoho, 2006; Marshall, 2004; Theoharis et al., 2009). It is this perspective that explicitly needs to be addressed in the context of leading P-12 schools through disasters.

Equity-focused leaders are those who focus on providing the resources and support for students whose identities include those that have been historically and currently marginalized. In his definition for social justice leadership Theoharis

Fig. 7.1. Practical Steps to Lead Through Disaster.

(2007) stated, "these principals make issues of race, class, gender, disability, sexual orientation, and other historically and currently marginalized conditions in the United States central to their advocacy, leadership, practice, and vision" (Theoharis, 2007, p. 223). Other researchers have created frameworks for equity-focused leaders, with the following practices "prioritizing equity leadership, preparing for equity, developing equity leadership teams, building equity-focused systems, and sustaining equity" (Radd et al., 2021, p. 6). Key to implementing equity-focused practices is understanding why equity is needed and then emphasizing equitable practices. In the context of environmental injustice and natural disasters, students of color and those who live in poverty experience a more severe negative impact (Esnard et al., 2017; Lee et al., 2008).

The practical steps for school leaders that have been previously discussed do not need to change for a school leader whose focus is equity. Instead, the steps should be enhanced to explicitly place those students whose identities align with those groups of historically and currently marginalized individuals. For example, while creating a comprehensive crisis response plan, the school leader and team should prioritize the students and families who live in poverty and those who come from groups that have been historically and currently marginalized. This could be realized through knowing the students and families and making pre-disaster plans to prioritize their physical and psychological needs. Other examples include ensuring equitable distribution of resources, fostering strong partnerships, and creating open communication and collaboration to those vulnerable student populations and their families. To further emphasize this point, it is important to recognize that an equity-focused approach does not force school leaders to recreate already existing plans, it is opening another lens to see another way of providing support and resources to those who are the most vulnerable to crises and have a greater need of support from school leaders.

Conclusion

While it may be unrealistic to expect any individual school leader to be fully equipped to handle every potential disaster scenario, this should not serve as a justification for neglecting crisis and disaster planning altogether (Jenkins & Goodman, 2015). Instead, we argue for a strategic focus on bolstering the capabilities of school leaders to effectively respond to unexpected disruptions such as climate disasters. By elucidating the historical context and academic data illustrating the impact of environmental factors on educational outcomes, we underscore the imperative for school leadership to prioritize supporting recovery following natural disasters.

Central to this discussion is the recognition of the disproportionate effects of climate disasters and environmental injustices on historically marginalized groups, highlighting systemic issues of racism, poverty, and social inequality that heighten vulnerability to disasters. Within this framework, we outline the evolving roles and responsibilities of school leaders in disaster response, showcasing their emergence as crucial figures in guiding communities through crises. From managing the immediate aftermath of disasters to advocating for equitable recovery efforts, school leaders are portrayed as playing multifaceted roles that extend beyond traditional educational duties.

Finally, we underscore the urgency of equipping school leaders with the necessary skills and knowledge to navigate the complexities of climate disasters and environmental injustices. We call for a reimagined approach to leadership education that prioritizes equity-focused practices and sustainability initiatives, empowering school leaders to effectively support their communities in times of crisis. By recognizing the pivotal role of school leadership in mitigating the impacts of climate disasters and environmental injustices, stakeholders can work toward building more resilient and equitable educational systems that prioritize the well-being of all students and communities.

References

Acevedo-Garcia, D., McArdle, N., Noelke, C., Huntington, N., Huber, R., & Sofer, N. (2020). Opportunity hoarding linked to racial and ethnic inequities in children's neighborhoods. *Diversity Data Kids.* https://www.diversitydatakids.org/research-library/data-visualization/opportunity-hoarding-linked-racial-and-ethnic-inequities

Ainsworth, J. W. (2002). Why does it take a village? The mediation of neighborhood effects on educational achievement. *Social Forces, 81*(1), 117–152.

Akbaba-Altun, S. (2005). Turkish school principals' earthquake experiences and reactions. *International Journal of Educational Management, 19*(4), 307–317.

Anderson, W. A. (2005). Bringing children into focus on the social science disaster research agenda. *International Journal of Mass Emergencies and Disasters, 23*(3), 159–175.

Barrett, E. J., Ausbrooks, C. Y. B., & Martinez-Cosio, M. (2012). The tempering effect of schools on students experiencing a life-changing event: Teenagers and the Hurricane Katrina evacuation. *Urban Education, 47*(1), 7–31.

Bathi, J. R., & Das, H. S. (2016). Vulnerability of coastal communities from storm surge and flood disasters. *International Journal of Environmental Research and Public Health, 13*(2), 1–12.

Bowman, M. (2008). Rebuilding schools, rebuilding communities: The Civic role of Mississippi's public schools after Hurricane Katrina. *The Mississippi Law Review*, (2007–08), 711–730.

Brooks, M. C. (2014). School principals in Southern Thailand. *Educational Management Administration & Leadership, 43*(2), 232–252.

Brymer, M., Layne, C., Jacobs, A., Pynoos, R., Ruzek, J., Steinberg, A., Vernberg, E., & Watson, P. (2006). Psychological first aid field operations guide. *National Child Traumatic Stress Network*. https://www.nctsn.org/resources/psychological-first-aid-pfa-field-operations-guide-2nd-edition

Changon, S. (2010). Trend analysis: Are storms getting worse?. *Weatherwise, 63*(2), 38–43.

Chetty, R., Hendren, N., & Katz, L. F. (2016). The effects of exposure to better neighborhoods on children: New evidence from the moving to opportunity experiment. *The American Economic Review, 106*(4), 855–902.

Davis, C. R., Berke, P., Holloman, D. E., Griffard, M. R., Haynes, S., Johnson, E. M., Warraich, Z., Crisostomo-Morales, L., Golda, D., Benissan, G., Gillespy, C., Butterfield, W., & Rakes, E. (2021). *Support strategies for socially marginalized neighborhoods likely impacted by natural hazards*. Coastal Resilience Center and U.S. Department of Homeland Security. https://coastalresiliencecenter.unc.edu/wp-content/uploads/sites/845/2021/07/Support-Strategies-for-Socially-Marginalized-Neighborhoods.pdf

Davis, S., Darling-Hammond, L., LaPointe, M., & Meyerson, D. (2005). *Review of research. School leadership study. Developing successful principals*. Stanford University, Stanford Educational Leadership Institute.

De Silva, M. M. G. T., & Kawasaki, A. (2018). Socioeconomic vulnerability to disaster risk: A case study of flood and drought impact in a rural Sri Lankan community. *Ecological Economics, 152*, 131–140.

Derakhshan, S., Hodgson, M. E., & Cutter, S. L. (2020). Vulnerability of populations exposed to seismic risk in the state of Oklahoma. *Applied Geography, 124*, 102295.

Dettinger, M. (2011). Climate change, atmospheric rivers, and floods in California: A multi-model analysis of storm frequency and magnitude changes. *Journal of the American Water Resources Association, 47*(3), 514–523.

Esnard, A. M., Lai, B. S., Wyczalkowski, C., Malmin, N., & Shah, H. J. (2017). School vulnerability to disaster: Examining school closure, demographic, and exposure factors in Hurricane Ike's wind swath. *Natural Hazards, 90*(2), 513–535.

Fletcher, J., & Nicholas, K. (2016). What can school principals do to support students and their learning during and after natural disasters? *Educational Review*, *68*(3), 358–374.

Fothergill, A., & Peek, L. (2015). *Children of Katrina*. University of Texas Press.

Frankenberg, E., Sikoki, B., Sumantri, C., Suriastini, W., & Thomas, D. (2013). Education, vulnerability, and resilience after a natural disaster. *Ecology and Society: A Journal of Integrative Science for Resilience and Sustainability*, *18*(2), 16.

Fuller, S. C. (2014). The effect of prenatal natural disaster exposure on school outcomes. *Demography*, *51*(4), 1501–1525.

Furman, G. (2012). Social justice leadership as praxis: Developing capacities through preparation programs. *Educational Administration Quarterly*, *48*(2), 191–229.

Gaffney, D. A. (2006). The aftermath of disaster: Children in crisis. *Journal of Clinical Psychology*, *62*(8), 1001–1016.

Gainey, B. S. (2010). Educational crisis management practices tentatively embrace the new media. *The handbook of crisis communication*, 301–318.

Gardiner, S. M. (2006). The Perfect moral storm: Climate change, intergenerational ethics, and the problem of corruption. *Environmental Values*, *15*(3), 397–413.

Goswick, J., Macgregor, C. J., Hurst, B., Wall, P. J., & White, R. (2018). Lessons identified by the Joplin school leadership after responding to a catastrophic tornado. *Journal of Contingencies and Crisis Management*, *26*(4), 544–553.

Gouwens, J., & Lander, D. (2008). School leadership in changing cultural contexts: How Mississippi superintendents are responding to Hurricane Katrina. *Journal of Education for Students Placed at Risk*, *13*(2–3), 273–296.

Greenberg, M. T., Domitrovich, C. E., Weissberg, R. P., & Durlak, J. A. (2017). Social and emotional learning as a public health approach to education. *The Future of Children*, 13–32.

Griffard, M. K. R. (2022). *Principal leadership as a moderator of teacher turnover following natural hazard exposure*. Doctoral dissertation. The University of North Carolina at Chapel Hill.

Grissom, J. A., & Condon, L. (2021). Leading schools and districts in times of crisis. *Educational Researcher*, *50*(5), 315–324.

Hayes, K. J., & Taylor, L. L. (1996). *Neighborhood school characteristics: What signals quality to homebuyers?* (pp. 2–9). Economic Review-Federal Reserve Bank of Dallas.

Howell, J., & Elliot, J. R. (2019). Damages done: The longitudinal impacts of natural hazards on wealth inequality in the United States. *Social Problems*, *66*, 448–467.

Imberman, S. A., Kugler, A. D., & Sacerdote, B. I. (2012). Katrina's children: Evidence on the structure of peer effects from hurricane evacuees. *American Economic Review*, *102*(5), 2048–2082.

Jacobs, F. (2019). Black feminism and radical planning: New directions for disaster planning research. *Planning Theory*, *18*(1), 24–39.

Jeffers, E. K. (2014). Discipline for students with disabilities in the recovery school district (RSD) of New Orleans. *Policy Futures in Education*, *12*(8), 1070–1077.

Jenkins, S., & Goodman, M. (2015). 'H e's One of Ours': A Case Study of a Campus Response to Crisis. *Journal of Contingencies and Crisis Management*, *23*(4), 201–209.

Johnson, C. E., & Hackman, M. Z. (2013). *Leadership: A communication perspective* (7th ed.). Waveland Press, Inc.

Kanter, R. K., & Abramson, D. (2014). School interventions after the Joplin tornado. *Prehospital and Disaster Medicine, 29*(2), 214–217.

Kates, R. W. (1971). Natural hazard in the human ecological perspective: Hypotheses and models. *Economic Geography, 47*(3), 438–451.

Konakli, T., & Kaplan, P. (2019). Emergency management in nursery schools: An analysis of experiences and opinions of administrators in Turkey. *European Journal of Educational Research, 8*(1), 73–85.

Kraft, M. A. (2020). Interpreting effect sizes of education interventions. *Educational Researcher, 49*(4), 241–253.

Kuntz, J. R., Näswall, K., & Bockett, A. (2013). Keep calm and carry on? An investigation of teacher burnout in a post-disaster context. *New Zealand Journal of Psychology, 42*(2).

Kusumasari, B., & Alam, Q. (2011). Bridging the gaps: The role of local government capability and the management of a natural disaster in Bantul, Indonesia. *Natural Hazards, 60*(2), 761–779.

Lamb, J., Gross, S., & Lewis, M. (2013). The Hurricane Katrina effect on mathematics achievement in Mississippi. *School Science and Mathematics, 113*(2), 80–93.

Leadbeater, A. (2013). Community leadership in disaster recovery: A case study. *Australian Journal of Emergency Management, 28*(3), 41–47.

Lee, D. E., Parker, G., Ward, M. E., Styron, R. A., & Shelley, K. (2008). Katrina and the schools of Mississippi: An examination of emergency and disaster preparedness. *Journal of Education for Students Placed at Risk, 13*(2–3), 318–334.

Levine, A. (2005). *Educating school leaders*. The education schools project. Washington, D.C. https://files.eric.ed.gov/fulltext/ED504142.pdf

Lin, Y., Kelemen, M., & Kiyomiya, T. (2018). The Role of community leadership in disaster recovery projects: Tsunami lessons from Japan. *International Journal of Project Management, 35*(5), 913–924.

Llorente-Marrón, M., Díaz-Fernández, M., Méndez-Rodríguez, P., & Gonzalez Arias, R. (2020). Social vulnerability, gender and disasters. The case of Haiti in 2010. *Sustainability, 12*(9), 3574.

Lugg, C. A., & Shoho, A. R. (2006). Dare public school administrators build a new social order? Social justice and the possibly perilous politics of educational leadership. *Journal of Educational Administration, 44*(3), 196–208.

Marino, E. K., & Faas, A. J. (2020). Is vulnerability an outdated concept? After subjects and spaces. *Annals of Anthropological Practice*, 1–13.

Marshall, C. (2004). Social justice challenges to educational administration: Introduction to a special issue. *Educational Administration Quarterly, 40*(1), 3–13.

Masten, A. S., & Narayan, A. J. (2012). Child development in the context of disaster, war, and terrorism: Pathways of risk and resilience. *Annual Review of Psychology, 63*, 227–257.

McGrath, B. B. (2006). *The Storm: Students of Biloxi, Mississippi, remember Hurricane Katrina*. Charlesbridge Publishing.

Mower, L. (2019). Why are 20,000 Hurricane Michael insurance claims unpaid? State officials are asking. *Miami Herald*. https://www.miamiherald.com/news/politics-government/state-politics/article234323522. Accessed on November 21, 2022.

Mutch, C., & Gawith, E. (2014). The New Zealand earthquakes and the role of schools in engaging children in emotional processing of disaster experiences. *Pastoral Care in Education, 32*(1), 54–67.

Mutch, C. (2015). Leadership in times of crisis: Dispositional, relational and contextual factors influencing school principals' actions. *International Journal of Disaster Risk Reduction, 14*, 186–194.

Nastasi, B. K., & Jayasena, A. N. (2014). An international partnership promoting psychological well-being in Sri Lankan schools. *Journal of Educational and Psychological Consultation, 24*(4), 265–282.

NOAA. (2018). U.S. Tornado climatology: Historical records and trends. https://www.ncdc.noaa.gov/climate-information/extreme-events/us-tornado-climatology/trends

Norris, F. H., Tracy, M., & Galea, S. (2009). Looking for resilience: Understanding the longitudinal trajectories of responses to stress. *Social Science & Medicine, 68*(12), 2190–2198.

O'Connor, P. (2013). Pedagogy of love and care: Shaken schools respond. *Disaster Prevention and Management, 22*(5), 425–433.

O'Toole, V. M. (2018). My emotional reservoir isn't filling as fast. Teachers' exhaustion 18 months post-earthquake. https://ir.canterbury.ac.nz/server/api/core/bitstreams/f0fdd3fb-5fc6-4b5e-8385-8d2ef2ad5f10/content

Ozmen, F. (2006). The level of preparedness of the schools for disasters from the aspect of the school principals. *Disaster Prevention and Management: An International Journal, 15*(3), 383–395.

Pane, J. F., McCaffrey, D. F., Kalra, N., & Zhou, A. J. (2008). Effects of student displacement in Louisiana during the first academic year after the hurricanes of 2005. *Journal of Education for Students Placed at Risk, 13*(2–3), 168–211.

Peek, L., & Stough, L. M. (2010). Children with disabilities in the context of disaster: A social vulnerability perspective. *Child Development, 81*(4), 1260–1270.

Potter, P. D., Pavlakis, A. E., & Roberts, J. K. (2021). Calming the storm: Natural disasters, crisis management, and school leadership. *Journal of Cases in Educational Leadership, 24*(2), 96–111.

Prinstein, M. J., La Greca, A. M., Vernberg, E. M., & Silverman, W. K. (1996). Children's coping assistance: How parents, teachers, and friends help children cope after a natural disaster. *Journal of Clinical Child Psychology, 25*(4), 463–475.

Radd, S. I., Generett, G. G., Gooden, M. A., & Theoharis, G. (2021). *Five practices for equity-focused school leadership*. ASCD.

Reid, M. (2013). Disasters and social inequalities. *Sociology Compass, 7*(11), 984–997.

Rousmaniere, K. (2013). *The principal's office: A social history of the American school principal*. State University of New York Press.

Ruiz, L. D., McMahon, S. D., & Jason, L. A. (2018). The role of neighborhood context and school climate in school-level academic achievement. *American Journal of Community Psychology, 61*(3–4), 296–309.

Seyle, D. C., Widyatmoko, C. S., & Silver, R. C. (2013). Coping with natural disasters in Yogyakarta, Indonesia: A study of elementary school teachers. *School Psychology International, 34*(4), 387–404.

Sherrieb, K., Louis, C. A., Pfefferbaum, R. L., Betty Pfefferbaum, J. D., Diab, E., & Norris, F. H. (2012). Assessing community resilience on the U.S. coast using school principals as key informants. *International Journal of Disaster Risk Reduction, 2*, 6–15.

Shorr, P. W. (2006). The longest days: Leadership during rebuilding and recovery from a disaster. *Threshold, 4*(3), 20–23.

Skousen, J. D. (2020). Hegemony, principal preparation, and the language of the oppressor: The elusive preparation of socially just school leaders. In *Handbook on promoting social justice in education* (pp. 1085–1111). Springer.

Slettebak, R. T. (2012). Don't blame the weather! Climate-related natural disasters and civil conflict. *Journal of Peace Research, 49*(1), 163–176.

Smith, A. B. (2020). *2010–2019: A landmark decade of U.S. billion-dollar weather and climate disasters*. National Oceanic and Atmospheric Administration.

Smith, L., & Riley, D. (2012). School leadership in times of crisis. *School Leadership & Management, 32*(1), 57–71.

Straub, A. M. (2021). Natural disasters don't kill people, governments kill people: Hurricane Maria, Puerto Rico–recreancy, and risk society. *Natural Hazards, 105*(2), 1603–1621.

Sturgis, S. (2018). Recent disasters reveal racial discrimination in FEMA aid process. *Facing South*. https://www.facingsouth.org/2018/09/recent-disasters-reveal-racial-discrimination-fema-aid-process

Swenson, C. C., Saylor, C. F., Powell, M. P., Stokes, S. J., Foster, K. Y., & Belter, R. W. (1996). Impact of natural disaster on preschool children: Adjustment 14 months after a hurricane. *American Journal of Orthopsychiatry, 66*(1), 122–130.

Theoharis, G. (2007). Social justice educational leaders and resistance: Toward a theory of social justice leadership. *Educational Administration Quarterly, 43*(2), 221–258.

Theoharis, J., Alonso, G., Anderson, N. S., & Su, C. (2009). Our schools suck: Students talk back to a segregated nation on the failures of urban education. In *Our schools suck*. New York University Press.

Tian, X. L., & Guan, X. (2015). The impact of Hurricane Katrina on students behavioral disorder: A difference-in-difference analysis. *International Journal of Environmental Research and Public Health, 12*(5), 5540–5560.

Tierney, K. (2019). *Disasters: A sociological approach*. John Wiley & Sons.

Tschakert, P., Zimmerer, K., King, B., & Baum, S. (2020). What is a natural hazard? https://www.e-education.psu.edu/geog30/node/378

Urick, A., Carpenter, B. W., & Eckert, J. (2021, March). Confronting COVID: Crisis leadership, turbulence, and self-care. In *Frontiers in Education* (Vol. 6, p. 642861). Frontiers Media SA.

Ward, M. E., & Shelley, K. (2008). Hurricane Katrina's impact on students and staff members in the schools of Mississippi. *Journal of Education for Students Placed at Risk (JESPAR), 13*(2-3), 335–353.

Ward, M. E., Shelley, K., Kaase, K., & Pane, J. F. (2013). Hurricane Katrina: A longitudinal study of the achievement and behavior of displaced students. *Journal of Education for Students Placed at Risk, 13*(2–3), 297–317.

Chapter 8

Mindful Leadership: Cultivating Awareness, Wisdom, and Connection

Sharon D. Kruse[a] and David E. DeMatthews[b]

[a]Washington State University, USA
[b]University of Texas at Austin, USA

Abstract

Mindful leadership offers a powerful antidote to the stress and burnout facing many school leaders today. This chapter integrates three key streams of mindfulness research and practice – contemplative, cognitive, and organizational mindfulness – to present a more caring and compassionate model of educational leadership.

Drawing on the experiences of focal school leaders, the chapter explores how mindful leadership practices can transform schools by cultivating awareness of self and others. In addition, this chapter explores how leaders can situate themselves within and the larger school-community environment, developing equanimity and resilience in the face of challenges, adopting a stance of curiosity and openness to multiple perspectives, nurturing authentic relationships and emotional attunement, and navigating paradoxes of purpose and identity with wisdom.

Rather than a fixed technique, mindful leadership is presented as an ongoing practice and way of being – purposeful, present, and openhearted. By starting where they are and committing to continual growth, educational leaders can become leaders in fostering cultures of well-being and transformative learning. The chapter concludes with suggested mindfulness practices for individuals and organizations to support this lifelong journey. Mindful leadership is ultimately a courageous and pragmatic path to more clearly see reality, embrace vulnerability, and wholeheartedly engage in positive change.

Keywords: Mindful leadership; contemplative mindfulness; cognitive mindfulness; organizational mindfulness; school leadership

Introduction

In today's complex and rapidly changing world, school leaders face unrelenting challenges and pressures that can lead to individual and collective burnout (Gonzalez-Morales et al., 2012; Urien et al., 2021). Mindful leadership offers a powerful antidote, providing principals and education leaders with practices to lead with greater clarity, resilience, and care for themselves and others (Mahfouz, 2018; Wells, 2015). As DeMatthews et al. (2021), Lane et al. (2021), and Mahfouz (2020) emphasize, job-related stress and burnout have become exceedingly prevalent in schools. Characterized by emotional exhaustion (i.e., psychological and physical depletion as a result of accumulated stress), depersonalization and cynicism (i.e., the development of a more callous, dehumanized perception of others, often paired with an inability to express empathy), and a sense of reduced personal accomplishment and efficacy (i.e., loss of feelings of confidence and competence, dissatisfaction regarding professional achievements) as a result of one's work environment, burnout has significant consequences for educators' well-being, performance, and retention (Capone et al., 2019; Ford et al., 2019). Of these, exhaustion has been suggested to be most damaging (Urien et al., 2021) to individuals in the short- and long-term.

While individual factors play a role in how one experiences job-related stress and burnout, research increasingly points to organizational conditions as key drivers of burnout. Heavy workloads, lack of autonomy and support, and misalignment between individual and organizational values can all contribute to a toxic stew of stress (Bunjak et al., 2021; Kruse & Edge, 2023; Van Droogenbroeck et al., 2021). Crucially, burnout is often communicable, with exhaustion and negativity spreading between colleagues and eroding collective capacity (Gonzalez-Morales et al., 2012). When burnout becomes enmeshed in the culture, even well-intentioned improvement efforts can backfire by layering on additional demands. As Weiss (2020) argues, meaningfully addressing burnout requires a systems perspective.

This is where mindful leadership comes in – offering a way to disrupt the vicious cycle of burnout by cultivating individual and collective awareness, well-being, and resilience. This chapter explores how mindful leadership can transform the organizational conditions that enable burnout into sources of individual and collective renewal. Drawing from research (Kruse, 2023) conducted with school principals and district office leaders during the 2020–2021 school year, the chapter provides insights into how mindful leadership was evidenced in the leadership practice of 20 school leaders. In sum the vignettes suggest how awareness, wisdom, and compassion can radiate from leadership practice to curate a culture of well-being.

The Three Traditions of Mindfulness

While often reduced to a technique for quieting the mind, mindfulness in fact represents a rich body of theory and practice with roots in both Eastern contemplative traditions and Western psychology and philosophy.

Contemplative mindfulness focuses on cultivating focused attention and awareness of one's subjective, moment-to-moment experience, including thoughts, emotions, and sensations. With roots in Buddhist meditation practices, contemplative mindfulness emphasizes nonjudgmental present moment awareness as a path to equanimity and liberation from habitual patterns of reactivity (Brown et al., 2007; Kabat-Zinn, 2003). Contemplative mindfulness practices like meditation can reduce stress, enhance emotional regulation, and promote a sense of groundedness (Kabat-Zinn, 2003). Moreover, the research is clear, practicing contemplative mindfulness produces salutary effects including stress and anxiety reduction (Hoge et al., 2013; Lomas et al., 2017), decreased blood pressure (Koike & Cardoso, 2014), emotional health (Goyal et al., 2014; Pathath, 2017), enhanced self-awareness and attention span (Dahl et al., 2015; Sood & Jones, 2013), increased creativity (Capurso et al., 2014), and the ability to lead with insight, compassion, and authenticity (Brown, et al., 2007; Lomas et al., 2017). In fact, there is growing evidence that, when applied in workplace settings, contemplative mindfulness is associated with increased well-being, more skillful leadership, and organizational effectiveness (Felver et al., 2013; Good et al., 2016; Janssen et al., 2018). These outcomes have been found to foster a leader's clarity about their perceptions of the world, their relationship to challenge and difficulty, and decrease worries about future events or issues (Good et al., 2016; Mendelson et al., 2010).

Cognitive mindfulness, pioneered by researchers like Ellen Langer, explores how actively noticing novelty and distinctions in one's environment can lessen mindless, rigid thought patterns. The practice of cognitive mindfulness encourages school leaders to broaden their perspectives, see their schools with fresh eyes, and use what they learn as tools for their leadership practice. By centering learning as a primary feature of leadership, theories of cognitive mindfulness emphasize that leadership is less about knowing and more about discovery and understanding (Brown et al., 2007; Donoon & Langer, 2011; Langer, 1989, 2014; Lee, 2019). The practice of cognitive mindfulness encourages school leaders to become curious about the organizations they lead and the world in which they live.

In this tradition, mindful activity is focused on actively noticing when and how our environment changes and resisting the tendency to view things as static and inflexible (Donoon & Langer, 2011; Langer & Molodoveanu, 2000; Lee, 2019). Importantly, cognitive mindfulness emphasizes that for any situation there are always multiple explanations and perspectives, and that issues and ideas are experienced and understood differently by different stakeholders. Leading within the tradition of cognitive mindfulness assumes that no matter how smart we are, how well educated, or well-positioned, our understandings are unavoidably, only partial. Therefore, cognitive mindfulness is a dynamic quality, one in which leaders remain open to new signals in and from the environment including, and perhaps privileging, those that are at odds with our prior experiences and understandings.

Organizational mindfulness, based on Karl Weick's research in high reliability organizations, looks at how collectives foster resilience by attending to small errors and anomalies before they escalate. It involves balancing success and failure through practices like reluctance to simplify, sensitivity to operations, and deference to expertise (Vogus & Sutcliffe, 2012; Weick & Sutcliffe, 2006). Vogus and Sutcliffe (2012) define organizational mindfulness as, "the extent to which an organization captures discriminatory detail about emerging threats and creates a capability to swiftly act in response to these details" (p. 723). However, capturing "discriminatory detail" and focusing on "emerging threats" does not happen by chance. Nor does swift action. Instead each is the result of attention to what the organization needs to accomplish *and* what it should never allow to happen. Research (Rerup, 2005; Vogus & Rerup, 2017; Vogus & Sutcliffe, 2012) suggests that *highly reliable organizations* purposefully organize to balance success (i.e., achieving goals) and failure (i.e., disastrous mistakes and errors). Therefore, organizational mindfulness offers leaders a buffer against burnout by enabling recovery, learning, and care (Weick & Sutcliffe, 2006).

While each mindfulness tradition has distinct elements, they share a common focus on developing clear, flexible, responsive, and nuanced attention and awareness, at the individual, interpersonal, and organizational levels. Together, they provide complementary lenses and practices for reimagining leadership (Ehrlich, 2017; Hunter & Chaskalson, 2013). Furthermore, research (Colzato et al., 2012; Shapiro et al., 2006) suggests that the ability to do what is right *and to do it for the right reason* is enhanced by the practice of mindfulness. Table 8.1 draws distinctions between the constructs of burnout and mindfulness suggesting that there are significant impacts for individuals, organizations, and leadership theorizing when they are considered in tandem.

The Centrality of Awareness

At the heart of mindful leadership is the capacity for awareness – of self, others, and the larger environment. Awareness goes beyond just paying attention to cultivating consciousness of one's subjective experience, perceptions, and meaning-making processes (Brown et al., 2007; Silsbee, 2010). Awareness involves developing self-knowledge, emotional attunement, and the ability to notice subtle cues and shifts. As an elementary school principal suggested,

> When I'm aware, really paying attention, I clearly know, what I'm dealing with and how I can use whatever resources I have in that moment to work with the issue. [For example], this year, it's been stressful, I know that teachers, they're all exhausted, and they're still trying, but it's just hard. So when I'm talking with them, I try to put myself in their shoes. [I ask myself], what is the issue, the real issue, here? Who is the person I know them to be? What is it that matters in this moment and how can I offer some direction? You notice, I didn't say tell them what to do. I said offer direction. Because I know that's not necessarily what they want, usually what they want is to be seen. To have me know that I'm aware

Table 8.1. Burnout and Mindfulness Contrasted (Brown et al., 2007; Ehrlich, 2017; King & Badham, 2018; Kruse, 2023; Kruse & Edge, 2023; Langer, 1989, 2014; Mahfouz, 2020; Weick & Sutcliffe, 2006).

	Burnout	**Mindfulness**
Definition	A state of emotional exhaustion, depersonalization, cynicism, and reduced self-efficacy	A way of cultivating awareness, equanimity, curiosity, and care for oneself and others
Origins	Largely driven by organizational conditions such as heavy workloads, lack of autonomy and support, and misalignment between individual and organizational values	Can be developed through individual practices and organizational routines that promote wellbeing, recovery, and resilience
Impact on self	Leads to stress, negativity, and a sense of depletion. Can erode one's sense of purpose and effectiveness	Enhances emotional regulation, groundedness, and the ability to approach challenges with balance and grace
Impact on others	Can be communicable, spreading exhaustion and negativity to colleagues and eroding collective capacity	Promotes genuine connection, mutual support, and a culture of care. Leaders model vulnerability and compassion
Organizational implications	Can become enmeshed in the culture, creating a vicious cycle that undermines even well-intentioned improvement efforts. Requires a systems perspective to address meaningfully	Transforms organizational conditions to support individual and collective wellbeing. Involves questioning assumptions, learning from challenges, and aligning structures with values of sustainability
Leadership actions and outcomes	Can lead to a culture of individualistic heroism, shame and blame, and unsustainable work habits	Balances compassion and accountability, treats self-care as mission-critical, and views people's humanity as the path to shared success
Paradigm		Represents a shift toward leadership as a humanizing,

(Continued)

Table 8.1. *(Continued)*

Burnout	Mindfulness
Reflects inadequate systems and structures that fail to meet the needs of educators	healing endeavor that embraces the full potential of educators

of what they're dealing with. If I can do that, and maybe offer something else, like maybe take a kid for a bit or make it okay to have an extra recess, that's the icing, what I really try to be aware of is who they are and what it takes to make them as whole as they can be so that they can do the job I know they are able to do.

These thoughts were echoed by a district office curriculum leader who remarked,

You know, when I pay attention, really work to be aware of what's happening in buildings, our work seems to make more of an impact. It's just so easy from where I sit to say, we can add this one more thing. It'll be good for kids. But you know, when we do that, all we really do is exhaust teachers. There is just too much for them to do. So when I sit back and truly ask myself do we need to do this? Can it wait or is there a way to weave it into something we're already doing, it just goes better. It took me awhile to learn this but I know that I get more done when I think about it wholistically and pay attention to how it fits into the whole system, not just trying to do this one thing.

Crucially, mindful awareness is not just an individual process but also an interpersonal and organizational one. When school leaders, like the ones quoted above, incorporate practices like generous listening, humble inquiry, and dialog, trust is built and collective efficacy enhanced (Bandura, 1997; Goddard et al., 2004; Schein, 2013). Therefore, at the organizational level, awareness is enhanced by mindful organizing – designing roles, routines, and systems to detect and respond to emerging issues and opportunities (Ray et al., 2011; Vogus & Sutcliffe, 2012). This could involve empowering frontline staff, creating feedback loops, and promoting candid upward communication. The goal is, to sense the real needs and dynamics of the school as a living system, not an inert machine. In turn, developing deeper awareness of the school as creates a channel for school leaders to cultivate stronger systems for listening, recognizing and celebrating of expertise, and identifying and remedying issues before they fester.

The Path of Equanimity

Mindfulness is sometimes misunderstood as detachment or indifference. But equanimity cultivated through mindfulness is not aloofness but rather stability, balance, and poise in the midst of turbulence (Desbordes et al., 2015). Equanimity involves meeting joys and sorrows with an evenness of mind, rather than grasping and fixating on pleasure and pain. In the pressure cooker of school leadership, equanimity is essential for avoiding burnout and reactivity (Mahfouz, 2018). Leading from a stance of equanimity asks leaders to be ambitious while being prepared for things to go wrong, to need adjustments, and to create space for teachers, staff, and student to grow and learn. As a middle school principal suggests,

> I try to accept that [stuff] happens. Things look great on paper. Then it hits classrooms and it changes. I've learned to roll with that. I've learned not to react and to correct. I tell them they should be doing it differently. But in the end our job is to educate kids, no matter the circumstances, no matter how it gets done... I try hard to let teachers figure it out themselves, it's not like I abandon them. It's more like, I'm less tied to having whatever it is look exactly alike in every classroom... SEL [Social emotional learning] looks different in a math class than in a history or English class. It has to. Sometimes I'm surprised how things turn out, how that math teacher can model compassion when a kid is frustrated, you know, teaching SEL by example... but in another class a teacher might take it head on and have a really deep discussion about how someone could have acted differently in whatever the situation was. Did they both teach to the standard? I'd say so. Did they do it the same way. No way.

Importantly, creating space to "let others teachers it out themselves" builds collective capacity. Leading through the lens of equanimity emphasizes adopting a more tentative, provisional relationship to one's perceptions and beliefs. This suppleness prevents rigid mindsets and enables mental flexibility (Langer, 2014). At the same time, the equanimity of mindfulness is not detachment from reality but groundedness in what is most essential. As the school leader quote above noted remembering "our job is to educate kids" serves as an unwavering north star amid distraction and adversity. Paradoxically, nonattachment to outcomes combined with fierce commitment to purpose fosters courageous, principled leadership (Sinclair, 2007). The equanimity born of mindfulness enables leaders to dance with the inevitable paradoxes of organizational life – balancing change and stability, diversity and alignment, accountability and trust (Smith & Lewis, 2011). This balance provides ballast in the storm, allowing leaders to find their sea legs and chart a steady course. Over time, meeting difficulties with equanimity builds resilience at both the individual and collective levels (King & Badham, 2018).

Curiosity as a Leadership Stance

If awareness and equanimity form the core building blocks of mindful leadership, curiosity provides the animating spirit. Curiosity means adopting a beginner's mind, setting aside assumptions, and approaching situations with fresh eyes (Suzuki, 2011). It involves what the poet John Keats called "negative capability," the capacity to rest in uncertainty without grasping for premature conclusions (Rejack & Theune, 2019). A vivid example comes from an assistant superintendent, who describes her practice of meticulously unpacking an issue by seeking out contrasting perspectives. She started first with teachers, then parents, and finally panning out to the broader political context. She contemplated all she learned before forming any conclusions. This practice of "making space for understanding" yields richer insights. As quoted in Kruse (2023, p. 87), she states,

> I learned, when I'm looking at something new or something that will change our schools in some way, that I needed to just soak in the information I can get from other folks. It's about reaching for understanding. I know I can't assume I know where other people are coming from. Typically, what I will do is spend time unpacking an issue from a variety of different contexts. I learned, okay, say first start with a teacher because they're in a different space than me. So, what might a teacher think? What are the commonalities between them and me? It's like as I listen to them, I'm highlighting and coding and figuring, okay, where are the similarities and the differences between those stories and how they take place? Then it's almost like I'm unpacking the teacher as well. Why do they believe what they believe? Is it typical of other teachers? Are they unique? I try to really hear them. I sit with all that and try to understand what there is to be learned. I work at not coming to a conclusion too soon. Then I do that with a parent as well. Okay so let's unpack the parent. Where are they coming from? Are they a new parent? Do they come from a different context? Maybe they've been here for five years and they're on the PTA and they have some political affiliation to that space. What does that mean for my understanding? Then I try to really go broad, I'm also thinking, what is the general nature of where we're at right now, politically, socially in our world? All these things play out in my head as the person is talking and I am just, okay, what is there to be learned here? Usually, I need to talk to five or six people before I begin to develop any conclusions. Sometimes more, sometimes a lot more, especially if I'm getting really different thinking. I try to get a rounded picture of the issue, so that I can really understand what's going on. Only when I've done that do I start to make plans. It's really important for me to know what I'm walking into where the landmines might be and where it won't be so bad.

Curiosity flows naturally from the practices of cognitive mindfulness like openness to novelty, multiple perspectives, and active differentiation. Rather than lumping people and situations into simplistic preexisting categories, mindful leaders ask: What distinctions or angles am I missing? What new questions could reframe this situation? How can I surface disconfirming data? (Langer, 1989). Importantly, curiosity is more than just an individual attitude but an interpersonal stance and organizational norm. Curiousity involves regularly seeking feedback, encouraging dissent, and rewarding experimentation (Edmondson, 1999). When curiosity becomes a leadership stance, it shifts power dynamics and identity. Rather than having to be the smartest one in the room with all the answers, the leader becomes chief question-asker and learner (Schein, 2013). Moreover, when leaders adopt a stance of curiosity, they acknowledge the complexity of change and challenge. In turn, leaders are able offer tangible evidence that they care and are willing to create opportunities that foster connection, growth, and learning.

The Relational Heart of Leadership

While mindfulness begins with self-awareness, it naturally extends to interpersonal attunement. Mindful leaders recognize that leadership is inherently relational and that authentic human connection is the foundation for collective action and impact (Dutton & Heaphy, 2003). Many of the focal leaders illustrate how mindfulness builds their emotional and social intelligence. Mindful communication is essential for forging trust and belonging. More than just transmitting information, it involves deep listening, authentic self-expression, and cocreating shared meaning (Scharmer, 2016). Building healthy relationships of course does not mean avoiding tough issues. In fact, mindful leaders are more equipped to skillfully navigate conflict by balancing care and candor (Boyatzis & McKee, 2005; Scott, 2004). An elementary school principal gives a clear example of generous listening when dealing with an angry parent, reflecting back the parent's concerns and committing to follow-up, which "lowers the emotion" and allows forward movement. As quoted in Kruse (2023, pp. 197–198), the principal describes,

> Seek first to understand then to be understood. It sounds great. To do it is really hard. I think the first step is I have to really understand where that person is coming from, and I have to be able to say it back to them so that they feel I completely understand them. For example, if I would have a parent come in that was really fired up, and really angry. The first thing that I would do is I would greet the parent, sit down. I would say, "Do you mind if I take some notes because I want to make sure that I fully understand your concern?" 99.9%, absolutely. So, they're talking. I'm writing notes, really trying to keep eye contact. And then when we're done, I say, 'I want to read back to you the

concerns that you shared, and I really want you to tell me have I fully captured it. "I'll go back... not censoring anything. I will just say, 'This is what I'm hearing." Many times, they will correct me and say, "No, no, I didn't mean that." So, I'll go back [and ask them to clarify.]

The principal explains the outcomes of listening in this way,

... Just doing that lowers the emotion. They feel heard. They feel concern. I always say, 'It doesn't mean that we're going to come to an agreement but the one thing that is important to me is that you feel that your concerns are heard.' ... I don't want [anyone] walking out of here feeling like, '[Schapiro] didn't even listen to me. [Schapiro] didn't understand me.' ...I approach [situations like this] like I'm going to listen with the perspective that maybe my mind could be changed... At very first you have to really listen to understand, and that's hard. It's hard to hear what they are saying because your mind already is going. I'm already strategizing how I'm going to work my way out of this one. You've got to suspend that. That's where the mindfulness can be very beneficial because you're going to take a breath and say, 'Okay, in this moment I'm going to be fully present for this person. I'm going to be fully present.' I owe it to that person to be fully present for them in that moment where they need to share something important.

At a collective level, mindful leaders foster the relational conditions for organizational learning and adaptation. They foster these conditions by: (1) strengthening psychological safety so people can give honest feedback and take risks (Edmondson, 1999); (2) promoting healthy dialog skills so teams engage in generative thinking not defensive posturing; and (3) designing structures and routines that enable collaboration across boundaries (Kruse & Louis, 2009). Crucially, mindful leaders understand that relationships exist within larger systems and power dynamics. Rather than take a solely individualistic view, they consider how the organization's roles, incentives and culture shape relational patterns, and work to create enabling conditions for everyone to contribute and thrive (King & Badham, 2018; Ospina & Foldy, 2010).

The Paradoxes of Purpose and Positionality

One of the key insights of mindfulness is that leaders must grapple with seeming paradoxes. The role of a leader inherently involves making hard choices between competing priorities and perspectives. Mindfulness can help leaders avoid simplistic framings of issues and challenges and instead navigate tensions with more nuance and wisdom (Smith & Lewis, 2011). A central leadership paradox is balancing commitment to personal values and vision with openness to the needs and perspectives of others. Mindful leaders anchor themselves in their "north star purpose" while flexing in how it manifests. This points to the crucial theme of positionality. As a long-standing superintendent suggests,

> For me, student learning is my north star purpose. It's what I think of every time I make a decision. Everyone around me knows that. But... I've also become aware what I think student learning looks like and what [someone else] thinks it is can be very, very different... Sometimes, especially when I'm dealing with the board, I can get really wrapped up in things like our test scores or how many students are in A.P. [advanced placement] classes. Those are priorities for me. No doubt, they matter. But, [others] rightfully, define student learning differently... I have to take those perspectives into account also. Learning, it can look like a lot of things, a kiddo who doesn't lose it on the playground, a really cool art project, an awesome paragraph by a struggling reader. It's not always the big, measurable things... the things that get us in the newspaper. And, I know, if I don't include those examples when I tell our stories of success, I'm not showing the full picture of what we do. It's not honoring all the work. It's not seeing all the things everyone is busting their butts to do for our kids. And that's not fair. I need to speak for all kids and all of our teachers. They need recognition too...

Our identities and social locations inevitability shape what we perceive and prioritize, in both limiting and empowering ways. Mindful leadership demands a reflexive awareness of one's own positioning and active work to de-center dominant perspectives in favor of other voices and viewpoints. When accomplishment is defined in broad and inclusive ways, people feel valued and in turn, they can be more resilient in times of stress and challenge (Capone et al., 2019; Weiss, 2020).

Embracing the Beginner's Mind

In promoting a new way of leading, it would be easy to replace one idealized model with another. But the practice of mindful leadership is not about achieving some static state of perfection, but rather embracing the path of continual growth and wakefulness. At its heart, mindful leadership means approaching oneself, others, and the work with a beginner's mind – openness, humility, and care (Suzuki, 2011). At the same time, mindful leadership is ultimately pragmatic and engaged. Awareness and equanimity are not ends in themselves but capacities to better serve others and act in the world. True mindfulness has an activist edge, it enables leaders to see reality, name what is essential, and wholeheartedly engage more clearly in change (Boyce, 2018). As one mindful leader put it, "Mindfulness isn't just navel-gazing, it's taking responsibility." They went on to add,

> Knowing what I don't know, that's a big deal for me. I've been doing this for a long time. Schools have changed. A lot. So every year, I need to show up and see what is new. I need to stay involved and not count on what worked last year working again this year. I have to take that responsibility seriously every year.

The path of mindful leadership is simple but not easy. It demands vulnerability, a willingness to not know, and the patience to attend to small moments. Yet this commitment to presence is perhaps the most radical act of leadership. In a world of unrelenting doing and fractured attention, purposefully cultivating awareness and connection is a courageous stance. The stories and reflections of the focal leaders make a compelling case for reimagining leadership through the prism of mindfulness. By cultivating awareness, wisdom, and authentic connection, mindful leaders are better equipped to navigate the complexities of 21st century school leadership. But beyond just a set of skills, mindfulness offers a way of being – purposeful, present, and openhearted. In the words of poet Mary Oliver (2017, p. 104), "Instructions for living a life: Pay attention. Be astonished. Tell about it." This is the essence of the art of mindful leadership.

Practices and Next Steps

Cultivating the qualities of mindful leadership is a lifelong journey. Yet research has shown that even short-term mindfulness interventions can yield meaningful benefits for leaders' well-being, performance, and relationships (Felver et al., 2013; Hoge et al., 2013; Janssen et al., 2018; Lomas et al., 2017; Pathath, 2017). We suggest that the response to increased teacher and school leader burnout should not be one that suggests that individuals ought to be able to rise to the challenges of schools today. Rather, the response should be to find ways to provide support for and sustain individuals in ways that contribute to individual and organizational health and effectiveness. In short, school leaders need to identify when the system has created conditions that fail to value individuals and the work that they do. We suggest that attentive, proactive, and preemptive mindful action can go far to reduce disengagement and burnout. As the leaders quoted here evidence, leadership responses can be evidenced in many ways, including attention individual and organizational awareness, personal equanimity and curiosity, building relationships, purpose, and positionality, and adopting a beginner's mind.

Physical health and sleep are areas we did not address in this chapter but is related to mindful leadership and burnout. To date, professional educational leadership standards do not include an emphasis on physical, social, or emotional well-being. Consequently, those who recognize the complexity and demands of school leadership should not be surprised that many school leaders are not taking care of themselves and can often find themselves in poor physical condition. Healthy sleep is one key area of well-being that is often overlooked, yet sleep is essential for performance in many professions and a lack of sleep can negatively impact one's cognition and ability to make decisions (Charest & Grandner, 2022; Harrison & Horne, 2000; Maki et al., 2022). In a recent study focused on principal sleep, Su-Keene et al. (forthcoming) found that school leaders experienced job-related stresses and were often not getting enough high-quality sleep especially during the school year. These principals reported feeling tired and that this continued state likely impacted their ability to do their jobs well. Thus, mindful leadership also necessitates healthy sleeping habits to ensure school leaders are prepared to attend to individual and organizational conditions, maintain a steady sense of curiosity, and building relationships.

We believe a series of practical steps can be taken to strengthen mindful leadership and the health and well-being of school leaders. First, districts and principal supervisors need training and support in ensuring school leaders are prepared and support in managing their workloads, dealing with stress and uncertainty, and engaging not only in instructional leadership practices, but also practices that foster individual and organizational mindfulness. This work might include redeveloping some school leader workload expectations, adopting policies where school leaders can have release time to reflect or consult with a health professional, and cocreating a campus plan where administrative duties are delegated on certain days/times so a school leader can maintain a healthy work-life balance or engage in mindful leadership activities (DeMatthews et al., 2021). We also recognize that school leaders may not always have district support, so we believe it is important for school leaders to self-educate themselves using freely available resources, such as the American Psychiatric Association's (2020) Well-Being Resources, which includes TED Talks, proactive coping strategies, assessment tools, and other helpful resources. We also encourage school leaders to create their own delegation plans and annual calendars. Such planning activities can create time and structure for check-in and mentoring activities and opportunities to engage in peer-check-ins and other support activities.

Research on positive psychology may also be a body of knowledge researchers, practitioners, and other stakeholders consider in strengthening school leader mindfulness. Positive psychology emerged from the field of psychology in part to shift away from a focus on repairing or curing mental health diseases (Meyers et al., 2013). Instead, positive psychology focuses on human strengths and assets. Many positive psychology interventions have been found to improve mental health for individuals (Sin & Lyubomirsky, 2009). Su-Keene and DeMatthews (2022) described the potential benefits of one positive psychology intervention – savoring, which is the psychological process of attending to, appreciating, and enhancing positive experiences in one's life (Bryant & Veroff, 2007). Su-Keene and DeMatthews point out that school leadership is often filled with many joys and accomplishments, but the natural tendency of human beings is to focus and pay greater attention to threats and uncertainties. Some potential savoring activities for school leaders includes finding a recent sacred moment that reaffirms one's passion and purpose in their work and attending to that sacred moment by building it into a daily routine. For example, a school leader might enjoy eating lunch with students or welcoming them each day, so it would be important for that leader to prioritize that activity regularly and also be present in those moments – not distracted by what is happening next in the day.

Conclusion

Mindful leadership is both a personal practice and collective aspiration. School leaders cannot afford to ignore the toll of job-related stress and the potential harmful professional, physical, and personal impact of burnout. We believe school leaders care deeply about their work, which means they must care deeply about themselves or risk reaching only a portion of their leadership potential. Hopefully, school leaders find support from within their organizations, but the reality is many school leaders do not have that luxury. By starting where we are and taking the next step with awareness and care, we plant seeds for a more compassionate and awakened model of leadership. We hope that those who traverse the path of mindful leadership be nourished by presence, connection, and purpose. More importantly we hope that our efforts radiate out to transform our schools, communities, and world.

References

American Psychiatric Association. (2020). Well-being resources. https://www.psychiatry.org/psychiatrists/practice/well-being-and-burnout/well-being-resources

Bandura, A. (1997). *Self-efficacy: The exercise of control.* W.H. Freeman and Company.

Boyatzis, R. E., & McKee, A. (2005). *Resonant leadership: Renewing yourself and connecting with others through mindfulness, hope, and compassion.* Harvard Business Press.

Boyce, B. (2018). *The mindfulness edge: How to rewire your brain for leadership and personal excellence without adding to your schedule.* John Wiley & Sons.

Brown, K. W., Ryan, R. M., & Creswell, J. D. (2007). Mindfulness: Theoretical foundations and evidence for its salutary effects. *Psychological Inquiry, 18*(4), 211–237.

Bryant, F. B., & Veroff, J. (2007). *Savoring: A new model of positive experience.* Lawrence Erlbaum Associates.

Bunjak, A., Cerne, M., Nagy, N., & Bruch, H. (2021). Job demands and burnout: The multi-level boundary conditions of collective trust and competitive pressure. *Human Relations.* https://doi.org/10.1177/00187267211059826

Capone, V., Joshanloo, M., & Park, M. (2019). Burnout, depression, efficacy beliefs, and work-related variables among school teachers. *International Journal of Educational Research, 95*(9), 97–108. https://doi.org/10.1016/j.ijer.2019.02.001

Capurso, V., Fabbro, F., & Crescentini, C. (2014). Mindful creativity: The influence of mindfulness meditation on creative thinking. *Frontiers in Psychology, 4*(10120), 1–2. https://doi.org/10.3389/fpsyg.2012.00116

Charest, J., & Grandner, M. A. (2022). Sleep and athletic performance: Impacts on physical performance, mental performance, injury risk and recovery, and mental health: An update. *Sleep Medicine Clinics, 17*(2), 263–282.

Colzato, L. S., Ozturk, A., & Hommel, B. (2012). Meditate to create: The impact of focused-attention and open-monitoring training on convergent and divergent thinking. *Frontiers in Psychology, 3*(116). https://doi.org/10.3389/fpsyg.2012.00116

Dahl, C., Lutz, A., & Davidson, R. (2015). Reconstructing and deconstructing the self: Cognitive mechanisms in meditation practice. *Trends in Cognitive Sciences, 19*(9), 515–523.

DeMatthews, D., Carrola, P., Reyes, P., & Knight, D. (2021). School leadership burnout and job-related stress: Recommendations for district administrators and principals. *The Clearing House: A Journal of Educational Strategies, Issues and Ideas, 94*(4), 159–167. https://doi.org/10.1080/00098655.2021.1894083

Desbordes, G., Gard, T., Hoge, E. A., Hölzel, B. K., Kerr, C., Lazar, S. W., Olendzki, A., & Vago, D. R. (2015). Moving beyond mindfulness: Defining equanimity as an outcome measure in meditation and contemplative research. *Mindfulness, 6*(2), 356–372. https://doi.org/10.1007/s12671-013-0269-8

Donoon, D., & Langer, E. (2011). Mindfulness and leadership: Opening up to possibilities. *Integral Leadership Review, 11*(5), 1–15.

Dutton, J. E., & Heaphy, E. D. (2003). The power of high-quality connections. In K. S. Cameron, J. E. Dutton, & R. E. Quinn (Eds.) *Positive organizational scholarship: Foundations of a new discipline* (pp. 263–271). Berrett-Koehler Publishers.

Edmondson, A. (1999). Psychological safety and learning behavior in work teams. *Administrative Science Quarterly, 44*(2), 350–383.

Ehrlich, J. (2017). Mindful leadership: Focusing leaders and organizations. *Organizational Dynamics, 46*(4), 233–243.

Felver, J. C., Doerner, E., Jones, J., Kaye, N. C., & Merrell, K. W. (2013). Mindfulness in school psychology: Applications for intervention and professional practice. *Psychology in the Schools, 50*, 531–547.

Ford, T., Olsen, J., Khojasteh, J., Ware, J., & Urick, A. (2019). The effects of leader support for teacher psychological needs on teacher burnout, commitment, and intent to leave. *Journal of Educational Administration, 57*(6), 615–634. https://doi.org/10.1108/JEA-09-2018-0185

Goddard, R., Hoy, W., & Hoy, A. (2004). Collective efficacy beliefs: Theoretical developments, empirical evidence, and future directions. *Educational Researcher, 33*(3), 3–13.

Gonzalez-Morales, M. G., Peiro, J. M., Rodriguez, I., & Bliese, P. D. (2012). Perceived collective burnout: A multilevel explanation of burnout. *Anxiety, Stress & Coping, 25*(1), 43–61. https://doi.org/10.1080/10615806.2010.542808

Good, D. J., Lyddy, C. J., Glomb, T. M., Bono, J. E., Brown, K. W., Duffy, M. K., & Lazar, S. W. (2016). Contemplating mindfulness at work: An integrative review. *Journal of Management, 42*(1), 114–142.

Goyal, M., Singh, S., Sibinga, E. M., Gould, N. F., Rowland-Seymour, A., Sharma, R., Berger, Z., Sleicher, D., Maron, D. D., Shihab, H. M., Ranasinghe, P. D., Linn, S., Saha, S., Bass, E. B., & Haythornthwaite, J. A. (2014). Meditation programs for psychological stress and well-being: A systematic review and meta-analysis. *JAMA Internal Medicine, 174*(3), 357–368.

Harrison, Y., & Horne, J. A. (2000). The impact of sleep deprivation on decision making: A review. *Journal of Experimental Psychology: Applied, 6*(3), 236.

Hoge, E., Bui, E., Marques, L., Metcalf, C., Morris, L., Robinaugh, D., Worthington, J., Pollack, M., & Simon, N. (2013). Randomized controlled trial of mindfulness meditation for generalized anxiety disorder: Effects on anxiety and stress reactivity. *Journal of Clinical Psychiatry, 74*(8), 786–792.

Hunter, J., & Chaskalson, M. (2013). Making the mindful leader: Cultivating skills for facing adaptive challenges. In *The Wiley-Blackwell handbook of the psychology of leadership, change, and organizational development* (pp. 195–219). https://doi.org/10.1002/9781118326404.ch10

Janssen, M., Heerkens, Y., Juijer, W., van der Heijden, B., & Engles, J. (2018). Effects of mindfulness-based stress reduction on employees' mental health: A systematic review. *PLoS One, 13*(1), 1–37.

Kabat-Zinn, J. (2003). Mindfulness-based interventions in context: Past, present, and future. *Clinical Psychology: Science and Practice, 10*(2), 144–156. https://doi.org/10.1093/clipsy.bpg016

King, E., & Badham, R. (2018). Leadership in uncertainty: The mindfulness solution. *Organizational Dynamics, 47*(2), 100–106.

Koike, M. K., & Cardoso, R. (2014). Meditation can produce beneficial effects to prevent cardiovascular disease. *Hormone Molecular Biology and Clinical Investigation, 18*(3), 137–143.

Kruse, S. D. (2023). *Mindful educational leadership: Contemplative, cognitive, and organizational systems and practices*. Routledge.

Kruse, S. D., & Edge, K. (2023). Is it just me? Organizational burnout and efficacy. *Journal of Educational Administration, 61*(3), 272–286. https://doi.org/10.1108/JEA-10-2022-0187

Kruse, S. D., & Louis, K. S. (2009). *Building strong school cultures: A guide to leading change*. Corwin Press.

Lane, J., Everts, S., Hefner, Y., Phillips, R., & Scott, K. (2021). Crises of care: School leaders and narratives of compassion fatigue. *Journal of Organizational Psychology, 21*(1), 16–31.

Langer, E. J. (1989). *Mindfulness*. Addison-Wesley.

Langer, E. J. (2014). *Mindfulness 25th anniversary edition*. Hachette.

Langer, E. J., & Molodoveanu, M. (2000). The construct of mindfulness. *Journal of Social Issues, 56*(1), 1–9.

Lee, S. F. (2019). Psychology's own mindfulness: Ellen Langer and the social politics of scientific interest in "active noticing". *Journal of the History of the Behavioral Sciences, 55*, 216–229. https://doi.org/10.1002/JHBS.21975

Lomas, T., Medina, J. C., Ivtzan, I., Rupprecht, S., Hart, R., & Eiroa-Orosa, F. (2017). The impact of mindfulness on wellbeing and performance in the workplace: An inclusive systemic review of the empirical literature. *European Journal of Work & Organizational Psychology, 26*(4), 492–513.

Mahfouz, J. (2018). Mindfulness training for school administrators: Effects on well-being and leadership. *Journal of Educational Administration, 56*(6), 602–619. https://doi.org/10.1108/JEA-12-2017-0171

Mahfouz, J. (2020). Principals and stress: Few coping strategies for abundant stressors. *Educational Management Administration & Leadership, 48*(3), 440–458. https://doi.org/10.1177/1741143218817562

Maki, K. A., Fink, A. M., & Weaver, T. E. (2022). Sleep, time, and space—Fatigue and performance deficits in pilots, commercial truck drivers, and astronauts. *Sleep Advances*, *3*(1), 1–21.

Mendelson, T., Greenberg, M. T., Dariotis, J. K., Gould, L., Rhoades, B. L., & Leaf, P. J. (2010). Feasibility and preliminary outcomes of a school-based mindfulness intervention for urban youth. *Journal of Abnormal Child Psychology*, *38*, 985–994.

Meyers, M. C., van Woerkom, M., & Bakker, A. B. (2013). The added value of the positive: A literature review of positive psychology interventions in organizations. *European Journal of Work & Organizational Psychology*, *22*(5), 618–632. https://doi.org/10.1080/1359432X.2012.694689

Oliver, M. (2017). *Devotions*. Penguin Books.

Ospina, S., & Foldy, E. (2010). Building bridges from the margins: The work of leadership in social change organizations. *The Leadership Quarterly*, *21*(2), 292–307.

Pathath, A. W. (2017). Meditation: Techniques and benefits. *International Journal of Current Research in Medical Sciences*, *3*(6), 162–168.

Ray, J. L., Baker, L. T., & Plowman, D. A. (2011). Organizational mindfulness in business schools. *The Academy of Management Learning and Education*, *10*(2), 188–203.

Rejack, B., & Theune, M. (2019). *Keats's negative capability: New origins and afterlives*. Liverpool University Press.

Rerup, C. (2005). Learning from past experience: Footnotes on mindfulness and habitual entrepreneurship. *Scandinavian Journal of Management*, *21*, 451–472.

Scharmer, C. O. (2016). *Theory U: Learning from the future as it emerges*. Berrett-Koehler Publishers.

Schein, E. H. (2013). *Humble inquiry: The gentle art of asking instead of telling*. Berrett-Koehler Publishers.

Scott, S. (2004). *Fierce conversations: Achieving success at work and in life one conversation at a time*. Penguin.

Shapiro, S. L., Carlson, L. E., Astin, J. A., & Freedman, B. (2006). Mechanisms of mindfulness. *Journal of Clinical Psychology*, *62*(3), 373–386.

Silsbee, D. (2010). *The mindful coach: Seven roles for facilitating leader development*. John Wiley & Sons.

Sin, N. L., & Lyubomirsky, S. (2009). Enhancing well-being and alleviating depressive symptoms with positive psychology interventions: A practice-friendly meta-analysis. *Journal of Clinical Psychology*, *65*(5), 467–487.

Sinclair, A. (2007). Teaching leadership critically to MBAs: Experiences from heaven and hell. *Management Learning*, *38*(4), 458–472.

Smith, W. K., & Lewis, M. W. (2011). Toward a theory of paradox: A dynamic equilibrium model of organizing. *Academy of Management Review*, *36*(2), 381–403. https://doi.org/10.5465/amr.2009.0223

Sood, A., & Jones, D. T. (2013). On mind wandering, attention, brain networks, and meditation. *Explore*, *9*(3), 136–141.

Su-Keene, E., DeMathews, D. E., & Keene, A. (forthcoming). Are principals really tireless? Conceptualizing the role of sleep in school leadership. *Management in Education*. https://doi.org/10.1177/08920206241251404

Su-Keene, E., & DeMatthews, D. E. (2022). "Savoring" the joy: Reducing principal burnout and improving well-being through positive psychology interventions. *The Clearing House, 95*(5), 210–219.

Suzuki, S. (2011). *Zen mind, beginner's mind*. Shambhala Publications.

Urien, B., Rico, R., Demerouti, E., & Bakker, A. (2021). An emergence model of team burnout. *Journal of Work and Organizational Psychology, 37*(3), 175–186.

Van Droogenbroeck, F., Spruyt, B., Quittre, V., & Lafontaine, D. (2021). Does school context really matter for teacher burnout? *Educational Researcher, 50*(5), 290–305. https://doi.org/10.3102/0013189X21992361

Vogus, T. J., & Rerup, C. (2017). Sweating the small stuff: High reliability organizing as a foundation for superior performance. *Strategic Organization*. https://doi.org/10.1177/1476127017739535

Vogus, T. J., & Sutcliffe, K. M. (2012). Organizational mindfulness and mindful organizing: A reconciliation and path forward. *The Academy of Management Learning and Education, 11*(4), 722–735.

Weick, K. E., & Sutcliffe, K. M. (2006). Mindfulness and the quality of organizational attention. *Organization Science, 17*(4), 514–524. https://doi.org/10.1287/orsc.1060.0196

Weiss, L. (2020). Burnout from an organizational perspective. *Stanford Social Innovation Review*. https://doi.org/10.48558/9CV0-C436

Wells, C. M. (2015). Conceptualizing mindful leadership in schools: How the practice of mindfulness informs the practice of leading. *Education Leadership Review of Doctoral Research, 2*(1), 1–23.

Chapter 9

Conclusion: Reflections and Lessons Learned

David E. DeMatthews[a] and Sharon D. Kruse[b]

[a]University of Texas at Austin, USA
[b]Washington State University, USA

Abstract

School leaders face increasing challenges in recent years, from the COVID-19 pandemic to political attacks on public education. Despite concerns about principal turnover and stress, effective school leadership is critical for navigating current difficulties and enabling schools to be transformative spaces for students and communities to thrive. This edited volume explores how school leadership can be reimagined for greater effectiveness and sustainability in uncertain times, through evidence and insights from leaders in the US and globally. Key implications discussed include revising professional standards to prioritize principals' self-care and long-term, holistic student outcomes beyond standardized testing. Investing in research on principals' job-related stress and health and providing training on coping strategies. Empowering distributed leadership among school staff and proactive crisis management plans. The authors conclude by calling for adequate supports and resources for principals, and a societal commitment to public education's role in democracy and human potential, to enable the reimagining of school leadership amid current challenges and opportunities.

Keywords: Distributed leadership; crisis management; professional standards; school staff training; proactive management

Introduction

School leaders have always confronted challenges as they sought to improve the education of the children within their schools and communities. Over the past 120 years, school leaders contended with the pressure and challenges of new bureaucracies and regulations, navigated economic recessions and depressions, dealt with the aftermath of wars and natural disasters, and implemented new laws and practices that grew out of the civil rights era victories (Tyack, 1974). For the past 40 years, school leaders have led through a neoliberal era of schooling bringing new pressures for students of all backgrounds to perform well on standardized tests and compete for students with charter management organizations. Additional pressures emerged as new principal standards, evaluation tools, and pay-for-performance models became increasingly popular, despite serious limitations in capturing the contributions, strengths, and areas of growth associated with leading a school.

Our Argument

Some have argued that the principalship has become a less desirable and more physically, emotionally, and psychologically draining (Beausaert et al., 2016; Darmody & Smyth, 2016). Given these concerns, more researchers have turned their attention to principal turnover and the implications of schools with higher-than-average rates of principal turnover (DeMatthews et al., 2022; Grissom & Bartanen, 2019; Yan, 2020). The last 5 years has only increased concerns about instability in the principal position as many schools were ill-prepared for the transition to distance learning at the beginning of the COVID-19 pandemic (Kaufman et al., 2022) or the level of toxic politics and attacks on public education from right-wing politicians that followed soon after. The murder of George Floyd reignited international calls for racial justice, but several years later, a right-wing counterattack emerged seeking to undue progress through antidiversity, equity, and inclusion legislation (DEI), book bans, mostly fabricated stories of critical race theory in pre-k through 12 schools, and attempts to whitewash curriculum. School leaders managed these challenges, while their students (and teachers) were trying to make sense of a world increasingly struggling with climate disasters and other significant world events, such as increased political polarization and regional wars in the Ukraine and Israel/Palestinian Territories.

While school leaders have always confronted challenges and uncertainty, the present situation appears daunting – especially if public education is to continue to play a role in improving the lives of children from all walks of life and remaining as a cornerstone to democracy and civility in the decades to come. Around the world, school leaders are reporting high levels of stress (Arastaman & Çetinkaya, 2022; Leksy et al., 2023; Upadyaya et al., 2021), which professional standards do not provide any expectation for self-care as they do in many other helping professions. Yet, despite all these concerns, school leadership has never been more important – especially if that leadership is effective, consistent, and forward looking with sustainability in mind. We believe, amid these concerns, an important opportunity is upon the field of educational leadership – one where the current challenges and disruptions can lead to a more flexible, adaptable, and resilient leadership practice. We see this opportunity partly in the fact that even amid attacks on public education and civil rights legislation, school leaders remain among the most trusted citizens in society (Gramlich, 2022). The chapters of this book add to our conclusion that school leaders matter regardless of the difficult and circumstances. Their role within communities and positional authority on campuses can still enable them to foster a powerful sense of shared purpose and priorities within their schools and communities. They can still provoke a forward-looking and sustainable pathway for continuous school improvement, which we believe educators, school personnel, students, and families are desperately seeking in these difficult times.

In this volume, we curated research and other scholarly contributions that document the ways school leadership can be more responsive and effective at navigating the emergent challenges and difficulties of our times. The contributions include evidence and insights from school leaders within the US and around the world confronting climate disasters, inequitable power dynamics, outdated modes of discipline, and long-standing racial injustices. The authors of these chapters thought deeply about the unique challenges school leaders confronted within their current and future contexts, the practices and approaches they took to support transformation within their schools, and how more innovative organizational structures and leadership practices could enable more effective responses to uncertainties and challenges in real time. Importantly, each of these important contributions clarified that school leadership is not simply about fostering organizational efficiency or improving student outcomes of standardized tests. Though efficiency and achievement measured by scores have some merit in orienting leadership practice, these chapters make clear that the true power and purpose of school leadership is in establishing schools that are vibrant, inclusive, and transformative spaces. Rather than rigid test preparation factories, such transformative spaces enable teachers, students, and families to thrive, learn about their potentials, and develop the sense of agency that enables them to have a positive impact on their own lives, the people around them, and the world. Of course, such spaces raise student achievement and other traditionally measured outcomes.

As we conclude this edited volume, we view this body of work not as a definitive guide to leadership practice in schools for sustainability in uncertain times, but instead as a starting point and a call for reimaging school leadership. The authors in each chapter covered an array of important territory which we hope has stimulated in our audience a renewed commitment to questioning existing practices and pushing forward with innovative leadership that promotes more effective and equitable schooling environments. However, we also want to leave readers with some recommendations for next steps, because more scholarship, research, and practical application is necessary. In what follows, we discuss implications for school leadership preparation, policy, and practice before concluding with our final remarks.

Implications for School Leadership Preparation, Policy, and Practice

To reimagine school leadership, we believe professional standards must change. Professional standards in the US and abroad shape leadership development programs as well as school leader evaluation tools. They signal to practitioners, faculty, instructors, and policymakers what the evidence-base within the field says about effective school leadership. In many contexts, these standards are used to heavily emphasize core principles of instructional leadership, which when overemphasized can create a false sense that school leaders should prioritize or over-prioritize student achievement over all other areas of education. The goal of school leadership cannot be short-term gains on standardized tests that do not translate into positive schooling experiences and long-term outcomes for students, but too often this is the case. Leading and teaching to the test is deprofessionalizing and demoralizing for teachers and disengaging and unproductive for students.

Standards are important and informative to the field when used thoughtfully and in recognition of their imperfections, but they can also mask just how unique each nation, state, region, community, and school really are and how adaptive and locally responsive effective and equitable school leaders must be in their daily work. Reimagining school leadership means rejecting one-size-fits-all approaches and also thinking more broadly about what these standards include, especially if new concerns arise. One clear concern that has gone entirely unaddressed in professional standards is that of job-related stress, burnout, and high rates of turnover. We are unaware of any professional school leadership standards that include self-care. Thus, if standards inform policy and preparation, it is likely all or most school leaders receive little or no training or support in managing the complexities of their job. We are not surprised to see a growing body of literature documenting higher levels of burnout, a decrease in an ability to maintain a creative and engaging approach to leadership, and an increased likelihood of premature turnover that can disrupt improvement efforts.

We implore the field – faculty, researchers, graduate students, policymakers, nonprofits – to expand their thinking about the nature of school leadership with an orientation toward sustainability, both for the principal but also for the campus and community. Professional standards need to clarify the importance of continuous improvement, but not with a focus solely on incremental improvements. Rather, continuous improvement must be oriented toward longer term goals because creating a schooling environment that allows children to thrive cannot be accurately evaluated by measuring annual test scores. The way principals recruit, hire, induct, and provide training to teachers must be oriented toward long-term student outcomes that include academic achievement, but also other important social, emotional, physical, and psychological goals. Likewise, these efforts should emphasize the importance of establishing long-term partnerships with communities and families – which is increasingly threatened as rates of principal and teacher turnover spike.

To reimagine school leadership, the field must also take principal self-care more seriously and invest in research and development to support a healthy lifestyle. An adage sets the stage for the importance of school leaders' self-care: You can't take care of others until you take care of yourself. On airplanes, flight attendants remind those onboard to put their mask on first before helping others. In schools, the old saying goes, "If you don't feed the teachers, they eat the kids." School leaders must\take care of themselves to ensure they can continue to do their jobs and make sustainable improvements on their campuses. Policymakers should consider revising the standards to include self-care. In addition, research is needed to better understand work-related stress and health conditions for school leaders and appropriate pro-active coping strategies and planning activities can strengthen principal well-being (DeMatthews et al., 2021; Su-Keene et al., forthcoming). Research and interdisciplinary collaborations with public health experts can help advance the knowledge base and ensure school leaders are adequately prepared and supported as they engage in their daily work. In addition, principal supervisors and evaluation tools should take into account the pressures of the job and the importance of maintaining a healthy lifestyle.

Finally, to reimagine school leadership, school leaders need to be prepared to embrace uncertainties by ensuring they have well-crafted crisis management plans and by maintaining an intentional approach to developing proactive leadership among teachers, staff, students, and families within the school community. At the onset of the pandemic, many principals reported being unprepared to manage a crisis and without an adequate crisis plan in hand (DeMatthews et al., 2023). The pandemic caused a need for a quick pivot to distance learning and to ensure students and families with varying needs were well supported. Those schools with strong relationships and strong leadership not just in the principalship, but among teachers and families were most likely to make a seamless transition and continue to meet the diverse needs of their students. Those without such ties and assets likely struggled. The pandemic did help generate prescriptive writings on school leadership crisis management and field-wide recognition of how important educators and school personnel can be when a crisis emerges (Grissom & Condon, 2021; Schechter et al., 2022). Thus, one bright spot of the pandemic is a clear point that preparedness and empowerment of faculty and staff is essential.

Final Remarks

In this edited volume, we explored leadership practices across the US and around the world with the intention of better understanding how the field can reimagine school leadership amid a time of great uncertainty. We believe the topic to be timely and that the current moment creates an important opportunity to think more innovatively about the way schools are led now and in the future. We see a clear need for reimaging school leadership in full recognition of the uncertainty principals confront, but also with the opportunities that come about in moments of great change and disruption. However, we would be remiss if we did not also acknowledge that principals are not superheroes and are constrained by the realities of their bureaucracies and contexts. Without adequate training, resources, and supports, principals cannot fully deploy their skillsets or deliver on the many goals and purposes of education. So, while we call for a reimagining of school leadership, we also call for a reimagining of how we fund and prioritize education within society. We also call for a politics that can remain rooted in different perspectives, but that must be universally committed to democracy, truth, and the role education must play in tapping the full human potential. The growing economic inequality, the rise of authoritarianism, a proliferation of misinformation on social and traditional media, and increasing polarization among segments of society threaten to undermine public education writ large and the important role of principals, teachers, counselors, and other school personnel seeking to positively impact the lives of their students. Thus, we conclude with a call for all readers to recognize the important role they play in helping all school leaders reimagine their work while simultaneously engaging in efforts large and small to make our societies, economies, and political bodies more inclusive, democratic, and just.

References

Arastaman, G., & Çetinkaya, A. (2022). Stressors faced by principals, ways of coping with stress and leadership experiences during the COVID-19 pandemic. *International Journal of Educational Management*, *36*(7), 1271–1283.

Beausaert, S., Froehlich, D. E., Devos, C., & Riley, P. (2016). Effects of support on stress and burnout in school principals. *Educational Research*, *58*(4), 347–365.

Darmody, M., & Smyth, E. (2016). Primary school principals' job satisfaction and occupational stress. *International Journal of Educational Management*, *30*(1), 115–128.

DeMatthews, D., Carrola, P., Reyes, P., & Knight, D. (2021). School leadership burnout and job-related stress: Recommendations for district administrators and principals. *The Clearing House: A Journal of Educational Strategies, Issues and Ideas*, *94*(4), 159–167.

DeMatthews, D. E., Knight, D. S., & Shin, J. (2022). The principal-teacher churn: Understanding the relationship between leadership turnover and teacher attrition. *Educational Administration Quarterly*, *58*(1), 76–109.

DeMatthews, D., Reyes, P., Solis Rodriguez, J., & Knight, D. (2023). Principal perceptions of the distance learning transition during the pandemic. *Educational Policy*, *37*(3), 653–675.

Gramlich, J. (2022, Febrauary 24). *Republicans' confidence in K-12 principals has fallen sharply during the pandemic*. Pew Research Center. https://www.pewresearch.org/short-reads/2022/02/24/republicans-confidence-in-k-12-principals-has-fallen-sharply-during-the-pandemic/

Grissom, J. A., & Bartanen, B. (2019). Principal effectiveness and principal turnover. *Education Finance and Policy*, *14*(3), 355–382.

Grissom, J. A., & Condon, L. (2021). Leading schools and districts in times of crisis. *Educational Researcher*, *50*(5), 315–324.

Kaufman, J. H., Diliberti, M. K., & Hamilton, L. S. (2022). How principals' perceived resource needs and job demands are related to their dissatisfaction and intention to leave their schools during the COVID-19 pandemic. *AERA Open, 8.* https://doi.org/10.1177/23328584221081234

Leksy, K., Wójciak, M., Gawron, G., Muster, R., Dadaczynski, K., & Okan, O. (2023). Work-related stress of Polish school principals during the COVID-19 pandemic as a risk factor for burnout. *International Journal of Environmental Research and Public Health, 20*(1, 805), 1–17.

Schechter, C., Da'as, R. A., & Qadach, M. (2022). Crisis leadership: Leading schools in a global pandemic. *Management in Education.* https://doi.org/10.1177/08920206241251404

Su-Keen, E., DeMatthews, D. E., & Keene, A. (forthcoming). Are principals really tireless? Conceptualizing the role of sleep in school leadership. *Management in Education.* https://doi.org/10.1177/08920206241251404

Tyack, D. B. (1974). *The one best system.* Harvard University Press.

Upadyaya, K., Toyama, H., & Salmela-Aro, K. (2021). School principals' stress profiles during COVID-19, demands, and resources. *Frontiers in Psychology, 12,* 731929.

Yan, R. (2020). The influence of working conditions on principal turnover in K-12 public schools. *Educational Administration Quarterly, 56*(1), 89–122.

Index

Ableism, 50
Abolish Chronic Truancy (ACT) program, 74
Adaptability, 24–25
Adaptive leadership, 2–3, 26
Adults in schools, 41–42
Agism, 105–106
Alternatives to punitive discipline, 83
Ambiguity, 32
Approaches to Learning (ATL), 63
ATLAS.ti qualitative software, 94
Autonomy, 52–54
Awareness, 136–138

Bias, 2–3, 93–94
Black students, 78
Brokering with outside agencies and organizations, 120
Burnout, 118–119, 134, 137

Canadian Council of Montessori Administrators (CCMA), 56–57
Centrality of awareness, 136–138
Challenges, 3–4, 32
Classism, 50
Climate disasters, 104
 historical and contextual factors, 105–111
Coalitions of progress, 8, 95–96, 98
Cognition, 36
Cognitive mindfulness, 135
Collaboration, 20–21
Collaborative approach, 90, 100, 124
Communication, 19–20
Community, 43
Community needs, 119
Complex adaptive system, 17
Complexity, 32

perspective in educational leadership, 17–18
 theory, 33
Conferences, 72
Connection, 54, 123
Consonance, 95
Contemplative mindfulness, 134–135
Content analysis, 93–94
Copley Public Schools (CPS), 8, 90
 lessons learned from, 95–99
 partnering with, 91–92
Courage, 5
COVID-19 pandemic, 2
Crisis and disaster management as gap in leadership preparation, 120–121
Crisis leadership, 19
Crisis management, 155
Cult of Pedagogy, 94
Cultural positioning, 38
Cultural responsiveness, 23
Culturally relevant frameworks, 22–23
Culturally relevant pedagogy, 95
Culturally responsive leadership, 24–25
Curiosity, 5
 as leadership stance, 140–141

Decentralization of race, 90
Deep knowledge, 44
Dilemma identification, 15
Disasters, 103–105
 location and experiences, 105–106
 management, 120–121
 school leadership in disaster response, 111–121
 on student outcomes, 106–111
Discipline, 80–81, 153
Discomfort, 36
Disproportionality, 77–78, 81

Disproportionate impact, 2, 111
Dissonance, 95
Distributed leadership, 24
District-level leaders, 81–82
Diverse perspectives, 42
Diversity, 3–4
Diversity, equity, and inclusion legislation (DEI), 152

Earthquakes, 19, 104
Education leadership, 4–5
Education Review Office (ERO), 15–16
Educational leaders, 34
Educational leadership, 14–15, 36, 40
   complexity perspective in, 17–18
   landscape in Aotearoa New Zealand, 15–17
Educators, 3, 36–37
Educultural Wheel, 22–23
Effective leadership, 33, 43
Emergence, 18
Emotion, 44
Emotional support to students and teachers, 117–119
Emotions, challenge of navigating, 36–37
Environmental injustice, 103–105
   historical and contextual factors, 105–111
   location and experiences, 105–106
   on student outcomes, 106–111
Equality, 52–54
Equanimity, path of, 138–139
Equity, 2, 52–54, 61–62, 92–93
   equity-focused leaders, 124–125
   leadership as theoretical lens for transformation, 93
Excellence for every student, 92–93
Exclusionary discipline policies, 77
Expulsion, 75–76

Fair Oaks Elementary School, 50–51
Fieldnotes, 57–59
"Fixing parts" approach, 33
Futures discourse, 35

Genuine inquiry, 39
Geography, 104
Gun-Free Schools Act, 74–75

7 Habits, 51
"Hearts and minds" approach, 96–97
Heterosexism, 50
Historical practices, 98–99
Holistic student outcomes, 9
Humility, 5
Hurricane Katrina, 110–112, 120–121
Hurricanes, 104

Inclusion, 92–93
Inequity in schools, 80
Informed decision-making, 99
Inquiry, 39
Instruction, 52, 54–55
Integrated respect, 54–55
International Baccalaureate educational system (IB educational system), 50, 61, 65
   analysis of dilemma, 63–65
   from field, 61–63
International Baccalaureate Organization (IBO), 61

Juvenile Justice and Delinquency Prevention Act of 1974, 73–74

Kotahitanga (ethic of bonding), 22–23

Leader in Me, 51
Leaders, 3–4, 43–44
Leadership, 31–32
   challenge of engaging voices of youth, 39–41
   challenge of interrupting problematic narratives, 37–39

challenge of navigating emotions,
36–37
challenge of navigating uncertainty,
34–35
complex challenges, 33–34
implications for school leadership,
41, 44
preparation, 80–82
Legal codification of zero-tolerance
policies, 74–76
Los Angeles Unified School District
(LAUSD), 73–74

Manaakitanga (ethic of caring), 22–23
Māori, 14
education, 21
Marginalization, 4–5
Marginalized communities, 97
Mātauranga Māori, 41
Mauri ora, 22–23
Mediation, 72
Mindful activity, 135
Mindful awareness, 138
Mindful communication, 141–142
Mindful leadership, 134
centrality of awareness, 136–138
curiosity as leadership stance,
140–141
embracing beginner's mind,
143–144
paradoxes of purpose and
positionality, 142–143
path of equanimity, 138–139
practices and next steps, 144–146
relational heart of leadership,
141–142
traditions of mindfulness, 134–136
Mindfulness, traditions of, 134–136
Mississippi schools, 119
Mitigating uncertainty, 104
Mixed-methods study, 15–16
Montessori educational system, 50, 56,
60
analysis of dilemma, 59–60
fieldnotes, 57–59
Mudslides, 104

Mutual respect, 50, 54–55
definitions and examples, 53
as dilemma-fraught, 55–56
framework for, 50
framework for examining
interactions, 52
leading for symmetry across
languages, 56–60
leading for symmetry across
socioeconomic status, 61–65
presenting framework for, 52–56
problem, 50–52

Narratives, 37
Natural disasters, 105–107, 109
Negative capability, 140
Networks, 14–15, 43
New Zealand, 13–14
collaboration and trust as emergent
processes, 20–21
complexity perspective in
educational leadership,
17–18
education system, 14
educational leadership landscape in
Aotearoa New Zealand,
15–17
flow of interaction and
communication, 19–20
implications, 25–26
leading in times of uncertainty, 18
recognizing culturally relevant and
complex leadership
practices, 21–25
New Zealand Ministry of Education,
15

Ontological security, 36–37
Open-mindedness, 38
Organization, 24–25, 97
Organizational mindfulness, 135–136
Organizational transformation, 99

P-12 school leaders, 124
Pākehā, 14
Pandemic, 2, 122

Peer counseling, 72
Peoplehood, 43
Personhood, 43
Physical environment, 104
Political attacks, 9
Postcolonial theories, 40
Potentiality clause, 73–74
Poverty, 104
Power, 5
Preferable future, 35
Primary Years Programme (PYP), 62–63
Principal turnover, 9, 152
Principalship, 152
Probable future, 35
Problematic narratives, challenge of interrupting, 37–39
Professional standards, 154
Public schools, 73–74
Pumanawatanga (morale, tone, pulse), 22–23
Punishment, 73

"Race neutral" policies, 77, 80
Racial bias, 80, 82
Racial disproportionality, 78
Racial equity, 90
  equity leadership as theoretical lens for transformation, 93
  forming coalitions of progress, 96–98
  historical practices, 98–99
  implications for future research and practice, 100–101
  lessons learned from Copley Public School District, 95–99
  methodology, 93–94
  oscillations between dissonance and consonance, 95
  partnering with Copley Public Schools, 91–92
  principals and impact on student achievement, 92–93
  removing systemic barriers to improve outcomes, 99
  transformation, 94, 99

Racial justice, 2, 72
  adverse impacts of zero-tolerance policies and practices, 76–77
  implications for school leaders, leadership preparation, and research, 80–82
  racial discipline gap, 77–78
  restorative practices as alternative to punitive and exclusionary discipline, 78–80
  school collaboration with law enforcement, 73–74
  school discipline, 72–73
  school discipline and legal codification of zero-tolerance policies, 74–76
Racial-discipline gap, 72, 77–78
Racism, 50, 96, 105–106
Rangatiratanga (teacher effectiveness), 22–23
Recovery, 20–21, 105
Reflexivity, 24
Reimagined school leader, portrait of, 121, 123, 126
Relational practice, 42–43
Relational trust, 43
Relationship (s), 19, 42–43
Reopening schools, 112–117
Research methods, 55–56
  animating framework, 56–65
Resilient leadership, 152–153
Respect, 50, 54
Restorative circles, 72, 79
Restorative conferences, 79
Restorative justice, 78–79
Restorative practices, 72
  as alternative to punitive and exclusionary discipline, 78–80
Risk, 36–37
Routines, 17, 99

School climate, 7–8, 72, 79–80
School collaboration with law enforcement, 73–74

School communities, 41–42
School counselors, 82
School discipline, 72–73
  and legal codification of zero-tolerance policies, 74–76
School leaders, 20, 32, 104, 151–152
  evolving role for, 122–123
  implications for, 80–82
School leadership, 2–3, 35, 43, 66, 92, 104, 139
  in disaster response, 111–121
  implications for, 41–44
  implications for school leadership preparation, policy, and practice, 153–156
  scholarship on, 113–116
  target audience and key themes, 4–6
School principals, 92, 105
School psychologists, 82
School social workers, 82
Schools, 17
Self-care, 152–153, 155
Self-organization, 18
Sensemaking, 18–19, 122
Sexism, 50, 105–106
Shared instructional leadership, 92
Social capital, 104, 124
Social change, 22–23
Social inclusion, 22–23
Social justice, 5–6
Social relations, 52, 54–55
Social-emotional learning, 50–51
Sociocultural theory, 91
Socioeconomic status, 61–65
Socioeducational transformation, 23
Standard deviations (SDs), 110
Standards, 154
Storm: Students of Biloxi, Mississippi Remember Hurricane Katrina, The, 117–118
Stress, 8–9, 152–153
Student achievement, 110
Student achievement, principals and impact on, 92–93

Student agency, 62–63, 100
Student outcomes, 5–6, 153
Student voice, 40
Students of color, 90
Substance Abuse and Mental Health Services Administration, 124
Superintendents, 105
Suspension, 75–76
Sustainability, 3, 5, 154
Symmetry, 61–65
Synergy, 64
System, 20
Systemic barriers, 99
Systems thinking approach, 33

Te Kotahitanga project, 40–41
Thoughts, Questions, Epiphanies protocol method (TQE protocol method), 94
"To-do" lists, 33
Toronto District School Board (TDSB), 59
Transformation, 2–3
Transformational leadership, 92
Transformative spaces, 5–6, 9
Treaty of Waitangi, 13–14
Trust, 20–21
Tsunamis, 104

Uncertainty, 32
  challenge of navigating, 34–35
United Nations Convention on the Rights of the Child (UNCROC), 40

Voice, 40
Voices of youth, challenge of engaging, 39–41
Volatility, 32
Volcanic eruptions, 104
Vygotsky's Zone of Proximal Development (ZPD), 91

Weather, 104
Wellbeing, 41

Whanaungatanga (building
    relationships), 22–23
Willful defiance, 75
Wisdom, 8–9

Xenophobia, 105–106

Youth voices, 39–41

Zero tolerance, 75
    adverse impacts of zero-tolerance
        policies and practices,
        76–77
    policies, 72
    school discipline and legal
        codification of, 74–76
Zero Tolerance Task Force, 76

Printed and bound by CPI Group (UK) Ltd, Croydon, CR0 4YY
16/01/2025

14627476-0005